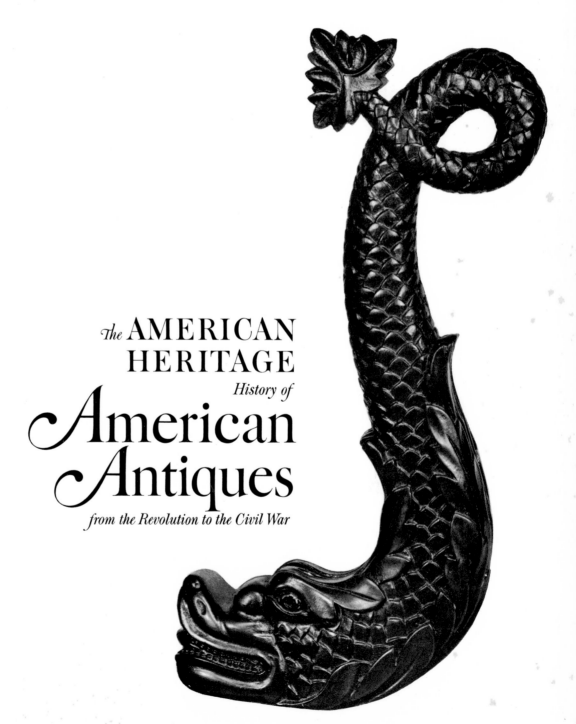

The AMERICAN HERITAGE
HERITAGE
History of
American
Antiques
from the Revolution to the Civil War

By the Editors of
AMERICAN HERITAGE
The Magazine of History

Author and Editor in Charge
Marshall B. Davidson

Published by
American Heritage Publishing Co., Inc.

Book Trade Distribution by
Simon and Schuster

The AMERICAN HERITAGE
HERITAGE
History of
American
Antiques
from the Revolution to the Civil War

American Heritage
Book Division

EDITORIAL DIRECTOR
Richard M. Ketchum

GENERAL EDITOR
Alvin M. Josephy, Jr.

Staff for this Book

EDITOR
Marshall B. Davidson

MANAGING EDITOR
Beverley Hilowitz

ART DIRECTOR
Marcia van Dam

ASSOCIATE EDITOR
Mary B. Durant

PICTURE EDITOR
Robert Bishop

ASSISTANT EDITOR
Audrey N. Catuzzi

ASSISTANT COPY EDITOR
Susan Breitling

ASSISTANT PICTURE EDITOR
Anne Palmbaum

EDITORIAL CONSULTANT
Nancy Lindemeyer

American Heritage
Publishing Co., Inc.

PRESIDENT
James Parton

CHAIRMAN, EDITORIAL COMMITTEE
Joseph J. Thorndike

EDITOR, AMERICAN HERITAGE MAGAZINE
Oliver Jensen

SENIOR ART DIRECTOR
Irwin Glusker

PUBLISHER, AMERICAN HERITAGE MAGAZINE
Darby Perry

Contents

Preface

In 1787 Benjamin Rush, signer of the Declaration of Independence and member of the Second Continental Congress, counseled his countrymen not to confuse the War of Independence with the American revolution. "The American war is over," he wrote, "but that is far from being the case with the American revolution. On the contrary, nothing but the first act of the great drama is closed." By the time the Civil War once again put the destiny of the American people in serious question, the sense of those remarks was clearly apparent. In the course of the intervening years Americans had indeed revolutionized the land of their colonial forebears. They had trekked and sailed and fought their way to the westernmost limits of the continent and in the process had taken over the vast territory that lay between the two coasts. The "inexhaustible" wilderness was already being replaced by the works of man in large and sometimes ugly patches. Democratic principles had been carried out in practice far beyond any intentions of the Founding Fathers, many of whom were loathe to believe that the common man could be trusted with a say in matters of government. By the 1850's, also, it seemed clear that the industrial nations would inherit the earth, and by then the United States already showed promise of becoming the greatest industrial country of them all. A nation that had been early schooled in homespun frugality was fast being re-educated to machine-made prodigality, and hopeful people from many lands were swarming into this new world of peace and plenty and of promise.

The drift of immigrants across the Atlantic, which was halted during the War of Independence, resumed immediately with the cessation of hostilities and, with only occasional abatements, gradually developed into an unprecedented migration of people. From the first days of independence there were among those hopefuls trained craftsmen who in their new homes produced what have since become treasured American antiques. The Scot, Duncan Phyfe, the Frenchman, Charles Honoré Lannuier, and the German, John Henry Belter were only three of such immigrant artisans whose work is reproduced on the following pages. Although these men, naturally, brought with them the traditions and practices of their separate homelands, they adapted their working habits to the tastes and preferences of the localities where they settled in the New World. More often than not, that required no serious adjustment, since even in periods of the most self-conscious and assertive nationalism, Americans continued to keep an attentive eye on style and fashion developments abroad. In any case, without documentary evidence it is often impossible to distinguish between the work of immigrant and native craftsmen.

Over the years covered by this book, from 1783 to 1860, the western world in general hunted the past more intently than it ever had before for models of design and ornament. The arts of every age have been more or less derivative, but the nineteenth century had wider opportunities than any previous period to gather evidence from other cultures and of other times. Far-reaching archaeological adventures, more extensive travel and trade about the globe, and the proliferation of printed reports and reproductions all provided a rich and novel vocabulary of design drawn from ancient Egypt, Greece, and Rome, from the Middle Ages, the Renaissance, and the more recent European past of Elizabethan England and of France under the Bourbons. This wealth of fresh evidence, not always well understood, was used with a freedom of expression that constituted a complex new language of styles—styles that are usually labeled as historical revivals, but that tell us far more about the outlook of the nineteenth century than they do about any earlier times.

Those styles as they were followed in this country, at one long remove from their sources abroad, inevitably took on a separate character. In the first decades of the country's independence, American versions of the neoclassic style, in the manner of Hepplewhite and Sheraton, revealed marked regional characteristics. During this federal period, as in colonial times, each of the major urban areas, and some smaller ones, interpreted the prevailing fashions in a manner that was distinctively its own. As communications quickened within the nation such variations tended to be less apparent, as in the succeeding, Empire phase of the classical revival. When this style in turn gradually gave way to others derived from nonclassical sources, local differences were even less noticeable. As the American people surged westward in the decades following the War of 1812, large and small enterprises sprang up beyond the Alleghenies to meet the demands of that prospering hinterland. Pittsburgh, Wheeling, and other midwestern cities had already developed into important glassmaking centers early in the century, and their operations continued to grow as the years passed. In 1848 the Cincinnati Chamber of Commerce boasted that its numerous furniture-making plants, working with steam-driven machinery, were producing vast quantities of beds, tables, chairs, and other forms, much of which output, presumably, was shipped to various down-river ports. By the middle of the last century labor-saving processes were progressively intruding on the traditional domain of the individual craftsman, and distinctive styles and forms emerged reflecting the impact of mechanical aids to production. The development of mass-production methods in virtually all fields was essential if the continuing revolution in American life was to answer the needs and wants of the democracy's sovereign public.

M.B.D.

7

Republican
Modes

*The
Federal
Style
(1783-1815)*

"We must not expect, that a new government may be formed, as a game of chess may be played, by a skilful hand, without a fault...chance has its share in many of the determinations, so that the play is more like *tric-trac* with a box of dice." So wrote Benjamin Franklin to Pierre Samuel du Pont de Nemours in June, 1788. The new Constitution of the United States had not yet been ratified by the requisite number of states. That document may have been, as William Gladstone once remarked, "the most wonderful work ever struck off at a given time by the brain and purpose of man." But it had been composed in the heat of violent controversy and was bitterly opposed by a large number of the people, including Patrick Henry who warned his countrymen that it was "the most fatal plan that could possibly be conceived to enslave a free people." However, as Franklin observed, the die was cast. In any case, he added, in the end the fate of the new government would be determined by the temper of the American people.

In recent years many new nations have been conceived and born in various parts of the world. In the 1780's, when the federal government of the United States was established, the birth of a nation was an uncommon, even a sensational, event. To some this trial in government was a matter of surpassing importance; it promised a fresh start in the history of human affairs. "Next to the introduction of Christianity...," wrote Benjamin Franklin's English friend, the Reverend Dr. Richard Price, "the American revolution may prove the most important step in the progressive course of human improvement." Turgot, minister of finance under Louis XVI, in turn wrote Price that the new nation that issued from the conflict was "the *hope* of the human race." And, he added, it might become a model for mankind to emulate, a point of view solemnly echoed by George Washington in his first inaugural address several years later.

There were others, Americans among them, who doubted that the infant republic would survive at all. In undertaking their experiment in self-government the Founding Fathers had cast aside the institutions of royalty, aristocracy, and established church, which for so many centuries had been considered the necessary safeguards of European societies. Beyond that, it was held, the temper of the people and the nature of the land they occupied would quickly lead to a separation of interests. The Dean of Gloucester gloomily predicted the ex-colonists would remain "a disunited people till the end of time, suspicious and distrustful of each other, they will be divided and subdivided into little commonwealths or principalities, according to natural boundaries, by great bays of the sea, and by vast rivers, lakes and ridges of mountains." America, in short, would but repeat the history of Europe with its sorry tale of local rivalries and international wars.

At the time of the Constitutional Convention the American people numbered fewer than four millions, spotted and scattered over some eight hundred thousand square miles of territory, much of it covered with dark forests. There

Opposite: detail of silver sauceboat, shown above, by Anthony Rasch of Philadelphia

9

Overland travel on the commercial mail stage between New York and Boston, 1815

were only a handful of communities, strung along the Atlantic seaboard, large enough to be termed cities. In 1790 more than 90 per cent of all gainfully employed Americans were farmers. Until the end of the century the new republic did not have a single well-paved road to help bind its straggling parts together—or to reduce the discomforts and dangers of travel by coach or stage. In 1791, while Washington was touring the South, Jefferson wrote him with understandable concern: "I shall be happy to hear that no accident has happened to you in the bad roads." Five years later it took one stagecoach five days to get from Philadelphia to Baltimore over the winter roads.

The waterways—the sea, the bays, and the rivers—provided the principal avenues of travel and communication, as they had in colonial times. (Even after improved roads and, still later, the railroads had begun to ease the problems of overland travel and transportation, fresh eggs were for a time still delivered to the markets in Providence, Rhode Island, by sailing sloop.) Overseas trade had been drastically reduced during the Revolutionary War, but with the return of peace in 1783 American harbors quickly filled with ocean-going ships from abroad, principally from England, eager to discharge their cargoes of European merchandise at low prices. From those harbors American vessels sortied to find what markets they could all around the globe.

Political independence did not radically reduce America's reliance upon England either for manufactures or for cultural guidance. Men like Noah Webster called for a brand-new start toward a purely American way of life. America must be "as famous for *arts* as for *arms*," Webster insisted. "Unshackle your minds," he beseeched his countrymen, "and act like independent beings." They "must *believe*, and *act* from the belief," he continued to admonish his fellow Americans, "that it is dishonorable to waste life in mimicking the follies of other nations and basking in the sunshine of foreign glory." However, in 1784 the im-

A hazardous crossing of the Susquehanna River, painted by Paul Svinin, about 1813

ports from Great Britain were almost five times greater than the exports to that country, and greater than they had been before the Revolution. In that same year William Pynchon, of Salem, Massachusetts, observed that "all who can cross the Atlantic seem determined to go and procure their goods from England."

There were others who bewailed that "madness of foreign finery" which "rages and destroys...threatening convulsions and dissolution to the political body." But in spite of such complaints a large part of the American public, among the fashionable at least, found nothing incompatible between an "inveterate enmity" toward Britain and a respect for the manners and customs of the Britons. At a different level, even Noah Webster's famous blue-backed speller, first issued in 1783 (and which would become one of the best sellers of all time), had to compete for a while with a British spelling book reprinted by the celebrated American printer Isaiah Thomas of Worcester, Massachusetts.

During the troubled years of the Revolutionary period a separate and peaceful revolution had been brewing in the British Isles—a revolution that within a score of years or so remarkably changed the style of English furniture, furnishings, and architectural decoration. Actually, this radical change in fashion might better be called another renaissance, for it developed largely out of a search for "ideal" designs among the ruins and remains of classical antiquity. There had already been one classical revival in England, which found its most eloquent expression in the earlier decades of the eighteenth century. But that had been a revival of a revival, a retarded English interpretation of the Italian Renaissance that left the British Isles sprinkled with Anglicized versions of the Italian villas of Andrea Palladio who, several centuries earlier, had published his own adaptations of ancient Roman structures.

The new "correct" classicism in design found its first inspiration in the revelations at Herculaneum and Pompeii when excavations of those buried Roman cities were undertaken before the middle of the century. Then the ruins of Rome, Athens, Palmyra, Baalbek, Split, and other ancient cities and sites were examined with a fresh interest and enthusiasm. An archaeological fever swept over most of western Europe, and in the remaining years of the century a large shelfful of books was published in Italian, German, French, and English describing and illustrating the finds and the studies that were made. Among those who could afford such an indulgence, collecting antiquities of every kind—statuary, coins, cameos, or whatever—became a sort of mania, a persistent mania that early in the next century brought the Elgin marbles from Athens to London, and among other things, the *Venus de Milo* to Paris.

As a direct and relatively quick reaction to such excitements, the spell of the rococo was broken. The robust exuberance of the Louis XV and the Chippendale styles gave way to the delicate grace of the Louis XVI and Adam styles with their preference for motifs and ornament of a generally classical character. The range of the literature published in various languages resulted in a greater uniformity of style throughout western Europe than had ever before prevailed, a uniformity that was in time and to a degree shared by America.

But America had to wait until it settled its quarrel with Great Britain before feeling the impact of the new vogue. Just before the Revolution, in 1773, the first volume of *The Works in Architecture of Robert and James Adam, Esquires* was issued in London. Robert Adam was the leading exponent of the new style in England. This Scottish architect had earlier toured Italy and Dalmatia and studied at firsthand their classical remains. After his return to England he won

The English antiquarian, Charles Towneley, in his gallery. Painting by Johann Zoffany

the patronage of numerous wealthy and aristocratic clients with his light and graceful adaptations of Roman forms and ornament. But it was the publication of his *Works* that provided architects and designers with material they could and did copy, and that brought his stylish innovations to the attention of a much wider audience. Some years later, in a lecture before students of the Royal Academy of Arts, Sir John Soane could truthfully state that "To Mr. Adam's taste in the Ornaments of his Buildings, and Furniture, we stand indebted, in-as-much as Manufacturers of every kind felt, as it were, the electric power of this Revolution in Art."

Adam's designs covered every kind of household equipment, from inkstands and fire grates to sideboards and bookcases, as well as buildings. However, all his projects were undertaken as commissions from individual—and moneyed—patrons, and all his plans were for particular houses, and specific rooms in them. On the other hand, those who followed him, adopting and adapting his designs, had in view the public salesrooms and markets and somewhat less exclusive customers. It was the published manuals intended to guide the cabinetmaking and other trades toward those wider outlets that gave the neoclassic fashion its ultimate broad popularity in England and America.

Among the most influential of such manuals, or trade catalogues, were those by George Hepplewhite and Thomas Sheraton. Hepplewhite's *The Cabinet-Maker and Upholsterer's Guide*, first published posthumously in 1788 and issued in two subsequent editions, illustrated about three hundred items, most of them showing a debt to Adam's designs. Sheraton's *The Cabinet-Maker and Upholsterer's Drawing-Book* appeared in four parts between 1791 and 1794 and, as one indication of its merit and usefulness, about six hundred furniture makers throughout England subscribed to it. This was a more original work and was followed by two other publications prepared by the same author. These and other guides published about the same time probably represent the furniture that could be had at the best English workshops in the later eighteenth century.

They also represented the type of furniture that England was exporting to other countries. For, as Hepplewhite asserted in his first edition, "English taste and workmanship have, of late years, been much sought for by surrounding nations." According to British customs records the value of English furniture exported from the country in 1800 was considerably more than thirty-eight thousand pounds, even though war was raging in Europe that year and America was embittered by the British impressment of American seamen. The exports shipped to America were sent either directly to private customers or to cabinetmakers to copy or resell. One of the most prominent furniture shops in London—it employed four hundred apprentices in 1786—was operated by George Seddon, "a man of genius...," according to a German tourist in England that year, "with an understanding for the needs of the needy and the luxurious;...a man who has become intimate with the quality of woods from all parts of the earth...and is for ever creating new forms." One of Seddon's American customers was the beautiful, gracious, enormously wealthy Mrs. William Bingham (the former Anne Willing) of Philadelphia who, supported by her indulgent husband's large fortune, displayed a "passion and thirst after all the luxuries of Europe," and who ruled Philadelphia society during the decade, from 1790 to 1800, the city remained the national capital. "Less money and more years may make her wiser," observed Abigail Adams, who was a witness of that scene, "but she is so handsome she must be pardoned."

A design for a pier table, from George Hepplewhite's Guide, *third edition, 1794*

Young Charles Bulfinch, on his way to becoming New England's most prominent and fashionable architect, thought the Bingham city house was "far *too* rich for *any* man in this country," with its great "white marble staircase, valuable paintings, the richest furniture and the utmost magnificence of decoration." An English visitor to Philadelphia in 1794 noted that among the "superb furniture" in the house was a set of drawing-room chairs from Seddon's, "of the newest taste; the back in the form of a lyre, adorned with festoons of crimson and yellow silk, the curtains of the room a festoon of the same."

Meanwhile, upper-class Englishmen were becoming acquainted with the new styles in furniture and decoration that were developing across the Channel. In 1802, with the short-lived Peace of Amiens ending nine years of war, they swarmed off their little island and over to Paris, as ever to savor the delights of that gay and beautiful city. By September, 1803, ten thousand of them were there, introducing Parisians to the benefits of vaccination, which had been successfully developed in England while the two countries were at war, and taking home memories of the brilliant social scene. This included—for some of the more distinguished tourists—the celebrated *salon* of the beautiful and "ever-virginal" Juliette Récamier and the elaborate receptions of the First Consul, Napoleon Bonaparte, and memories of the new styles in furniture and decoration that could be seen at those occasions. During those years of war America was harboring, particularly in Philadelphia, a large number of French *émigrés*, refugees from the insurrections in Santo Domingo (Haiti) and from the terror of the French Revolution, and later from the absolutism of Napoleon. Some of these early *émigrés* planned to establish a special retreat, a settlement on the banks of the Susquehanna, named Asylum, for Louis XVI and Marie Antoinette. But those unfortunates lost their heads to the guillotine before they could make such a move, and their distant, faithful subjects never quite succeeded in mastering the wilderness. Talleyrand came to Philadelphia in 1793 to rehearse international intrigue on the shores of the Schuylkill. The gastronomist Anthelme Brillat-Savarin came to the same exile and took notes on the American cuisine that he later incorporated into his *Physiologie du Goût*. Also came Médéric Moreau de Saint-Méry, onetime *de facto* president of the Paris Commune, who introduced contraceptives to America and, when he returned to Paris, took with him the Philadelphia system of street numbering—with even addresses on one side, odd addresses on the other. The system is still followed in Paris.

Among still other eminent personages came the Duc d'Orléans who, as Louis

Mrs. William Bingham, by Gilbert Stuart

The Duc d'Orléans and his two brothers picnicking at the Genesee Falls, N.Y.

13

Philippe, a generation later became the Citizen King of France but whose future at the time was uncertain. Following an itinerary prepared for him by George Washington, the duke and his two younger brothers made a tour of the western country, which took them to such remote outposts as Pittsburgh and Niagara Falls and thus back to Philadelphia. When he asked for the hand of the Binghams' daughter in marriage William Bingham, with the solid assurance of a Philadelphia aristocrat, is said to have replied: "Should you ever be restored to your hereditary position you will be too great a match for her; if not she is too great a match for you." Several of these highborn Frenchmen professed to be shocked by the conspicuous luxury of Philadelphia life. The Duc de La Rochefoucauld-Liancourt described entertainments as stylish and splendid as any that he had seen in Europe; and his countryman, Jacques Pierre Brissot de Warville, observing two young ladies at a formal dinner with "very naked" bosoms, was scandalized by "this indecency among republicans." (Others were more concerned that ladies so extremely décolleté would suffer illness from exposure.)

Just what effect, in turn, these French visitors had on America is not easy to determine. One French veteran of the American Revolution, Pierre Charles L'Enfant, stayed on and undertook the remodeling of New York's old City Hall into the first Capitol of the United States, the structure on whose balcony Washington was inaugurated on April 30, 1789. However, when L'Enfant's changes were completed, the structure was more American than French in the character of its elements and the style of its decorations. The grateful citizens offered L'Enfant ten acres of Manhattan real estate as a gift, but this he declined, feeling he had no need to stoop to petty gains. He then proceeded to plan the future capital city of Washington, keeping in mind the great radial avenues and carefully placed principal structures of the royal complex at Versailles.

Almost a century passed before this "capital without a city," this "little village in the midst of the woods," began to resemble L'Enfant's vision. However, the White House—or the President's House as it was first called—was far enough advanced for the Adamses to move into shortly before John Adams' term of office expired in the spring of 1801. "The house is upon a grand and superb scale," Abigail wrote her daughter in the autumn of 1800, "requiring about thirty servants to attend and keep the apartments in proper order, and perform the ordinary business of the house and stables...; lighting the apartments, from the kitchen to parlours and chambers, is a tax indeed; and the fires we are obliged to keep to secure us from daily agues is another very cheering comfort. To assist us in this great castle, and render less attendance necessary, bells are wholly wanting, not one single one being hung through the whole house, and promises are all you can obtain. This is so great an inconvenience, that I know not what to do, or how to do.... The house is made habitable, but there is not a single apartment finished.... We have not the least fence, yard, or other convenience, without, and the great unfinished audience-room I make a drying-room of, to hang up the clothes in.... [But] It is a beautiful spot, capable of every improvement, and, the more I view it, the more I am delighted with it."

When he succeeded Adams as President, Thomas Jefferson gave serious attention to furnishing and finishing the mansion. This epicure and connoisseur, who employed a French chef and steward and whom, because of his love of such alien delights as macaroni in the Italian manner and French wines, Patrick Henry labeled "a man unfaithful to his native victuals," had brought back from Paris in 1790 eighty-six cases of French furniture for his own use. (During his two

Federal Hall, New York, as redesigned by L'Enfant

The east façade of the President's House in Washington, D.C. Drawing by Latrobe, 1807

terms in office Jefferson spent more than ten thousand dollars for wine to be served at his table.) Also, in 1801 he was asked to consider other French pieces for the President's House. "This furniture is elegant," the financier Robert Morris advised him, "and well suited to your apartments, perhaps better than any other in America." No doubt his taste in these matters led to a French accent in the equipment and decoration of the building, although the precise nature of his acquisitions can never be known since in 1814 the British put a torch to them—and to the additions that had been made by the Madisons in the next administration. It seems likely, in any case, that the interiors were taking on that air of elegance which recent presidential families have tried to restore to them.

For some years after the seat of government moved to Washington, Philadelphia remained the most important cultural center of the new nation and the most creative headquarters of the arts and sciences. It was there that Charles Willson Peale, a craftsman-artist of inexhaustible talents, organized America's first art school, which held a public exhibit as early as 1795. There, too, the naturalist William Bartram published his scientific and poetic description of the American scene, a literary masterpiece to which Coleridge, Southey, Chateaubriand, and Wordsworth turned to inform their romantic speculations on the world in general and America in particular. The first four Presidents of the United States quite naturally patronized Philadelphia craftsmen. Jefferson thought the city was more handsome than either Paris or London.

In later years the famous portraitist Gilbert Stuart, who had painted likenesses of all those early Presidents, mischievously stung the local pride of his fellow Bostonians by recalling the days he had spent in "the Athens of America," as he referred to Philadelphia. Others referred to the city as the "London of America." However, no city has ever been to the United States what London, Paris, and Rome so long have been to their respective countries: the main center, not only of government, but of wealth, fashion, population, and culture as well. At Boston, and no less at New York and Charleston, there also flourished a deeply rooted and distinctive urban culture. Each of the burgeoning American cities had been born of widely different circumstances; each had been shaped differently by its separate colonial experience; and the particular inheritance of each was marked in its physical appearance, the character of its population, and the nature of its enterprise. Before the end of the eighteenth century, Baltimore blossomed into another full-fledged city; and in 1803, with the Louisiana Purchase, New Orleans became a colorful addition to this roster of urban communities.

In and about several of those centers there developed a regional expression in the arts that, in the generation following the Revolution, was especially recognizable in cabinetwork. Although the designs that were characteristic of each area were based, sometimes quite literally, on English (and to some degree on French) precedents, in their different ways they took on obvious American attributes. Documentary evidence from this period makes it possible to identify more examples of the work of—and to detect the influence of—individual craftsmen than was true of the colonial period. Duncan Phyfe in New York, John Seymour in Boston, Samuel McIntire in Salem, Henry Connelly in Philadelphia, and John Shaw in Annapolis are just a few of the outstanding craftsmen in different cities who contributed to the creation of a Federal style in furniture—a term used to denote those American equivalents and variants of the neoclassic forms and fashions that prevailed abroad.

Following the Revolution overseas trade provided the main hope of recovery from war and of economic independence. From the time the British blockade was lifted until the Civil War, except for a brief period during the War of 1812, there were few parts of the earth where the Yankee sea trader was not a familiar figure. Sleighing across the winter snows of Russia to tap the inland markets of that vast country, gathering hides at Río de la Plata in South America, and whale oil from the Antarctic, peddling beads and bells for sea otter pelts with natives along the northwest coast of the American continent, and exchanging these and sea slugs, edible birds' nests, and tortoise shell, picked up among the islands of the Pacific, for tea and porcelain at Canton—wherever the waters of the seven seas would carry their sleek little vessels—American seamen went swapping and bargaining their way about the globe.

By 1790 the China trade alone accounted for approximately one seventh of the nation's imports. The first American ship to sail for Canton, the *Empress of China*, which left New York harbor on Washington's birthday, 1784, returned the next year with a mixed cargo that included 137 chests of porcelain. For scores of years to come porcelain remained a staple of that trade; because of its imperishable character, it customarily paid for its way by serving as ballast—and as protection from water damage for teas and silks that were piled on top for the long transit halfway around the world. Of all the exotic freight brought back from the Far East—the silks, lacquers, ivories, and other commodities—the most widely coveted trophies of that trade were those porcelains decorated with patriotic symbols or with designs reflecting the personal interests and enthusiasms of the owner. George and Martha Washington were only the most celebrated of a great number of prominent Americans who had services of such Chinese export porcelain bearing designs of their preference.

In 1793, when most European nations were at war, the United States remained the only important neutral trading country in the world, although neither France nor England, for their separate interests, would consider any trade with the enemy acceptable. Under the circumstances the risks of reaching any market through the gauntlet of hostile ships lining the trade routes rose sharply, but so did the profits from a successful venture. Armed and ready for action,

Engraved label of a looking-glass maker, 1806–10

American vessels kept to the seas until Jefferson imposed an embargo in 1807 in an effort to avoid outright war. Even then ways were found to get around the enactment. John Jacob Astor managed to get one ship off to China, under the pretext of accommodating a "distinguished" Chinese visitor who, he claimed, was needed at home to attend to family affairs. Astor's competitors asserted that the Oriental was but a petty Chinese merchant being used as a blind for Astor's highly private enterprise. Astor's ship, the *Beaver*, the first to reach New York in more than a year, returned with a small fortune in trade goods, to the consternation of rival merchants who had remained tied in port.

For most of a full generation after Americans had secured their independence they had to fit their destiny into a world at war. The outburst of the French Revolution shattered the peace of Europe, and until the final defeat of Napoleon the Continent was in an almost constant turmoil. In his Farewell Address to the American people George Washington had looked forward to the day when they would have grown powerful enough to repel any threat to their own peace from abroad. He knew well enough that since the time of King William's War in the seventeenth century America had been repeatedly involved in the major wars between European powers. He had fought with the English against the French and with the French against the English, each time because America was too weak to stand apart and alone in the protection of its own interests. While wars raged abroad he hoped the new nation might gain time "to settle and mature its yet recent institutions, and to progress without interruption to that degree of strength and consistency, which is necessary to give it, humanly speaking, the command of its own fortunes."

The United States had not yet reached that degree of strength and consistency when it undertook war with England in 1812. In the first year of the conflict the small American navy and a swarm of privateers won spectacular victories on the high seas. When the *United States* brought the British *Macedonian* into New London and the *Constitution* knocked out first the *Guerrière* and then the *Java*, England was stunned. One impudent American sea captain out of Baltimore sent ashore a proclamation, to be posted in Lloyd's Coffee House in London, announcing that the British Isles were blockaded. In the end, however, American men-of-war and the bulk of the American merchant marine were blockaded in their home ports by Britain's overpowering fleet. When the hostilities ended with Andrew Jackson's slaughter of the British forces at New Orleans (peace had already been negotiated, but the news had not yet reached this country) almost everyone rejoiced.

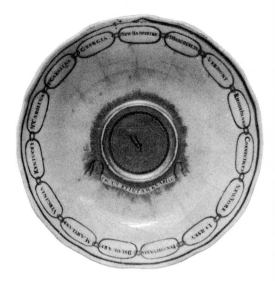

Chinese export porcelain saucer, from a service made for Martha Washington

The battle between the Constitution *and the* Guerrière *in 1812. Painting by Michele Corné*

Design of a Bracket and Vase with Branches
for Candles.
Dessein d'un Tasseau et d'un vase garni de deux
branches pour des Chandelles.

Design of a Glass and Commode Table, upon which is
placed a Clock and vase with Branches for Candles.
Dessein d'un glace et d'un commode avec des vases
garni des branches pour des Chandelles.

Design of a Bracket and Vase with Branches
for Candles.
Dessein d'un Tasseau et d'un vase garni de deux
branches pour des Chandelles.

Design of a Tripod with a Vase and Branches for three Candles.
Dessein d'un trepie et d'un vase portant trois Chandelles.

Design of a Tripod and Vase for Candles.
Dessein d'un trepie et d'un vase servant de Chandelier.

Robert Adam's legacy to the architects and designers of Great Britain was a rich assortment of examples and proposals that led to a complete reversal of taste in such matters over the last three decades of the eighteenth century. When, with his brother James, he issued *The Works in Architecture* in 1773, he noted therein that his ideas had already been imitated by others and that within a relatively few years there had been "an almost total change" in home decoration among the rich and fashionable of England. Thomas Chippendale, whose rococo and eclectic designs had won such wide favor earlier, did some of his finest work under Adam's guidance. The style so strongly associated with Chippendale's own name quickly became "wholly antiquated and laid aside."

Adam's insistence on complete harmony in the interiors of his buildings led him to design new forms of furnishings that would properly complement the architectural backgrounds he established. To create the variety of articles required by such highly co-ordinated schemes, Adam drew imaginatively from his memories of the late classical designs he had seen in Italy and Dalmatia, and from the drawings he had made there. "We flatter ourselves," he wrote, "we have been able to seize, with some degree of success, the beautiful spirit of antiquity, and to transfer it, with novelty and variety, through all our numerous works." The extreme elegance Adam specified put his designs beyond the reach of all but the very wealthy. Before his death in 1792 the furniture and furnishing trades in England had taken over the neoclassic forms and ornament that inspired Adam's designs and modified them to the point where it was practical to offer them to a larger public. As already mentioned, these adaptations were given wide currency by the pattern books of George Hepplewhite and Thomas Sheraton. Interestingly, neither of these authors was known as a distinguished craftsman in his own day. Hepplewhite kept shop in a very ordinary section of London and was not even listed in the city directories. Sheraton, who had worked in his youth as a journeyman cabinetmaker, spent the later years of his life as an impoverished drawing master and Baptist lay reader, scratching out his meager living through his publications. No single piece of furniture has ever been attributed to either of these men, but their names are linked for all time with the forms and motifs recorded in these several editions of their books.

These books quickly found their way to America where craftsmen and their patrons used them for guidance. At times, as in the case of the two chairs with carving by Samuel McIntire of Salem, Massachusetts, the printed designs were copied quite literally; one (2) followed a plate in Hepplewhite (3), the other (4) a plate in Sheraton (5). McIntire not only carved but provided the design (7) for the oval in the back of another chair (6) made by Benjamin Frothingham of Charlestown, Massachusetts, about 1780. By far the largest proportion of the furniture made in America during the federal period reveals a fairly free interpretation of the prevailing English styles as represented in the printed manuals. Very loosely speaking, furniture with straight, tapering legs square in section, with serpentine lines, and with flaring bracket feet (on case pieces) is referred to as being "in the Hepplewhite style," as are chairs with shield- or heart-shaped or oval backs and spade feet. Sheraton's influence is acknowledged in square-back seating furniture, tapering, reeded legs, and projecting elements. As in colonial days, in and about the major cities local preferences led to the development of distinctive regional schools of design, several of which are discussed on the following pages.

1. Opposite: illustration from The Works in Architecture *by Robert and James Adam*

Adam's Heirs

In Federal America

2

3

4

5

6

7

A
Capital City

—◄◆►—

Philadelphia

"Philadelphia may be considered the metropolis of the United States," wrote Jacques Brissot de Warville in 1788. "It is certainly the most beautiful and best-built city in the nation, and also the wealthiest, though not the most ostentatious. Here you find more well-educated men, more knowledge of politics and literature, more political and learned societies than anywhere else in the United States." Brissot was not alone in eulogizing Penn's "greene Country Towne." Every aspect of Philadelphia was hailed by European and American visitors.

One traveler praised the water front, "the largest merchant vessels being able to lie close alongside." Another admired the elegance of the private houses, the raised footways paved with red brick, and the uniformity of the tidy, poplar-shaded streets, which could vie with "the fashionable parts of London." The tranquillity of the market was commented upon, "no drivers and porters swearing at one another;...no madmen galloping at full speed." And Manasseh Cutler, a Massachusetts clergyman, was particularly impressed with the Philadelphia ladies who breakfasted "at half past five, when in Boston they can hardly see a breakfast table at nine without falling into hysterics."

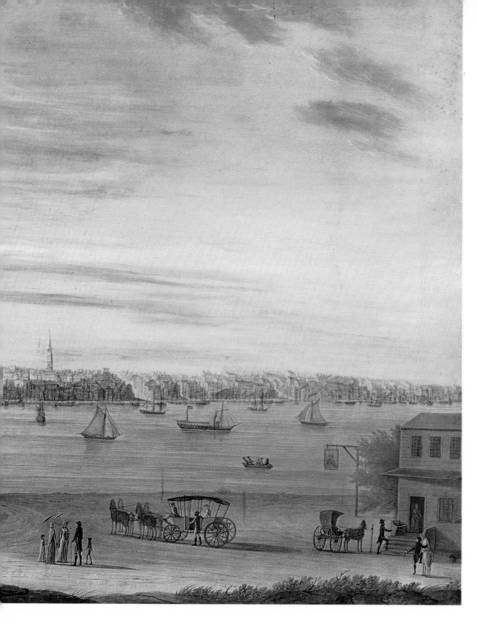

8. *Left: a water color view of Philadelphia as seen from Camden, New Jersey, painted by J. L. Bouquet de Woiseri, around 1810*

9. *Below: an oyster barrow in front of the Chestnut Street Theatre, "a place of fashionable resort," as painted by Paul Svinin*

Philadelphia, at the junction of the Schuylkill and Delaware rivers, held the shipping supremacy of the United States until about 1797, when its foreign trade was eventually surpassed by New York. The construction of the sixty-two-mile Lancaster Pike in the 1790's opened new routes to the West, increased domestic commerce, and sparked Pennsylvania's turnpike-building boom. The first American banks (the Pennsylvania Bank, 1780, and the Bank of North America, 1782) as well as the main branch of the Bank of the United States, 1791, were all in Philadelphia, thus underscoring the city's financial prestige—slowly and grudgingly relinquished to New York in the opening decades of the 1800's. A German traveler, speaking of this intercity rivalry, wrote: "If Philadelphia should become extinct, everybody in New York would rejoice, and vice versa. New York is the vilest of cities, write the Philadelphia journalists. In New York they speak no better of Philadelphia." Earlier in France, the aging Voltaire had rankled at the whims of royalty, mused on the wisdom and tolerance of the Pennsylvania Quakers, and expressed a longing to spend the rest of his life in the "city of brotherly love."

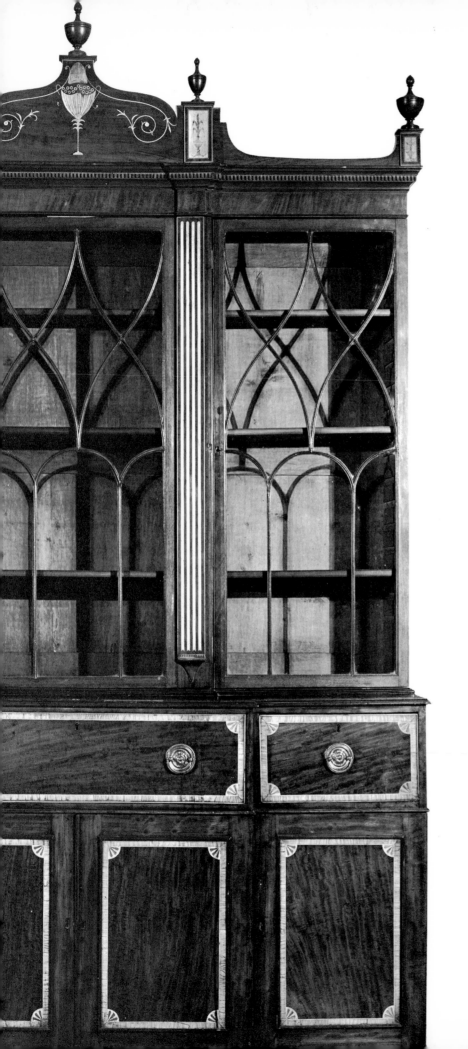

In the highly sophisticated and wealthy city of Philadelphia there was ample demand for furniture made in the latest styles, and there were artisans who were ready and able to satisfy the most exacting customers. As early as 1790 John Aitken, Philadelphia cabinetmaker to George Washington, remarked on "the completest and newest taste now prevailing in this city." The three pieces illustrated on these pages brilliantly display separate facets of that taste as it was interpreted in Philadelphia in the federal period. The kidney-shaped work table (11), made principally of satinwood with colorful inlays, follows no known published design, although it does follow Sheraton's prescription for such a "Table with a Bag, used by the Ladies to work at, in which bag they deposit their fancy needlework." In his *Drawing-Book* Sheraton also referred to the practice of painting and gilding chairs, which, he averred, gave them an effect that could hardly be suggested by his engraved pictures. Gilded furniture was in fact highly favored by John Adams, Thomas Jefferson, James Monroe, and other eminent Americans, all of whom had French examples in their homes and all of whom lived in Philadelphia at some point during the years when the city was the national capital. One rare Philadelphia armchair with upholstered back (12), of a type called "Drawing-Room Chairs" by Sheraton, has survived with such original decoration intact. The massive breakfront bookcase (10), with its satinwood inlay and banding, is one of a unique pair made in the Federal style for the Willings, one of the most prominent families of Philadelphia.

10. *Opposite: detail of one of a matching pair of inlaid mahogany breakfront bookcases*

11. *Above: a lady's work table of satinwood, with mahogany, rosewood, and ebony inlays and a bag for holding fancywork*

12. *Right: armchair painted white and gilded*

23

13. Left: secretary with oval mirrors

14. Above: a veneered and inlaid case for knives, made in the Sheraton style

During the quarter century preceding the Revolutionary War the furniture makers of Philadelphia won lasting acclaim with the exuberant, richly carved pieces they fashioned of solid walnut and mahogany in the Chippendale style. A few of those craftsmen continued to turn out such forms for a decade or two following the war. However, in the waning years of the eighteenth century, those past masters were largely replaced by a new generation of artisans, a number of whom came from far places to work in the largest city of America. As one observer pointed out in 1794, "No cabinet-maker can miss of employment there."

John Davey, who apparently worked in Philadelphia from 1797 to 1822, made the secretary shown here (13) and penciled his name on it, as did his son and probable collaborator. In his play of oval patterns and sharply contrasting, colorful veneers, principally of mahogany and satinwood, Davey was abreast of the latest fashion. The striking effects achieved with veneers of highly figured grains would have been impossible in solid woods. The lower doors conceal drawers, the upper doors, shelves; the middle panel drops forward to provide a writing surface. A knife case (14) from Ormiston, the Edward Burd mansion in Fairmount Park in Philadelphia, has variously grained maple veneers outlined by decorative strings of inlay, composed of contrasting woods, and mounted on a mahogany pedestal and topped by a mahogany finial. According to Sheraton, such pieces were not made in regular cabinet shops; they were, apparently, the work of specialists.

Such practices did not eliminate the use of solid woods or of carved decoration. However, as in the case of the mahogany tilt-top table, or candlestand (15), carving was reduced to relatively low relief in the federal period. The stylized leaf forms associated with reeding typifies such decoration in the Sheraton manner.

15. *A carved mahogany tilt-top table*

25

16. *Left: an armchair possibly made by Ephraim Haines*

17. *Above: detail from Henry Connelly's label, 1808–18*

18. *Lower left: portrait of Connelly, by Thomas Sully*

19. *Below: a sideboard made and labeled by Connelly*

20. *Opposite: mahogany card table in the Sheraton style*

In 1807 Ephraim Haines made a set of black ebony furniture for the French-born financier Stephen Girard, one of Philadelphia's most prominent citizens. These pieces—now preserved in Girard College—cost Girard over five hundred dollars. The bar-back mahogany armchair shown here (16) is very similar to one in that set. In 1811 Haines went into the lumber business and an immigrant cabinetmaker, Henry Connelly (18), took over Girard's patronage. The work of the two craftsmen had much in common: both were indebted to the plates of Sheraton for many of their patterns and both men may have used the same specialists for turning, carving, and other services. A kidney-shaped sideboard (19) in the Sheraton style is definitely Connelly's for it bears his label. The sideboard, a form new to this period, developed from Adam's designs for dining-room furniture. The card table with folding top (20) is similar to the work of both men.

In 1792 it was announced in New York that "the forte piano is become so exceedingly fashionable in Europe that few polite families are without it." Three years earlier George Washington had ordered an American-made piano for his stepgranddaughter, Eleanor Custis. About that time Charles Albrecht of Philadelphia made this instrument with its inlaid mahogany case (23). As might be expected, the cabinetwork reflected the prevailing modes of the period. The several pattern books that illuminated those modes provided an endless variety of designs for chair backs. Both the Philadelphia chairs illustrated (21, 22) owe a debt to Sheraton's *Drawing-Book*. In near-by Manheim, Jacob Eby made a clock (24) whose dial showed the moon's phases. The works are encased in curly maple with decorative inlays.

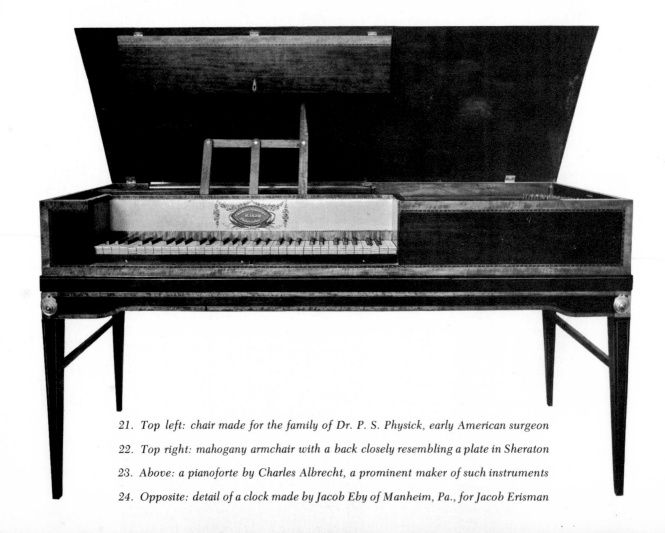

21. *Top left: chair made for the family of Dr. P. S. Physick, early American surgeon*

22. *Top right: mahogany armchair with a back closely resembling a plate in Sheraton*

23. *Above: a pianoforte by Charles Albrecht, a prominent maker of such instruments*

24. *Opposite: detail of a clock made by Jacob Eby of Manheim, Pa., for Jacob Erisman*

Maryland
Center

Baltimore

"Some forty years ago it consisted of several fishermen's huts," wrote Paul Svinin in his description of Baltimore about the time of the War of 1812. "Now it is one of the fairest cities of North America, in point of wealth and trade, occupying the first place after Philadelphia, New York, and Boston." Baltimore had indeed grown by prodigious leaps and bounds. From a mere village in the 1750's, with twenty-five dwellings, two taverns, and one church, the town's population had soared to over twenty-six thousand people by the 1800's. A European later commended the city's "American frankness and French ease."

Moreau de Saint-Méry spoke admiringly of Baltimore's spacious streets and handsome brick houses. He noted the many cotes for doves and swallows and the pleasant belief that these birds would "bring prosperity." He exclaimed at the diversity of church denominations, ten in all, "How admirable is this liberty of religion!" From the hill above the town he was charmed by a park, groves of trees, a stream with a windmill, and mused on "the combination of rustic simplicity with the nearby commerce and marine activity." In a final, approving word he said: "I ate green peas at Baltimore the eighteenth of May, 1794."

25. *Left: Baltimore in 1800, with the two-towered First Presbyterian Church, built in 1791, and the Courthouse "on stilts" over Calvert Street, painted by an unknown artist*

26. *Below: detail from a painting, by Francis Guy, of Perry Hall, the Baltimore home of Harry Dorsey Gough, a wealthy merchant*

The port of Baltimore, which now commanded shipping on Chesapeake Bay, had become a principal market town for the entire South as well as serving a good portion of Pennsylvania, the latter a commercial plum jealously sought by competing Philadelphia merchants. In further rivalry with the long-established ports in the North the Baltimore clippers—long, low, rakish schooners whose speed would win them fame as privateers during the War of 1812—not only enjoyed brisk coastal trade and European trade but also established a rising commercial exchange with South America.

"The merchants occupy the highest social position," wrote a German visitor to Baltimore in 1800. "The ship captains are just below. Many captains manage to accumulate large fortunes, profiting from their dauntlessness and their willingness to risk their lives wherever there is a prospect of making money." In strong contrast to bustling Baltimore was the patrician capital of Maryland, the small but highly social town of Annapolis with its venerable colonial flavor. "Many rich merchants who made their fortunes in Baltimore," continued the German visitor, "come here to enjoy their money in peace."

Baltimore's rocketing prosperity brought an influx of skilled cabinetmakers, many from Great Britain, and the school of design that arose in Maryland was closer to English patterns than any other in America. A London fashion gracefully expressed in Baltimore was painted furniture, or "fancy furniture," an imported fad that supported fifty-odd makers and painters of fancy chairs working in the city at the turn of the century. Among them were John and Hugh Findlay, Irish born and trained, who advertised caned furniture decorated with "real Views, Fancy Landscapes, Flowers, Trophies of Music, War,...Love."

27. Right: a painted settee from Baltimore

27a. Above: detail of Homewood, completed in 1809 for $40,000, and now on the campus of Johns Hopkins University

27b. Opposite, right: detail of the Baltimore building that housed the city's three banking firms. It was constructed about 1801.

This settee (27) is attributed to the Findlays, whose work was among the finest in Baltimore. (During Madison's administration, for example, Latrobe commissioned them to execute a suite of furniture for the President's House.) On the top rail, the left-hand oval (27a) depicts Homewood, built by Charles Carroll, son and namesake of the signer of the Declaration of Independence, as a wedding gift from his father. The center oval (27b) shows the Baltimore bank building. The right-hand oval represents Mount Clare, completed in 1760 by yet another Charles Carroll, which remains as Baltimore's oldest manor house.

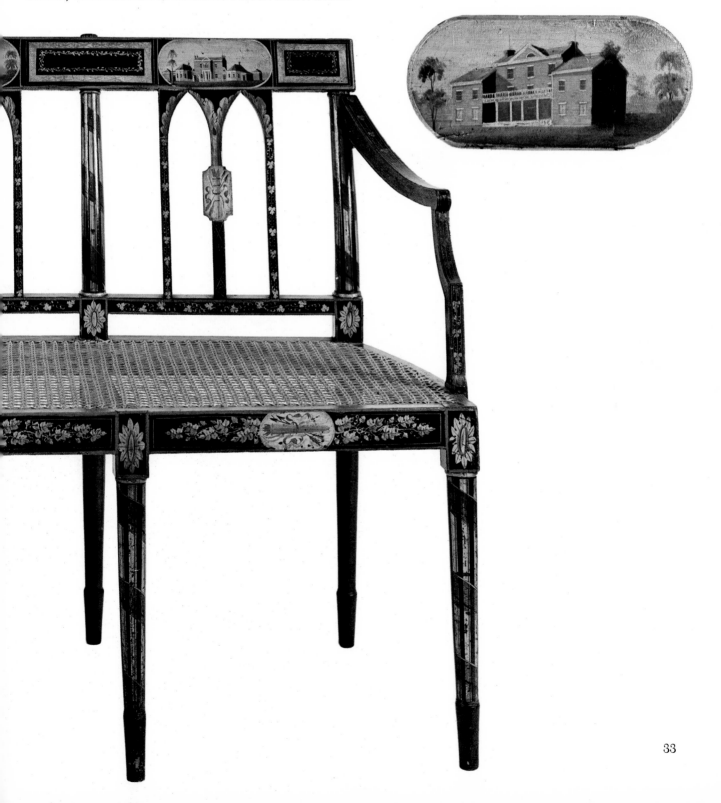

Possibly the most distinctive feature of Baltimore's Federal furniture was the use of painted glass, or *verre églomisé*, as decorative inserts. The word *églomisé* was derived from the name of an eighteenth-century French frame maker and designer, Jean-Baptiste Glomi. However, the technique of backing painted glass with silver or gold foil was an ancient one known in early Damascus, used during the Renaissance, and introduced into England from France late in the 1600's. In these Baltimore examples the figures on the skirt of the encoignure, or corner table (29), come from a design in Sheraton's *Accompaniment* (1802), "a faint moonlight scene, representing Diana in a visit to Endymion." The source of the figures on the mahogany and satinwood-veneered desk (30) is as yet unknown. The detail (28) from a similar desk is of "Temperance." In no other American city were English furniture styles interpreted with such exuberant ornamentation.

28. Above: a detail of an allegorical figure on a painted glass panel (from a desk not shown)

29. Left: a corner table in the Sheraton style

30. Opposite: "Cabinet and Writing Table"

36

Among decorative techniques employed by Baltimore's cabinetmakers the profuse and artful use of inlay became a regional characteristic in itself. The high degree of workmanship achieved by Maryland's craftsmen is illustrated in this detail (34) of oak leaves, ropes and tassels from the leg of a Hepplewhite card table. A distinctly regional touch was given the popular bellflower design by elongating the central petal, as shown on the legs of the pembroke table (31), a piece used for breakfasting or writing. Here the bellflower pendant is suspended by a loop, a fanciful device also used on two Baltimore chairs (38, 39) shown on page 38.

The inlaid mahogany card table (35), one of a pair, demonstrates the variety of contrasting woods which so frequently exemplifies Baltimore cabinetwork. Satinwood was used for the inlays on the legs, and rosewood for the urn, which is set in a background of curly maple. The sewing table (32), one of the new Federal fashions, is inlaid with satinwood and ebony. For the interior of the mahogany and satinwood secretary (33) zebrawood was used to face the four drawers and the doors to the side compartments. The pediment of this secretary was inspired by Sheraton's plate of "Pediments for Bookcases" in his *Drawing-Book*.

Many furniture makers, particularly in large cities, could buy inlay ready-made from masters of this exacting craft, and it is quite possible that some inlay and stringing were also imported from Europe.

31. Opposite, above: pembroke table with bellflower inlay

32. Opposite, below: oval Hepplewhite sewing table

33. Opposite: secretary by Joseph Burgess of Baltimore

34. Top: detail of inlay from a card table (not shown)

35. Above: a card table with inlay typical of Baltimore

36. *Above: a mahogany cupboard with flame-grained oval insets, holly borders on the doors, and neoclassic inlays on the top and on the skirt*

37. *Top right: chair by John Shaw.* 38. *Center right: Hepplewhite chair*

39. *Bottom right: Sheraton chair.* 40. *Opposite: Sheraton mixing table*

Among popular specialized forms of the federal period was the mixing table, a hospitable adjunct designed for serving drinks. In the White House inventory, 1809, Jefferson listed "an elegant Mahogany *drink Table* with a Marble Top." This one (40), with its decanter drawers and tamboured roll top, is handsomely inlaid in the Baltimore style; the "cuffs" on the legs were a typical regional device. Oval inlays set within mitered panels were also widely used, as on the doors of this cupboard (36). On the side chair (39), with the square back, the upholstery covers only half the rail (a detail found on many Baltimore sofas), there is beading at the upholstery line and a strip of inlay at the lower edge of the rail, and there are teardrop or carrot-shaped insets on the front legs. The side chair (38), with its oval back shaped in a favored Baltimore design, again shows the teardrop motif in the piercings of the splats. Scottish-born John Shaw, who practiced his craft in Annapolis and has been credited with initiating the Federal tradition in Maryland, made the side chair (37) which incorporates the eagle—a ubiquitous national symbol—within the carved splat.

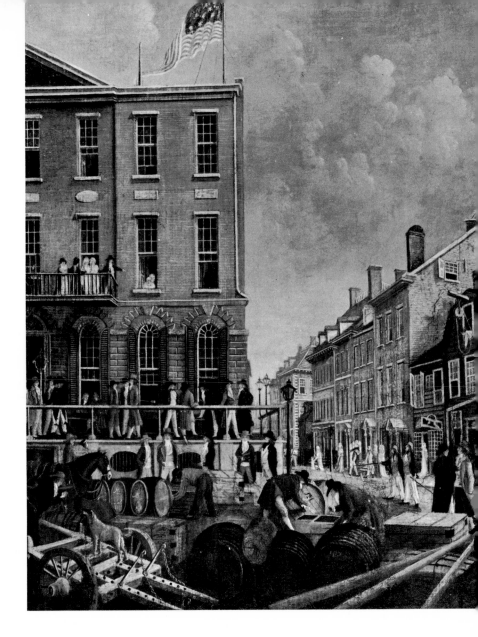

Metropolis on the Hudson

New York

Although British occupation forces had left New York warworn and fire-ravaged, the city quickly recovered its commercial footing and by 1797 had surpassed its rival ports, Boston and Philadelphia, in foreign trade. Between 1792 and 1807 New York's registered tonnage would treble, and the multitude of ships moored on the East River alone "looked like a Forest." As for the city itself, "On all sides houses are going up and streets are being laid out; everywhere I see workers filling land, excavating, building, laying pavements, erecting public pumps." One of the most important of the new buildings was the Tontine Coffee House where two books were kept, as at Lloyd's in London, of every ship's arrival and departure. Here merchants, brokers, bankers, and insurance agents met daily to transact their business, and here the New York stock exchange had its quarters—lately removed from its earlier alfresco site under a Wall Street buttonwood tree. The bloom of prosperity was pervasive. Albany, at the head of sloop navigation on the Hudson River, sent ships to Europe and the West Indies and became the hub for turnpikes radiating into New York State's frontier lands, to cities in Vermont, and to New England seaports.

41. *Left: the Tontine Coffee House, at Wall and Water streets, is the building at the left in this painting by Francis Guy, about 1798.*

42. *Below: the pump at Greenwich and Dey streets is shown below in a detail from a water color done on a January day in 1810 by the French Baroness Hyde de Neuville.*

The flavor of New York City was highly cosmopolitan, attracting prominent visitors both from home and abroad. In its brief but brilliant year as the nation's capital social activities reached dazzling heights. "Public dinners, public days, and private parties may take up a person's whole attention if they attend to them all," John Adams' daughter complained gently. But a young man visiting in Savannah, homesick for the city's whirl, wrote that he "would rather live in New York with 100 pounds than live here with as many thousands." Meanwhile, *The Boston Gazette* was gratified to note that "our beloved President stands unmoved in the vortex of folly and dissipation which New York presents."

For everyday folk, New York offered such amusements as balloon ascensions, waxwork museums, fireworks, tightrope dancers, band concerts, and tea gardens, not to mention such diversions as the city's some three hundred thirty taverns and grogshops or public hangings at the Fields (now City Hall Park), the gallows set in a "gaudily painted Chinese pagoda." A rural aura, however, had not yet been dispelled. Pigs and goats scavenged the streets, and cows ambled down Broadway at milking time. Porpoises still tumbled in New York's harbor.

43. *Above: a mahogany wing chair*

44. *Below: desk in the French manner*

The international commerce that brought such goods as English shoe buckles, Barcelona handkerchiefs, Canton fans, and Holland gunpowder to New York also brought rich crosscurrents of fashion. Mrs. John Jay gave dinners "à la mode Française." Women wore plumed hats "à l'Espagnole" and gowns trimmed "à la Henri IV." Uniforms copied from Frederick the Great's Prussian guard were worn by a troop of New York grenadiers in Washington's inaugural parade, while yet another company was in full Scottish regalia—with kilts and bagpipes. Washington's cream-colored state carriage was decorated with cupids and garlands, but his inaugural costume was an unadorned "republican" suit of brown broadcloth from a Hartford mill. The inauguration was held at Federal Hall (built in 1699 and formerly New York's second City Hall), newly remodeled in a classical design by Major Pierre L'Enfant, the French-born architect. The surviving furniture from that building, in keeping with L'Enfant's background, shows a decided kinship to the neoclassic styles of the Louis XVI period. In this mahogany desk (44), reputedly used by Washington, the legs are carved in stopped fluting and the corner blocks trimmed with disc-shaped ornaments, or paterae—both typical of Louis XVI design. The easy, or wing, chair (43), found on Long Island, offers an example of mingling fashions: the back in the Chippendale, the straight legs in the Federal style.

45. Right: detail from the speaker's desk that was used in New York's Federal Hall

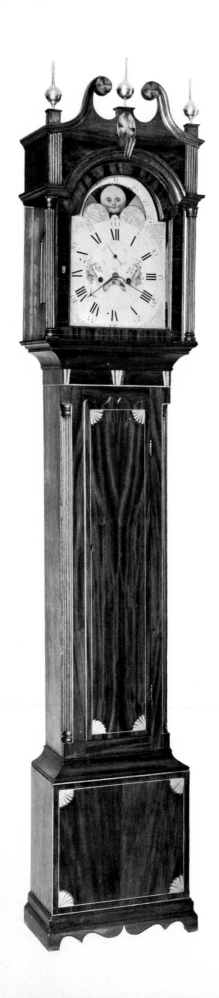

46. A Sheraton side chair

47. Hepplewhite side chair

As in Philadelphia, New York artisans also established a book of prices. In the 1802 edition the Sheraton side chair (46) is precisely described, at eighteen shillings and six-pence, as "A Square Back Chair, No. III., With gothic arch-es, and four turned columns...plain taper'd legs." The legs in this example curve outward in the French style. The shield-back chair (47), a favorite pattern in New York, is un-usual for its lavish combination of both inlay and carving, and in accordance with the price books each detail chosen by the patron raised the cost of the finished product. Fine furniture was also made in other areas of New York State. The tall case clock (48) comes from the village of Lansing-burgh, now part of Troy. Clocks remained a rarity even among the wealthy; between 1800 and 1820 inventories of ten well-to-do households listed four hundred eighty-two chairs, but only one clock. In Albany (which in 1792 had im-pressed Timothy Dwight, president of Yale, as little more than a Dutch river port with muddy streets) exceptionally beautiful looking glasses were being made, many with painted glass panels. This chimney glass (49), or overmantel looking glass, is of gesso, white pine, and wire, and overlaid with gold leaf—the handiwork of an unknown master crafts-man, about 1805. It originally belonged to Joseph C. Yates, mayor of Schenectady and later governor of New York.

48. *Left: a mahogany clock, the inlaid fans typical of New York*

49. *Opposite: chimney glass shown in a room of the federal period*

50. *Top: a tea chest veneered in mahogany and satinwood*

51. *Above: mahogany side table from a dining-room set*

52. *Right: an inlaid sideboard with matching veneers*

In 1789 Vice President and Mrs. John Adams lived on the outskirts of New York, in Greenwich Village, on an estate set in forests of oak and pine. "In front of the house, the noble Hudson rolls his majestic waves," wrote Mrs. Adams. "Beyond the Hudson rises to our view the fertile country of the Jerseys, covered with a golden harvest." The island of Manhattan abounded in such estates. "The rides in the neighbourhood of the city are for miles beautiful," wrote Governor John Drayton of South Carolina, during a visit to New York. "Every elevation of ground, presenting some handsome country seat."

Among the furnishings of such countryseats and New York's town houses, sideboards were a fashionable new fixture. "The convenience it affords renders a dining room incomplete without a sideboard," declared Hepplewhite's *Guide*, and Sheraton emphasized the "grand effect" sideboards produced in "spacious dining-rooms." This one (52), attributed to Matthew Egerton, Jr., of New Brunswick, New Jersey, has inner legs set on a diagonal, a characteristic of sideboards from the New York area. Architect John McComb, who built New York's City Hall, 1802–12, in collaboration with the French architect Joseph F. Mangin, designed his own dining-room furniture. The side table (51) is a piece from that set. The tea chest (50), also an example of the delicate elegance of the federal period, has an interior divided into three sections, which were shaped to hold three rectangular canisters for as many different kinds of tea.

53. *Right: a detail from Michael Allison's label*

54. *Below: Hepplewhite bureau with inlays*

55. *Opposite, top: Sheraton mahogany chair*

56. *Opposite, bottom: a Hepplewhite chair*

Among the innumerable chair patterns created by varying combinations of motifs this example (55) offers an array of designs favored in New York: the square back with its draped-urn splat and three feathers, the serpentine arms and supports, the carved rosettes at the junctures of arms and supports, and the reeded legs. The shield-back armchair (56) again illustrates the popularity of drapery motifs in splat designs. The carving of the leaves from which the drapery is suspended suggests that this chair, one of a pair, may possibly be the early work of Duncan Phyfe.

With the Hepplewhite bureau (54) there is no doubt either of its maker or of its owner. The top right-hand drawer bears the label of Michael Allison. Another drawer carries the inscription: "Maria Mayo Scotts chest of drawers given her by her mother." Although "chest of drawers" appears in this instance, the word "bureau" was coming into general use in America. In England, however, a bureau continued to mean a slant-top desk, and "dressing chest" was the designation for a chest of drawers.

Michael Allison, active from 1800 to 1845, was one of the leading cabinetmakers in New York during both the Federal and the Empire periods. His shop was on Vesey Street in the same section of the city as that of his contemporary Duncan Phyfe on Partition Street (later renamed Fulton Street). New York was moving uptown in the early years of the century, and both these craftsmen were handily situated to the fine town houses that lined Broadway and looked out across the four-acre park where the new City Hall was rising—its façade in the Louis XVI style, its walls of Massachusetts marble.

Across from City Hall Park was the Park Theatre, where New York's first families viewed performances from the tiers of gilt-trimmed boxes. One block south was St. Paul's, where the fashionable thronged to Sunday services. (One New York belle wrote that St. Paul's was *the* place to "ogle the beaux.") And on Broadway, near Vesey Street, stood the mansion that Senator Rufus King sold, about 1802, for the sum of $27,500 to a German butcher's son named John Jacob Astor, who was making his entering bid into the upper ranks of New York society.

The Hub
of
New England

—◆—

Boston

Proper Bostonians were not to be teased out of their own convictions by Gilbert Stuart's barbed reference to Philadelphia as "the Athens of America." As one of the Cabots observed in 1804, among the people of New England there were "more wisdom and virtues than in any other part of the world." And during the federal period, as before and after, Boston remained the hub of New England. The Crowninshields and Derbys of Salem and "Lord" Timothy Dexter and the other opulent merchants who lined Chestnut Street in Newburyport with their stately mansions might have liked to quarrel with that last statement. But Boston was still the largest and most important city north and east of New York, even though it was losing ground to other leading cities in the game of counting heads and in the race for size.

Boston lads acquired a taste for salt water with their mother's milk. Few of them could escape the temptation of going to sea, to make their fortunes if all went well, and then to settle down to manage their affairs from land. More than a few who thus made good commissioned the young Charles Bulfinch to build them new homes to match their important stations in the city's life. "The

57. Left: State Street, Boston, and the old State House, the seat of government until 1798; painting by James B. Marston, 1801

58. Below: detail of a painting showing a "stag" dinner at a well-equipped table in Boston; by Henry Sargent, early 19th century

great number of new and elegant buildings which have been erected in this Town, within the last ten years," remarked one returning visitor in 1808, "strike the eye with astonishment, and prove the rapid manner in which the people have been acquiring wealth."

In 1798 Bulfinch finished the new Massachusetts State House atop Beacon Hill, whose lofty gilded dome, covered with copper by Paul Revere and Son in 1802, almost threw a shadow on its venerable predecessor, shown above. Among many other splendid residences he also built three houses for the eminent lawyer and speculator Harrison Gray Otis who, after forty years of gout and at the age of eighty, continued to breakfast daily on *pâté de foie gras.* Another contemporary Bostonian, John Cushing, after profitable years in the China trade, settled back in the South End and surrounded his house with a fence of brilliantly colored Chinese porcelain, and his Cantonese servants wore their native dress. By the end of the eighteenth century Boston had lost most traces of its earlier Puritanism, even though in the 1790's the first plays to be staged in the city were advertised as "Moral Lectures" in an effort to avoid official censorship.

51

In 1809 Thomas Seymour, cabinetmaker of Boston, billed Mrs. Elizabeth Derby eighty dollars for a "Large Mahogany Comode" (59). The bill included another item of ten dollars paid to John Ritto Penniman, a Boston artist, for painting the sea shells on the top (59a). Although Mrs. Derby was the daughter of Elias Hasket Derby, the immensely wealthy Salem ship owner, she did not settle her account until 1812. On the same account there was a charge for carving furniture, "legs & orniment," performed for Seymour by Thomas Whitman. Whitman worked for several cabinetmakers, including John Doggett, who specialized in looking glasses and who in 1809 charged Mrs. Derby four dollars for "re-gilding 1 oval dressing glass frame"—possibly the one mounted on this little dressing stand (61). Like these two pieces, the inlaid, mahogany-veneered sideboard (60)—with its tambour doors, ivory vase-shaped escutcheons, and brass lion-head drawer pulls—is an eloquent translation of the Sheraton style into a Boston idiom.

59, 59a. Opposite: semicircular chest of drawers of satinwood and mahogany veneer with carved, painted, and inlaid decoration, from the Seymour shop

60. Below: carved and inlaid mahogany sideboard, made in or about Boston in the early 19th century

61. Bottom: satinwood and mahogany dressing glass with gilded frame, possibly made by Seymour

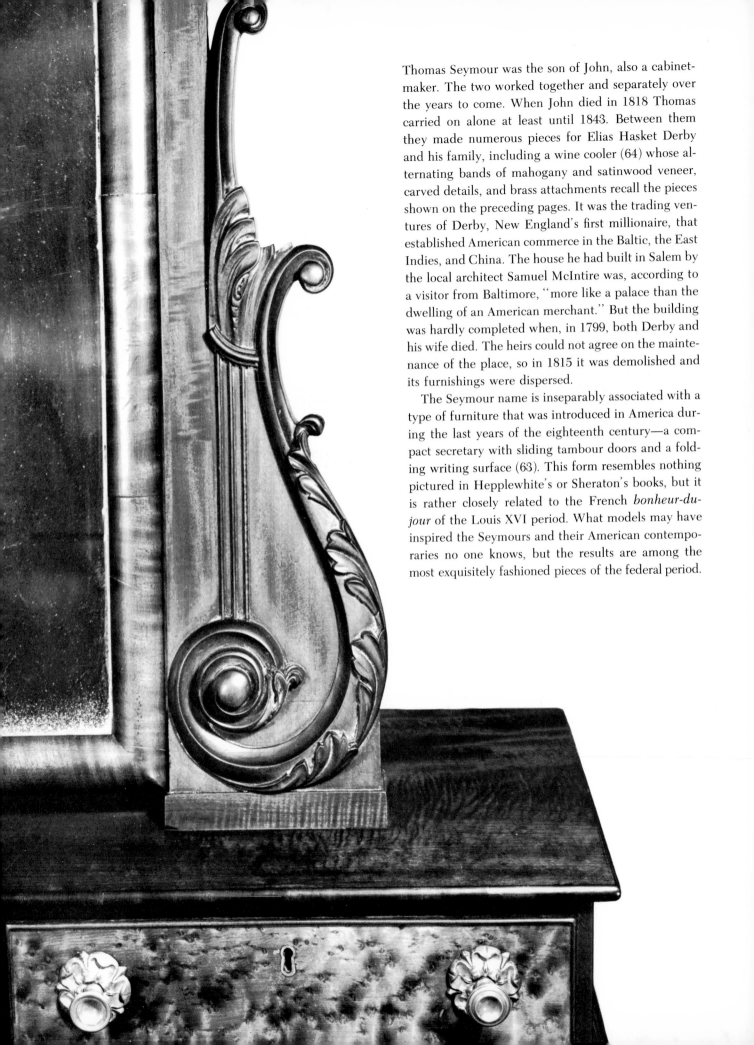

Thomas Seymour was the son of John, also a cabinet-maker. The two worked together and separately over the years to come. When John died in 1818 Thomas carried on alone at least until 1843. Between them they made numerous pieces for Elias Hasket Derby and his family, including a wine cooler (64) whose alternating bands of mahogany and satinwood veneer, carved details, and brass attachments recall the pieces shown on the preceding pages. It was the trading ventures of Derby, New England's first millionaire, that established American commerce in the Baltic, the East Indies, and China. The house he had built in Salem by the local architect Samuel McIntire was, according to a visitor from Baltimore, "more like a palace than the dwelling of an American merchant." But the building was hardly completed when, in 1799, both Derby and his wife died. The heirs could not agree on the maintenance of the place, so in 1815 it was demolished and its furnishings were dispersed.

The Seymour name is inseparably associated with a type of furniture that was introduced in America during the last years of the eighteenth century—a compact secretary with sliding tambour doors and a folding writing surface (63). This form resembles nothing pictured in Hepplewhite's or Sheraton's books, but it is rather closely related to the French *bonheur-du-jour* of the Louis XVI period. What models may have inspired the Seymours and their American contemporaries no one knows, but the results are among the most exquisitely fashioned pieces of the federal period.

62. *Opposite: a detail from a Seymour bureau*

63. *Above: mahogany tambour desk, which is virtually identical to a labeled Seymour piece*

64. *Below: a wine cooler in Hepplewhite style*

65. Sofa with carved eagle and drapery festoons

Of all the craftsmen called upon to give the Derby mansion fittings worthy of a merchant prince, Samuel McIntire was the most versatile. In the course of his life he was a carpenter and a carver, who worked on ships and buildings alike, a designer, an architect, a sculptor, and a musician of sorts. "His industry, usefulness and consistent virtues gave him an uncommon share of the affections of all who knew him," as one obituary recalled. "By his own well directed energies, he became one of the best of men."

For some reason, in spite of his varied skills, he seems to have done little or no cabinetwork, although he added decorative carving to the furniture made by a number of his neighboring contemporaries. In 1802 and again in 1803 McIntire billed the Salem cabinetmaker Jacob Sanderson for carving and "working" the top rails of sofas. Several years later it seems McIntire did similar work on a sofa, very closely resembling the one shown here and of a type known to contemporary designers as a "Square Sofa," for Nehemiah Adams, another Salem furniture maker. The design for this piece (65) is straight out of Sheraton's *Drawing-Book*, but the carved ornament (with raised elements set against a stippled background), like the motifs carved on the two chairs (66, 67), is in McIntire's individual style. The first of those two chairs is probably one of a set of six made for the Derby family.

66. *Above: a Hepplewhite chair carved by McIntire*

67. *Left: a side chair. The top rail is carved with a basket of fruit, a decorative motif favored by McIntire.*

68. *Above: a card table carved by McIntire;
one of a pair made for Elias Hasket Derby*

69. *Below: a work table carved by McIntire*

Among the many artisans, European, Asian, and American, whom the Derby family patronized for their various purposes were Paul Revere, silversmith and man of affairs in Boston, and one William Lemon, cabinetmaker of Salem. Lemon is best remembered for the elaborately carved chest-on-chest (70), or double chest of drawers, he made for Derby's daughter, Elizabeth, in 1796. On October 22 of that year McIntire billed Elizabeth directly for carving "a Case of Drawers Made by Mr. Lemon," undoubtedly this same one, with among other features its carved cornucopia spilling out fruit, flowers, and leaves (70a). About the same time, McIntire used an almost identical motif on a card table (68), one of a pair made for Elias Hasket Derby himself.

Meanwhile, from the end of the Revolution to his death in 1811, McIntire designed and worked on a score of buildings in and about Salem, native and personal versions of the Adam style that gave a new grace and dignity to the local scene. In the tradition of earlier fine craftsmen, he also tackled such modest jobs as mending fences and building pigsties. "Directed by an ear of exquisite nicety" he also performed on different musical instruments and repaired them when they were out of order. As one Salem minister stated the day McIntire died: "All the Instruments we use he could understand & was the best person to be employed in correcting any defects." As he further observed, there was no one left in Salem who could take the place of this versatile craftsman.

70. *Chest-on-chest made for Derby by Lemon and carved by McIntire*

70a. *Detail of carving from the above*

71. *Top: the Sargent family of Massachusetts, by an unidentified artist, 1800. Mrs. Sargent sits in a Martha Washington chair; two of the children stand before Hepplewhite chairs.*

72. *Left: a mahogany and maple bureau from Portsmouth, N.H.*

73. *Above: an open arm- or "lolling" chair from Portsmouth*

74. *Opposite: detail of a carved mahogany and satinwood sofa*

As in the colonial period, when craftsmen moved from one community to another, they carried with them the tricks of their trades and styles that were popular where last they worked. Although this tended to bring about a wide uniformity of style, local differences persisted. The designs of these pieces (72, 73, 74), for example, suggest they were made in Portsmouth, New Hampshire. In the federal period, it was said, there were more private carriages and liveried servants in Portsmouth in proportion to the population than in any other community in New England. When Washington visited the town in 1789, it was recalled some years later, the Portsmouth meetinghouse was filled with "ancient, venerable forms [that] loom out of the distant dimness, arrayed in all the splendor of the costume of the court of George the Third. Immense wigs, white as snow, coats trimmed with gold lace, embroidered waistcoats, ruffles...[and] cocked hats."

One of the most graceful, and most distinctively American, chairs ever made was developed in the federal period, the so-called Martha Washington chair (73). When and why it acquired that name no one knows; the form, with its high upholstered back and open arms was known as a "lolling" chair to contemporaries. To loll, according to the *Oxford English Dictionary* definition, means "to lean idly; to recline or rest in a relaxed attitude."

75. One of a pair of carved and gilded looking glasses

American craftsmen of the federal period occasionally offered imported wares for sale along with the products of their own workshops. This was particularly true of looking-glass makers. The making of the carved and gilded frames typical of the period was a specialized craft requiring skills in the use of composition and wired ornament and gold leaf. And it was costly work. In 1790 Abigail Adams wrote to her sister from her temporary residence in New York, then the national capital, asking for the "large looking glass" from her Massachusetts home, since she could not do without such a convenience and could not afford to buy another like it. In any case, she wrote, "this House is much better calculated for the Glasses, having all the Rooms Eleven foot high." In the 1788 edition of his *Guide* Hepplewhite observed that as many as nine looking glasses were hung on the walls of the "Dining Parlours of our first nobility." Twenty-

one years later, however, there were only two in the large dining room of the President's House in Washington. The example above (75), with its painted glass panel, side-bracket candleholders, and a carved eagle, is one of a pair that was made in Massachusetts. Writing of what he called a "Gentleman's Secretary," Sheraton explained that "this piece is intended for a gentleman to write at, to keep his own accounts, and serves as a library. The style of finishing is neat, and sometimes approaching to elegance." Forms of this general description seem to have won especial favor among the craftsmen of northeastern New England. A whole category of such secretaries, as a consequence, have been loosely termed "Salem secretaries." Among the most colorful and elegant examples in this group is one (76) with two oval mirrors and painted glass panels depicting vases with bouquets and fashionably clad ladies.

76. A "Gentleman's Secretary" with mahogany and satinwood veneers and decorative glass panels, from northeastern Mass.

Gilbert Stuart, Maker of Resemblances

"His canvas was ready on his easel," wrote Eliza Susan Quincy in 1824, in describing a visit to Gilbert Stuart's Boston studio where a portrait of her father, Josiah Quincy, was in progress. "A bold outline was sketched in chalk while conversing rapidly. Mr. Stuart began to put on his colors, apparently at random but of course every touch told." When she repeated a comment to Stuart that the portrait was worthy of the old masters, "he replied with a sharp glance of his piercing eye, 'And am I not an old master, Miss Quincy?'"

Gilbert Stuart was then sixty-nine years old (four years away from his death), heavily addicted to snuff and strong drink, and famed for his scathing wit, irascible disposition, and chronic insolvency. In poignant contrast to the youthful self-portrait at left is the picture of Stuart painted in 1825 by John Neagle, which shows the master in his

old age. "A passionate man and a great liar," wrote one of his students. An "indolent, thoughtless being," wrote Charles Willson Peale. "A vain proud man and withal quick tempered," wrote Henry Sargent. John Adams, however, that stern exponent of Puritan virtues, was so charmed by the artist's wit and conversation, he remarked that he "should like to sit to Stuart from the first of January to the last of December." And Dolley Madison kindly excused Stuart's erratic, imprudent ways by pointing out that as a "man of

genius, he of course does things differently from other people."

As to his genius, there was no disagreement, even among the severest critics of Stuart's personal eccentricities. Certainly Stuart himself never hesitated to proclaim his own talents. He was a master indeed, as he had sharply reminded Miss Quincy, and had been hailed as such during the fifty years of his international career.

Stuart was born on December 3, 1755, in North Kingston, Rhode Island, a town it later amused him to describe as "six miles from Pottawoone, and ten miles from Poppasquash." His boyhood was spent in Newport where his father, an easygoing Scottish immigrant, pursued his unsuccessful trade as a snuff grinder. Dr. Benjamin Waterhouse, a lifelong friend of Gilbert's, recalled him as "a self-willed boy, who, perhaps on that account, was indulged in every thing, being an only son; handsome and forward, and habituated at home to have his own way in every thing." The self-willed boy's artistic bent was recognized by a Newport physician, who gave him his first paints and brushes and then ordered a picture—a pair of spaniels under a table. And thanks to the doctor, Stuart became the apprentice of a Scottish artist, Cosmo John Alexander, who was painting portraits in America. Young Stuart returned with Alexander to Edinburgh in 1771, but with his master's abrupt death the following year the seventeen-year-old apprentice was left friendless and starving. He worked his way home on a collier, set himself up as a portraitist in Newport, and won an immediate patronage among the local gentry and merchants. His work at this time, in crude imitation of Alexander's stock compositions, shows Stuart's gift for catching a likeness, but his portraits bore the constrained, detailed mark of the primitive painter.

Buoyed by his success in Newport, Stuart once more sailed for Great Britain in 1775. But London, the brash young colonial discovered, was not so easily conquered. The naïve portraits that had suited his Newport patrons were trifling, stilted efforts next to the English style of portraiture—the Grand Style, as it has been called, richly decorative, monumental in feeling, a neo-classic reflection of Michelangelo, Raphael, Correggio.

He briefly sustained himself as an organist in a London church. (Stuart was always fond of music, dabbled in composition, and played a number of instruments.) He painted a few portraits but, driven by his own demons of despair, left others unfinished on his easel, or willfully accepted payment and then made no attempt to fulfill the commission. "With Stuart it was either high tide or low tide. In London he would sometimes lay in a bed for weeks, waiting for the tide to lead him on to fortune," wrote Waterhouse, then studying medicine in England. "Of my allowance of pocket-money he always had two thirds, and more than once the other third." Stuart was twice seized by bailiffs for his debts and was rescued from the "sponging-houses" (temporary quarters for debtors) by his patient friend. By the spring of 1777 Stuart was reduced to one meal a day and had no means to pay his landlord. In the depths of misery he wrote to Benjamin West, the Pennsylvania Quaker expatriate and court painter to George III, to implore West's pity and charity.

Stuart was taken into West's household, and here his studies began in earnest. Confident, irrepressible, and secure in the snug haven of West's studio, his brilliant knack for portraiture was released into the fluent, glowing style that distinguished his mature work. West once remarked to his other pupils: "It's no use to steal Stuart's colors; if you want to paint as he does you must steal his eyes." In 1782 Stuart's portrait, *The Skater*, was the sudden and unqualified hit of the Royal Academy art show. "A noble portrait. . .the most powerful effect." "Everyone is enchanted with it." Stuart, who two years earlier had looked "more like a beggar than a painter," was catapulted into the world of the rich, the famous, and the influential. He moved into fashionable quarters, charged fees surpassed only by Gainsborough and Reynolds, hired a French chef, entertained lavishly, and dressed in the costly attire of the dandy. "As he has said of himself, he was a great beau."

In 1786 Stuart married Charlotte Coates, the eighteen-year-old daughter of an English physician. Evidently an unprepossessing young woman, she was doomed to play the role of the long-suffering wife of an irresponsible genius. She would bear twelve children, of whom six survived, and would spend her life regretting her husband's reckless extravagance, "or what she called his folly." The telling comment would one day be made that Stuart's "family appeared to fear him."

In 1787, at the peak of his profession, Stuart's prodigal existence caught up with him. He fled London, his debts, and the bailiffs, sailed to Dublin, and again established himself as the leading painter of the social and political elite. Years later an admirer would say: "Ah, no one could paint a head like our Irish Stuart." It seems to have been a time of comparative peace. He and his family lived on a farm outside Dublin, where Stuart found enormous pleasure in his garden, his orchard, and his apple-fattened pigs. But the persistent specter of unpaid debts arose once more, despite his artistic triumphs. In 1793 he fled the bailiffs yet again, this time to the United States, leaving behind him a number of incomplete canvases which he lightly bequeathed to the artists of Dublin, suggesting with wry indifference that they would "get employed in finishing them."

Stuart arrived in America with all the prerequisites for success. He was a London celebrity, a *bon vivant*, and above all, a brilliant painter. There were no artists in America to rival him. Stuart, in short, became "all the rage," as a Philadelphia friend of Dolley Madison's expressed it. Stuart himself expressed it in equally superlative terms: "In England my efforts were compared to those of Vandyck, Titian, and other great painters—but, here they compare them to the works of the Almighty!" In less than two years after his return to America he painted more than thirty-five pictures and climaxed this burst of creativity with his portraits of the President. Washington posed for Stuart three times, the sittings diplomatically arranged through the intercession of such lights of the Republican Court as John Jay and Mr. and Mrs. William Bingham. Despite contemporary comments

of approval or disapproval of the likenesses caught by Stuart's brush, to posterity his images of Washington *are* Washington. As to Stuart's motives in securing the President as a model, they were apparently quite mercenary rather than patriotic. Before leaving Dublin he had boasted that in the United States he expected "to make a fortune by Washington alone. I calculate upon making a

plurality of his portraits." And this he proceeded to do, dashing off copies to which he coolly referred as his "hundred-dollar bills," the price he put on them. Ironically enough, for an artist so beset by financial headaches, one of Stuart's portraits of Washington was fated to be reproduced by the billions—on the dollar bill.

But Stuart was still driven to let any fortune within his grasp slip away. Although his five successive studios in New York, Philadelphia, Germantown, Washington, and Boston were besieged by patrons, Stuart's pattern of living did not alter. "He was a very capricious man, and would never paint unless he was in the humor," observed Thomas Sully. And as a Boston lady cautiously phrased it: "he loves a cheerful bottle and does no work in the afternoon;... he is said to be poor." The rumor was accurate. When Stuart died in Boston on July 9, 1828, he died in debt.

Fractious, egocentric, and dilatory though he was, his artistic reputation remained. In London Benjamin West, his teacher and benefactor, told an English diplomat about to depart for America: "Then, sir, you will find the best portrait painter in the world, and his name is Gilbert Stuart."

Queens of the Republican Court

The group of influential, often wealthy, persons who played important roles in the social life of the new nation was long ago dubbed the Republican Court. Most of the beautiful and cultured ladies of that group sat for Stuart. Louisa Carolina Matilda Stoughton (77), daughter of John Stoughton, the Spanish consul in Boston, was married in 1794 at the age of sixteen to the elegant, aristocratic, spendthrift Don Josef de Jaudenes y Nebot, Spanish chargé d'affaires in Philadelphia. In the summer of 1794 Stuart painted portraits of the young couple, who were described by a contemporary as being "as fine as little dolls." Another spoke of Matilda as "brilliant with diamonds." And thus, fittingly, did Stuart paint her.

The only woman with whom Stuart's name has been romantically linked was Sarah Wentworth Apthorp Morton (78), the wife of Perez Morton, a Massachusetts lawyer and legislator. The cultivated Mrs. Morton was famed not only for her beauty but also for her literary talents. She was known as the "American Sappho," but in her poems to Stuart she called herself the "Friend of Genius." Filled with ardent admiration for each other, they exchanged veiled sentiments in verse. "Stuart," Mrs. Morton wrote, "thy portrait speaks with skill divine....'Tis *character* that breaths, 'tis *soul* that twines round the rich canvas, trac'd in living lines." To which he replied: "T'was heaven itself that blended in thy face, the lines of Reason with the lines of Grace."

77. *Opposite: Matilda Stoughton de Jaudenes y Nebot*

78. *Above: an unfinished portrait of Mrs. Perez Morton*

When Stuart painted a sketch of Abigail Adams in 1800 he reportedly said that he wished he could have taken her likeness when she was young. He believed he would have had "a perfect Venus" for his model. This picture (79) was delivered in 1815 as a companion piece to her husband's portrait. Mrs. Adams, the first First Lady to live in the White House, was then seventy-one and one of the best-informed women of her time. "If we mean to have heroes, statesmen, and philosophers," she firmly believed, "we should have learned women." Her letters give a charming and keen commentary on the manners and mores of the period. Eleanor Parke Custis Lewis (80) was Martha Washington's granddaughter, "a very pleasing young lady." This portrait was painted about 1799, the year she married Washington's nephew, Lawrence Lewis. Mrs. Lewis, mistress of Woodlawn (near Mount Vernon), enjoyed poetry, music, and painting, and presumably played the piano with skill. As a girl she practiced four or five hours a day at the command of her grandmother, a gracious but exacting Virginia lady. Mrs. Washington's portrait (81) remained unfinished.

79. Opposite, top: Mrs. John Adams. 80. Opposite, bottom: Mrs. Lawrence Lewis. 81. Above: Martha Washington, 1796

Stuart's unfinished portrait of Anne Bingham (83),
"uncrowned queen of the Federalist group," offers a luminous example of the artist's technique.
Because he had never mastered line drawing or
the rudiments of draftsmanship, Stuart considered
such mechanics unnecessary and applied his paint
to the canvas with no preliminary outline or detail. To the art world of his day, this was a bold
and radical approach. Stuart blocked in a head
with opaque pigments and transparent hues. "The
well-charged brush went down upon the canvas
with an action like cutting into it with a knife,"
wrote his student John Neagle. "He always seemed
to avoid vexing or tormenting the paint when once
laid on, and this accounts partly for the purity and
freshness." Color was Stuart's forte, but "no
blending," he cautioned, " 'tis destructive of clear
and beautiful effect. It takes [away from] the
transparency and liquidity of coloring, and renders the flesh the consistency of buckskin." Flesh
tones, he further states, have "all the gaiety of a
silk-mercer's shop without its gaudiness and gloss."

During his student days in London Stuart had
mastered the English tradition of large-scale canvases with rich backgrounds, but it was not a style
of portraiture most congenial to him—nor were
full-length pictures. (An early critic once said that
Stuart could not paint "below the fifth button.")
Stuart preferred the directness and simplicity of
a head and shoulders against a plain background,
and much of his finest work was in this manner.
His spontaneous approach to a subject is clearly
revealed in his brilliant, unfinished sketches (78,
81, 83). An occasional portrait, however, suggested the European school, as does this one (82) of
Maria Morris (left) and her sister, Hester (right),
who are playing chess before billowing draperies,
rushing clouds, and a Tuscan pillar. The Morris
girls posed around 1795, when Stuart was at the
peak of his American success. Their father was
Robert Morris, who guided American government
finances through the Revolution and the founding
years of the nation, but so mismanaged his personal affairs, he went to debtors' prison in 1798.

82. *Above: the daughters of the financier Robert Morris*
83. *Opposite: an unfinished portrait of Anne Bingham*

Symbols of Fealty

"It is noteworthy that every American considers it his sacred duty to have a likeness of Washington in his home, just as we have images of God's saints," Paul Svinin observed during his tour of the United States. In 1827, more than a decade later, Mrs. Basil Hall, visiting from England, declared that in every inn there hung the "eternal picture" of Washington, "holding in one hand a roll of paper," the other hand "extended in a position which indicates what the Americans would call a very lengthy speech." Amusing as Mrs. Hall's caustic comment may seem today, her American readers in the 1800's were enraged. Washington was the "hero of freedom," he had become the symbol of constitutional liberty, equally revered in America and in Europe. His likeness appeared everywhere, from silver and bronze presentation medals to memorial cotton kerchiefs and wooden snuffboxes. In this reverse painting on glass (87) he is eulogized as the *Pater Patriae*, mourned by Columbia and a weeping soldier, while Minerva drapes his portrait with garlands, Fame blows her trumpet, and cupids carry the emblems of war and liberty. (The painting, by an unknown patriot, was taken from Enoch G. Gridley's engraving, issued in 1800, which was in turn derived from a painting by John Coles, Jr.)

Washington's portrait was used extensively on Chinese export porcelains. The picture on this toddy jug (86), made about 1805 for Edward Tilghman of Philadelphia, was from an engraving by David Edwin, based on a Stuart painting. The figure on the clock, made in Paris by Dubuc (1780–1819), was modeled on a John Trumbull portrait of Washington. In England potters in such centers as Liverpool and Newcastle, and throughout Staffordshire, produced shiploads of wares decorated with American historical scenes and symbols, imprinted by black transfers on creamware. Washington, of course, was a popular subject (85). This teapot, an example of the general term "Liverpool pottery," has a picture of Martha Washington on the reverse side (not shown).

84. *Top: a French clock, gilded bronze*

85. *Above: a Liverpool pottery teapot*

86. *Right: Chinese export porcelain jug*

87. *Opposite: a memorial to Washington*

88. *Top: painted and gilded pine eagle, New England*

89. *Left: a tilt-top candlestand with an inlaid eagle*

90. *Above: eagle detail from a speaker's desk, Maryland*

In 1782, by act of the Continental Congress, the bald eagle became the national emblem, a choice that prompted Franklin to comment that the eagle was "a bird of bad moral character." Franklin would have preferred the turkey: "He is a bird of courage, and would not hesitate to attack a grenadier of the British Guards." But this wry protest was to no avail. The eagle was firmly established as an American symbol and became the most popular of American motifs.

John Shaw, one of Maryland's finest cabinetmakers, used eagles in many of his designs. This example (90) is the eagle of the Great Seal, inlaid in the speaker's desk made by Shaw for the House of Delegates, Annapolis, about 1797. Another fine craftsman, probably in Connecticut, made the delicate candlestand (89), about 1805, with a soaring eagle inlaid on the cherry wood top. The eagle on the goblet (92) has fifteen stars twinkling above its head, which would indicate that this piece of glass was presumably engraved between 1792, when Kentucky became the fifteenth state, and 1796, when Tennessee became the sixteenth.

The eagle, however, did not always fly alone. Liberty frequently attended it. In this painting on glass (91), a Chinese export item at the turn of the century, Liberty holds a cup from which the eagle quenches its thirst. The goddess stands on Beacon Hill, behind her the British fleet leaves Boston harbor, above her a flagstaff carries the cap of liberty, beneath her foot are the badges of hereditary nobility and the key of tyranny (the key to the Bastille, given Washington by Lafayette in 1790). The scene was copied by Cantonese artists from an engraving, printed in Philadelphia in 1796, of Edward Savage's painting titled *Liberty. In the form of the Goddess of Youth; giving Support to the Bald Eagle.* Savage was apparently inspired by an earlier English water color by William Hamilton, in which Hebe held a cup for Zeus, guised as an eagle. But whatever the source Liberty and the eagle appeared for years to come in all aspects of American decorative arts.

91. *Above: a Chinese painting of Liberty on glass*

92. *Below: goblet with engraving of American eagle, possibly from J. Amelung's Maryland glass manufactory*

75

The Society of the Cincinnati, composed of American and foreign officers in the Continental Army, was formed in 1783 as a fraternal and patriotic organization. Its name recalled the Roman general Cincinnatus who returned victorious from war to resume the peaceful routine of his farm, as did Washington and most of his troops. Washington was its first president, Louis XVI its royal patron; membership was to be hereditary through eldest sons. Benjamin Franklin, among many others, was strongly opposed to such hereditary distinctions as being contrary to republican principles. The emblem of the society, designed by L'Enfant, displays the motto (in Latin): "He left all to save his country." The badge shown here (93), of gold and enamel, was made in France in 1784 and was worn by Major Samuel Nicholas, Philadelphia.

The most elaborate catalogue of symbols used in Federal design derived from Freemasonry. Throughout this period, as earlier, this order was almost the equivalent of a religion; to some it was as important as Christianity. Its membership included Washington (although he was not very active), Franklin (who was), Jefferson, Paul Revere, Lafayette, Audubon, and other personages. Masonic symbols appeared on every hand. The back of a gilded armchair (95) carried the all-seeing eye of God (also used on the dollar bill). On a dram glass (94) are such motifs broadly defined as the compasses of reason, the plumb line of truth, and the trowel that cements the social order with charity. On the snuffbox (96) are further examples, including a key symbolizing the importance of Masonic secrets and a G for God, suspended in Solomon's Temple.

93. Top: badge, Society of the Cincinnati

94. Left: dram glass with Masonic symbols

95. Opposite, top: detail from Masonic chair

96. Opposite: a brass snuffbox, silver inlay, engraved with various Masonic emblems

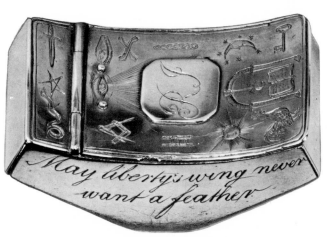

May liberty's wing never want a feather

Classics in Silver and Gold

From time to time while he was in service during the Revolutionary War, it is said, Paul Revere managed to slip back to his Boston shop to hammer up an occasional piece of silver. He loved his craft, and when his service was ended he happily returned to his forges and his anvils. As a newspaper advertisement he ran in 1786 stated, he made "all kinds of Plate...in the newest taste, and finished in the neatest manner." He also conducted a more general retail business, dealing in hardware, looking glasses, and other merchandise.

Immediately following the war the "newest taste" in silver, as in furniture, followed the delicate and restrained classicism initiated by the brothers Adam. Revere's teapot (98), elliptic in shape, with fluted sides, and decorated with engraved swags of tasseled drapery, is a "neat" realization of that style. In earlier times the different elements of a tea set were designed separately. By the 1780's and 1790's the entire set was customarily designed *en suite*. An urn-shaped sugar bowl (97a) and a helmet-shaped cream pitcher (97b) from another set echo the pattern of the teapot.

One of the most enduringly popular forms made by Revere is the barrel-shaped pitcher (99). The shape was an adaptation of the Liverpool pottery jugs which, decorated with patriotic and other appealing designs, were made in quantity for the American market around the turn of the century.

97a, b. Top: a sugar urn and cream pitcher from a tea set made by Revere

98. Left: Revere teapot and stand

99. *A pitcher used in Revere's home; a design that has been frequently reproduced*

100. Top: a silver teapot by J. Richardson, Jr.

101. Left: silver cake basket by Simon Bayley

102. Opposite, top: a Chinese porcelain teapot

103. Opposite: tankard given to Richard Devens, the special director of the Charles River Bridge

When Revere returned to his shop on Clark's Wharf he had as a neighbor a fellow silversmith, Benjamin Burt. In his own day Burt might have been more celebrated for his bulk than his silverwork, for apparently he weighed three hundred eighty pounds. However, his skills equalled Revere's, and the work of the two men was closely alike both in style and craftsmanship. In 1786 it was Burt whom the proprietors of the Charles River Bridge commissioned to fashion a tankard (103) to commemorate the completion of that enterprise. The bridge itself, pictured in an engraved panel on the tankard, was an engineering triumph. It was more than fifteen hundred feet long, with a railed passage for pedestrians on either side, a draw that could be raised by two men, and "forty elegant...lamps."

The tankard, so typical of colonial silverwork, was losing popularity in this period, partly as a consequence of a budding temperance movement. Teapots, on the other hand, were never more popular. Philadelphians favored a shape similar to that of the porcelain pots (102) made in China for the American market, which were often embellished with a pierced gallery about the lid. This one (100) is part of a nineteen-piece service made about 1790 by Joseph Richardson, Jr. Tea equipages as a whole were more elaborate than they had earlier been. In 1791 one lady visitor to a Connecticut home saw such an assortment of tea things as she had never before seen, from silver urns, waiters, and chafing dishes, kettles, pots, and sugar dishes, to "an elegant set of china." A cake basket such as the one shown here (101), by Simon G. Bayley of New York, with its restrained classical outlines and pierced and engraved decoration, might have been used with the tea service as well as at the dining table.

R. Devens Esq.... this Tankard...

...nted by Lily W. Devens to Richard Devens Great...

Inherited by Richard Devens

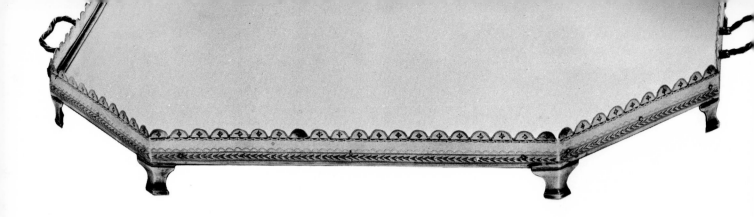

In 1789 Washington's secretary wrote that the President was "desireous of getting a sett of those waiters, salvers, or whatever they are called, which are set in the middle of a dining table to ornament it—and to occupy the place which must otherwise be filled with dishes of meat, which are seldom or never touched." He added that Robert Morris, William Bingham, and the French and Spanish ministers to the United States had such plateaus, but no one else that he knew of.

Very few of these mirrored table pieces appear to have been made in America. However, about the time the President received his pair from France in 1791, the New York smith Benjamin Halsted fashioned one (104) for Daniel Crommelin Verplanck, a prominent Duchess County landowner.

In 1784, following a traditional custom, the Corporation of the City of New York presented General Washington, Governor George Clinton, the Marquis de Lafayette, Baron von Steuben, and John Jay with the freedom of the city in recognition of their services to the nation. These acknowledgments were enclosed in gold boxes fashioned—at least four of them, including the one for Jay (108)—by Samuel Johnson, alderman on the presentation committee, and engraved by Peter Maverick with the arms of the city and suitable inscriptions.

Another prominent silversmith, Isaac Hutton of Albany (counselor, treasurer, and committee member of the Society for the Promotion of Useful Arts, among other things), made the pair of candlesticks (105) in the form of fluted classical columns—a consummately straightforward and simple expression of the prevailing style. In the same spirit an unknown silversmith made the urn-shaped nutmeg grater (106). The hinged base, front, and lid open to reveal the grating surface.

104. Above: a silver plateau by Benjamin Halsted, New York, 1790–1800

105. Below: candlesticks by I. Hutton

106. *Above: a hinged silver nutmeg grater*

107. *Left: an engraved trade card, 1808–9*

108. *Below: the gold freedom box presented to John Jay by the City of New York in 1784*

More varied and individual designs in silver were essayed in the federal period than in the years preceding the Revolution. Among many different forms of candleholders, for example, a distinctive piece (109) by Joseph Lownes of Philadelphia includes a stand with its scissor-snuffers and a conical extinguisher, along with the holder itself, all set within a boat-shaped tray. The tea or coffee urn was one of the new forms made by American silversmiths in the late eighteenth century. The earliest American example known was made in the Adam style. This one (111), made about 1805 by Anthony Simmons of Philadelphia, retains the vase shape

of classical fashion, but it is heavier and more squat than the designs directly inspired by Adam. In such forms a hot iron enclosed within a sheath in the vessel kept the liquid warm.

In 1814, with the hope of securing their aid in the war with England, Major General (later President) William Henry Harrison ceremoniously presented to the Wyandot, Delaware, and Shawnee tribes "each a large silver pipe, elegantly ornamented, and engraved with devices emblematic of the protection and friendship of the United States." On one of its four engraved panels the pipe given to the Delawares (110) pictures the actual presentation (110a).

109. *Upper left: candleholder by Lownes*

110, 110a. *Opposite: silver peace pipe with engraving of the presentation scene*

111. *Right: silver urn for tea or coffee*

Masters
&
Journeymen

From December, 1787, to July, 1788, as state after state ratified the new Constitution, a series of Federal Processions, each more elaborate than the last, paraded through the streets of major American cities to celebrate the occasion. Philadelphia staged its parade on the Fourth of July, with more than five thousand marchers and numerous gaily decorated floats, some drawn by as many as ten horses. The procession was a mile and a half long and when it wound up at the "Union Green" half the population of the city was gathered there. On several of the floats master craftsmen with their journeymen and apprentices worked at their various trades—the "Gentlemen Cabinet-and Chair-Makers," the carvers and gilders, the turners and Windsor-chair makers, along with the rest.

Later in the same month the New York demonstration was enlivened by a large flag, carried by the tailors, showing Adam and Eve all but naked, with the motto: "And they sewed fig leaves together." The brewers displayed a three-hundred-gallon cask of ale, topped by a tun of wine. On the tun they sat a "*living Bacchus*," a youngster clad in flesh-colored, skintight silk and wearing a cap decorated with hopvines and barley. With a silver goblet in his hand he kept "drinking and huzzaing the whole day with the greatest cheerfulness." The Windsor-chair makers' banner asserted that, with free trade and the new federal union, "O'er all the world our chairs are found," which was a forgivable exaggeration of the truth. Only three years later, in any case, four thousand Windsor chairs were shipped to the French West Indies, five hundred thirty-three to the Dutch West Indies, one hundred forty-four to the Danish West Indies, and twenty-four to Africa.

In the years shortly to come those expressions of solidarity and shared purpose among the crafts took on some disquieting overtones. As early as 1756 a group of cabinetmakers in Providence, Rhode Island, had agreed upon the prices they would charge for certain types of furniture and, apparently, how much they would pay journeymen for their services in making such pieces. The figures had to be revised the next year because of the depreciation of

Rhode Island currency. A similar effort by furniture makers to establish uniformity in prices and wages was made in Philadelphia in 1786, and others possibly earlier. None of those agreements was published, although one was printed in Hartford, Connecticut, in 1792. The evidence, in any case, suggests that price-fixing and wage-fixing were common practices in various American cities, as they were in England in the late eighteenth century. In 1794, to the annoyance of the master craftsmen, the Philadelphia journeymen took matters into their own hands and came out with the first major American book of rates to be published, which they reissued the following year under the title, *The Journeymen Cabinet and Chair-Makers Philadelphia Book of Prices*. In it they called for higher wages for, as they complained, the rising cost of living had not been taken into consideration in the masters' calculations. When their masters remonstrated, the journeymen, organized as the Federal Society of Philadelphia Cabinet Makers, called upon "their mechanical Fellow Citizens... throughout America" to support their cause in the interest of workingmen everywhere—an appeal which won them a sympathetic response from "respectable and independent Societies" representing other trades. They also refused to work with journeymen who would not observe their rules of fair practice. In addition, the Philadelphia "union" opened a warehouse where they offered for direct sale to the public furniture they themselves had made, planning to by-pass their former bosses on the way to market with their wares.

The two-year conflict, the strike in short, was not settled until the following year when still another book, *The Cabinet-Makers' Philadelphia and London*

Book of Prices, was issued with the approval of all parties concerned in the dispute. This publication, as the title indicates, was based on a similar English manual of rates. However, the Philadelphia workmen were to receive 50 per cent more than the rates prevailing in London. Furthermore, the book stipulated, "whenever the necessaries of life, house-rent, &c. shall rise above what they are at present, the Employers agree to advance the per centum to what shall be agreed on." This probably is the earliest instance of an escalator clause in a union contract.

In the end, the journeymen received on an average about one dollar a day (eleven hours) for their work, and the masters' retail prices were marked up anywhere from 100 to 400 per cent above the cost of labor. All of which was about what the workmen had proposed in the first place.

There were similar disputes and reconciliations in other cities in later years, and cabinetmakers' price books were issued until fairly late in the nineteenth century. The earlier American price books were sparsely illustrated if at all, but the English editions frequently contained engraved designs of both details and complete furniture forms—designs which, together with descriptive texts, probably had as much influence in America as those of Hepplewhite and Sheraton. A description of one type of chair in the 1802 edition of *The London Chair-Makers' and Carvers' Book of Prices for Workmanship* very closely corresponds to chairs that were being made five years later in New York by Duncan Phyfe (see page 107) and, no doubt, his contemporaries.

The furniture makers of the federal period were often as dependent upon one another as they were upon their journeymen. When, as earlier mentioned, Ephraim Haines of Philadelphia made a set of ebony chairs and a settee for Stephen Girard, he employed a sawyer to cut the logs and other independent craftsmen to perform special jobs: Barney Schumo to turn the spindles, legs, and feet; John Morris to carve the designs; George Brindenhart to upholster the seats; and Robert Pullen to plate the tacks of the chair seats. It is altogether probable that other local furni-

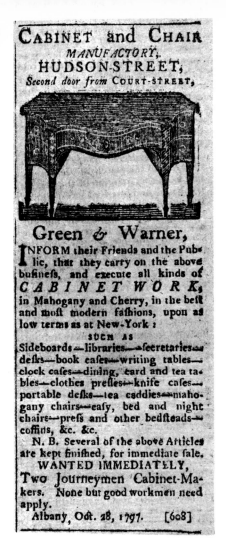

ture makers turned to these same specialists for similar work. In Salem, Massachusetts, Samuel McIntire carved furniture for a number of different makers, as did Thomas Whitman. Thomas Barrett of Baltimore provided finished inlays for fifteen different cabinetmakers. And so on. As a consequence, attributing furniture to some maker on the basis of the details is obviously not plausible. Some furniture makers provided furniture for others, as the slack and press of demands suggested. The day was passing when furniture was made to individual order and specifications by a single workman and his helper. Furniture warehouses, like the ones proposed by the striking Philadelphia journeymen, where the customer might shop as he does in a modern department store, were becoming common outlets for the goods made by craftsmen. Mail orders were increasingly solicited not only from the neighboring countryside but from far distant places.

At times cabinetmakers banded together in joint enterprises of consider-

able magnitude. In Salem at one point practically all the furniture makers of that general area, including Nehemiah Adams, Samuel McIntire, and some others already mentioned, were participating in a co-operative export business. As a group they shipped huge "venture cargoes" for sale up and down the coast, into the Caribbean and to South America, and to Africa and India. A series of lawsuits brought that undertaking to an end shortly before the War of 1812.

As Alexander Hamilton claimed in 1791 and as surviving examples make clear, American furniture makers of the federal period were on the whole turning out work of eminently fine quality, comparable at least to the work of their counterparts abroad. Even the best of them, however, at times also served their patrons as handy men, doing odd jobs in, on, or about the house and repairing broken chairs, tables, wheelbarrows, and anything else that needed mending. Job E. Townsend, who made expensive furniture for the fashionable folk of Newport, Rhode Island, also hung their looking glasses, put up their bedsteads, helped hang their window curtains, and when they died, made their coffins. (Making coffins for their customers was standard practice among cabinetmakers; David Evans, a prominent furniture maker of Philadelphia, made at least two thousand of them.)

The variety of such odd jobs undertaken by men who were responsible for the typical and best furniture of the time is both surprising and entertaining. Townsend also built hencoops, a cowpen, and, like Samuel McIntire, pigsties—and he mended cellar doors. Other reputable craftsmen in wood made washtubs and ironing boards, lime squeezers and crutches ("for walking with"), signposts, teapot handles, and cloth pounders. Such everyday services must have been especially invaluable to the housewife and well remembered when more impressive commissions were made; which recalls a verse from a song that was sung in the Federal Procession at Philadelphia:

Ye *Cabinetmakers!* brave workers
    in wood,
    As you work for the ladies,
    your work must be good.

112. *Top: mahogany card table with brass mountings, Lannuier*

113. *Left: a teapot, attributed to French-born Simon Chaudron*

114. *Above: label of Charles Honoré Lannuier's New York shop*

An Approach to Empire

In Europe at the turn of the century the neoclassic style was developing a richer and grander expression than it had been given in the earlier patterns of Hepplewhite and Sheraton. French Directoire and Empire fashions, typifying this trend, strongly influenced the character of English Regency designs. In America reflections of the new mode were derived from pattern books and were also introduced directly by French *émigrés*.

One of the latter was Charles Honoré Lannuier, a successful and an influential cabinetmaker, born in France in 1779, trained in Paris by his brother, Nicholas, a master *ébéniste*, and active in America from 1803 until 1819. The card table (112), one of his earliest-known pieces and typical of French styles at the time Lannuier left for New York, is embellished with applied gilt-brass, or ormolu. The bed (115) illustrates French fashions in its high, outcurving headboard and footboard, the posts carved with acanthus leaves, and the green and gold canopy rail with applied ormolu stars, eagles, and anthemia, or Greek honeysuckle, patterns.

This silver teapot (113), once owned by Auguste Chouteau, one of the founders of St. Louis, is representative of the work of another *émigré* craftsman, Simon Chaudron. The teapot's robust shape and animal-head spout again illustrate the departure from the slim delicate forms of the Federal style to the sturdier shapes of the Empire period. Chaudron's onetime partner was Anthony Rasch, who made the sauceboat shown on page 9.

115. *A bed in the French style made by Lannuier*

Duncan Phyfe, whose name is often mistaken as a synonym for Federal furniture, was one of America's cabinetmakers whose creative abilities profoundly influenced contemporary design. Years after his death another New York cabinetmaker wrote: "Duncan Phyfes chief merrit lies in the carrying out and Especially *improving* of the 'Sheriton' style." This side chair (119) exemplifies Phyfe's interpretation of English and French fashions prior to the full-blown forms of the Empire period. The lyre was a Greek motif popularized in England by Adam, Hepplewhite, and Sheraton, and one of the principal features of Regency designs, as were the lion-paw feet, adapted from Egyptian, Assyrian, Persian, and Roman designs. Although often considered as a Phyfe "trademark," the lyre was also used by any number of American cabinetmakers, as were acanthus carvings (shown on the chair legs), which Phyfe simplified into a pattern of formalized grooves and ridges. The sketch (118) and price list are believed to have been sent by Phyfe to Charles Nicoll Bancker, a Philadelphia patron.

Duncan Phyfe (or Fife, as it was originally spelled) was born in 1768 at Loch Fannich, Scotland. At fifteen he emigrated with his family to Albany, where he presumably received his training. In *The New-York Directory* for 1792 he was listed as a joiner, in 1794 as a cabinetmaker, and was soon known as one of the city's most talented craftsmen. This drawing (117), done by an apprentice, shows Phyfe's establishment on Fulton Street. The center building was his salesroom, where two ladies (117a) can be seen considering the comparative merits of a lyre-back chair and a chair with an ogee-cross splat. To the left was his workshop, to the right, his warehouse. His home was directly across the street. At his death in 1854 Phyfe's estate was valued at nearly half a million dollars, a considerable sum in those times, accrued not only through his distinctive skills, but also through his industrious, no-nonsense nature. Phyfe thought of little else but his work. "He was very strict in his habits," a later memoir would recall. "And all the members of the family had to be in bed by nine o'clock."

116. *Opposite: Duncan Phyfe's tool chest*

117. *Top: a water color of Phyfe's shop*

117a. *Right: detail of Phyfe's salesroom*

118. *Above: sketch attributed to Phyfe*

119. *Left: mahogany lyre-back side chair*

In this card table (121) stamped by Michael Allison, a contemporary and neighbor of Phyfe's, the so-called Phyfe trademarks were executed by another master cabinetmaker. Phyfe had, indeed, introduced this type of table (derived from Sheraton) with its vase pedestal, incurved legs, and clover-leaf shaped folding top. It seems likely that other furniture makers in New York also worked in the Duncan Phyfe style.

Caned furniture, so popular in late seventeenth-century England and America, was revived at the end of the eighteenth century because of its light, attractive appearance. Phyfe also used such caning as appears on this sofa (120). Among his preferred motifs was reeding, not only in vertical lines but in horizontal lines, as on the seat rail of the sofa, made around 1805. The carved designs on the top rail were also Phyfe favorites: reeds tied with ribbons (the outside panels) and swags

of drapery trimmed with tassels (the center panel).

In a description of Phyfe's workroom, it was said that motifs he liked best were drawn on paper and hung from the ceiling, and in giving orders to his men, Phyfe would point out a variety of hanging designs: "Use a combination of this and this and that." The combination of designs in the caned window seat (122), made about 1810 and attributed to Phyfe, clearly shows the imprint of French and English fashions with its brass paw feet, the scrolled top rails of the end pieces with their laurel carvings, and the crossed ogee splats (earlier pictured in the detail 117a, page 91). Window seats, known as French stools in the Chippendale period, had become enormously popular in England. Adam used them to enhance the formality of the great *salons* he furnished, and Hepplewhite's *Guide* described them as "peculiarly adapted for an elegant drawing-room."

120. *Left: a caned sofa, probably from Duncan Phyfe's workshop*

121. *Top: mahogany card table made by Michael Allison of New York*

122. *Above: caned window seat attributed to Phyfe, made about 1810*

Convex mirrors in circular gilt frames were introduced into England from France in the late 1700's; when decorated with branches for candles they were known as girandoles. (Girandole, which originally meant a branched candlestick, not necessarily backed by a reflecting surface, is a French term derived from the Italian *girandola*—a radiating and showy composition, such as a wheel of fireworks.) Convex mirrors became "universally fashionable," as Sheraton phrased it in his *Cabinet Dictionary* (1803), and he particularly remarked on the "agreeable effect" they produced. They were equally fashionable in America through both the Federal and Empire periods. This girandole (125), probably made in Boston early in the nineteenth century, is closely similar in design to those that were so popular throughout the English Regency period. It is topped by an eagle, the concave frame is lined with gilt balls, an ebonized molding lies next to the glass, the base is decorated with carved foliage, and the scrolled candle branches are hung with cut-glass drops. Most of these mirrors found in America were European imports.

The highly sophisticated double-chair-back settee, made about 1805, has the outflaring legs copied from Greek patterns. Attributed to the Seymours of Boston, the settee is carved mahogany with veneered birch panels, its overall design a graceful, New England approach to Empire patterns.

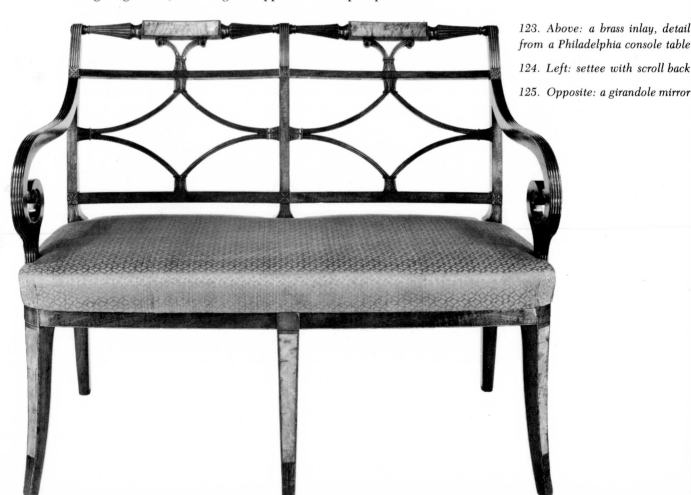

123. Above: a brass inlay, detail from a Philadelphia console table

124. Left: settee with scroll back

125. Opposite: a girandole mirror

American Empire

The Classic Summation (1815-1840)

The War of 1812 has been called the second war for American independence. Had England not been at death's grip with Napoleon's forces during those years of conflict, the consequences could have been very unfortunate for this country. As it was, with the ratification of the Treaty of Ghent in 1815, the nation jubilantly and with only a minimum of adjustment went about its peacetime business. That same year, following the Battle of Waterloo, war-weary Europe laid down its arms for a while and concerned itself with the serious problems of peace on the Continent. A generation of Americans had grown to manhood without ever having known a period when business was not conducted on a wartime basis. Now, for the first time in its history, this country felt free and able to consolidate its own latent resources without any interference from abroad, to take "command of its own fortunes," as Washington had hoped it might. In spite of the humiliations of the British blockade and the burning of the Capitol, Americans looked to the future with fresh confidence and new optimism. The blockade had practically stopped foreign trade, but the money that had earlier gone into shipping had been diverted to new and vital domestic manufactures to supply a public deprived of European goods.

With the war's end there was a prospect of expansion in all directions. "Peace and plenty" was a popular toast of the day. Beyond that, as Albert Gallatin observed, the war had "renewed and reinstated the national feelings and character which the Revolution had given....The people have now more general objects of attachment," he added, "with which their pride and political opinions are connected. They are more Americans; they feel and act more as a nation." Indeed, over the decades to come foreign visitors found the American's insistent and assertive pride in his Americanism a particularly offensive aspect of the national character, a bumptiousness they rarely could condone or understand. "It is impossible to conceive a more troublesome or more garrulous patriotism," wrote Alexis de Tocqueville, "it wearies even those who are disposed to respect it."

The first necessary step, both practical and symbolic, toward the assertion of that new sense of nationalism was to restore and finish the uncompleted Capitol in Washington, which the British had reduced to a charred near-ruin. This job was entrusted to Benjamin Henry Latrobe. Latrobe, a widely traveled, well-educated, British-trained architect, had come to America in 1796 and had been surveyor of the public buildings of the United States in the Jefferson and Madison administrations, until such work was discontinued in 1812 with the outbreak of war. Although there have been subsequent changes in its appearance, notably a higher central dome of cast iron completed in 1865, the Capitol as we know it today is largely Latrobe's building. For years still to come the surrounding city with its assortment of modest shops, homes, and boarding houses—some of them little more than shanties—offered an "awful contrast" to the few public

Opposite: detail of a carved and gilded figure from the card table, above, by Lannuier

buildings. In 1842 Charles Dickens compared the scene to a London slum suburb. But even the hypercritical Mrs. Frances Trollope was "struck with admiration and surprise" at the Capitol rising in its magnificence from that raw landscape when she visited Washington in 1827.

It was more than an imposing building; it was a symbol of the national spirit, one of those "objects of attachment" to which Gallatin referred. So, too, was the flag that rose from its roof—the "star-spangled banner" that Francis Scott Key celebrated in the verse he wrote after the British bombardment of Fort McHenry in 1814. Set to the tune of an English drinking song, it became immediately popular as a further expression of the current lusty patriotism.

When the capital was moved to Philadelphia in 1790, en route to the barren flatlands of the Federal City, it was dismally predicted that New York would be deserted "and become a wilderness, peopled with wolves, its old inhabitants." However, in less than a generation that city became the nation's largest center, surpassing Philadelphia in the number of its population and the scope of its commercial enterprise. Immediately after the peace of 1815 England made the city the major dumping ground for surplus goods that had been held at home during the war. In three months of 1815 almost four million dollars were paid in duties at New York; on one day, November 14, twenty square-rigged ships sailed up the bay together, bulging with freight.

New York had great natural advantages as a trading center. The waters of its matchless harbor push far past the city through the channel of the Hudson River, forming the greatest tidal estuary in the Western Hemisphere between the Río de la Plata and the St. Lawrence. That estuary, in turn, leads to the Mohawk Valley, the only water-level route through the coastal mountains which, from Georgia in the south to the St. Lawrence in the north, block off the interior mass of the continent. The Erie Canal, undertaken in 1817, followed that route, giving New York easy access to the vast western hinterland. Even to such a far-reaching mind as Thomas Jefferson's it seemed "little short of madness" to attempt cutting such a passage through more than three hundred and sixty miles of wilderness. It was indeed just that, but the job was finished in the

Below: the Capitol as it appeared in 1824

Right: the "bombs bursting in air" over Fort McHenry in the night of September 13, 1814

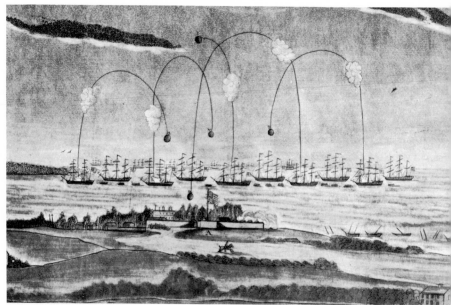

fall of 1825, shortly before Jefferson's death. And the nation swelled with pride at such an achievement. (Duncan Phyfe fashioned a wooden casket of a cedar log, brought from Lake Erie by the first canalboat, to enclose a bottle of canal water intended as a gift to the Marquis de Lafayette.) That "mighty ditch" was only four feet deep, but it quickly floated a tremendous burden of traffic between East and West. With the untold resources of the interior continent to tap and a huge, new, and growing market to supply, New York became "the great commercial emporium of America."

The lifting of the blockade not only brought flotillas of English ships to American harbors, but it released the pent-up American merchant marine from its own home ports, laden with cargoes of native products and produce destined for sale and exchange wherever a market might be found. For more than a quarter century after the war Boston owned more ships than New York; ships that carried ice from the ponds of Saugus, Massachusetts, to the West Indies and Calcutta, shirtings from the Lowell mills to Montevideo, and shoes made at Lynn from California hides back to California; ships that carried sugar from Cuba to Sweden and Russia, Peruvian bark to Tunis (by way of Boston), and sandalwood from Hawaii to China, in exchange for palm-leaf hats sent back to Hawaii.

The ship-lined water front of New York in 1828

As a consequence of such far-flung enterprise, necessities and luxuries from every corner of the earth soon found their way to American markets and American homes. Harriet Martineau, a visiting Englishwoman, noted during her stay in 1834–36 that the fruits of the Mediterranean appeared on every table in Salem, and, she might have added, pepper from Sumatra, coffee from Arabia, and tea from China. The seamen who manned the vessels of that little town were a cosmopolitan breed. "They have a large acquaintance at Cairo," wrote Miss Martineau. "They...have wild tales to tell of Mosambique and Madagasca....Any body will give you anecdotes from Canton, and descriptions of the Society and Sandwich Islands. They often slip up the western coasts of their two continents; bring furs from the back regions of their own wide land; glance up at the Andes on their return; double Cape Horn; touch at the ports of Brazil and Guiana; look about them in the West Indies, feeling there almost at home; and

Detail of a scene along the Erie Canal in 1831

A Chinese porcelain pagoda made for export to the West

land, some fair morning, at Salem, and walk home as if they had done nothing very remarkable." And there were few of the better homes without their Canton shawls and Smyrna silks, their Chinese porcelains and bits of lacquer, or parrots and pet monkeys from the remote ports of the world.

One of the most celebrated Salem ships was the luxurious, ocean-going pleasure yacht, *Cleopatra's Barge,* launched in October, 1816, and owned by that wealthy man of the world George Crowninshield, Jr. Such a vessel, with its paneled woodwork of mahogany and maple, its fashionable and costly furniture, and its glazed wall cupboards stocked with porcelain and silver, had never before been seen in American waters. The finest liquors and wines were served by smartly uniformed crewmen at tables covered with the best of linens; gold leaf edged the deck beams and red velvet wormed with golden cord covered the hand ropes. Surrounded by the splendor of such accommodations Crowninshield visited far places. Off the coast of Italy he was watched by guard ships, for a rumor had spread that he planned to rescue Napoleon from his exile in St. Helena. He did make a pilgrimage to Elba and visited Napoleon's sister Pauline in Rome, and wherever the *Barge* put in it caused excitement and wonder. After Crowninshield's death the vessel became the royal yacht of King Liholiho of the Hawaiian Islands, who soon managed to wreck it on a reef.

But the lure of the land was as great as the lure of the sea. Old cities were growing and new ones were sprouting up in the wilderness. In 1838 Captain Frederick Marryat, the English sea captain and widely traveled novelist who two years before had published his engaging story *Mr. Midshipman Easy,* found that the stores in Buffalo and Cleveland were better looking and better stocked than any shop in Norwich, England. The war and the blockade had stimulated domestic manufactures, and as the nation expanded and prospered more people wanted more of the comforts and conveniences of life. Also, as the urban communities became more specialized in their commercial interests and more dependent upon the surrounding countryside for provisions, the need for better roads became critical for townsman and countryman alike. During the war, when much of the coastal traffic was driven from the seas, that need was sharply emphasized. Half humorously the newspapers referred to the wagons that took over the hauling of freight by inland routes as "fast-sailing" vehicles and reported their progress under such headings as "Horse-Marine Intelligence." But the needs those "fleets" of wagons served were serious and not easily met. When Americans started moving westward in unprecedented numbers following the war, more and better communications were imperative if the social and political fabric of the nation were to hold together. "We are great, and rapidly—I was about to say fearfully—growing," remarked John Calhoun in 1817. "This is our pride and our danger; our weakness and our strength....Let us, then, bind the republic together with a perfect system of roads and canals."

The National Road, started as early as 1811 and leading from Cumberland, Maryland, through the mountains to the western waterways, was only the most ambitious of scores of thoroughfares that were constructed to meet those needs. Even before it was finished it attracted such great streams of traffic it looked more like the main street of a large city than a road through the back country. The success of the Erie Canal released a frenzy of canal building throughout the nation in the years following 1825, until America seemed to be developing into a Venice of interlocking waterways. Even that frenzy was surpassed by the excitement that attended the development of, first, steamboats and, then, railroads.

For, as one contemporary prophesied, steam "is going to alter, in a degree far more remarkable than any previous change, the condition of mankind....*Steam is union*. It connects minds....It will diminish the size of the globe."

From the beginning Robert Fulton's Hudson River steamboats offered accommodations and facilities that astonished the public by their elegance and efficiency. When Paul Svinin, a Russian visiting America in 1811–13, surveyed the *Paragon*, Fulton's third ship, he likened it to "a whole floating town," with its dining saloon serving one hundred and fifty passengers daily and its kitchens where cooking was done by steam. "Gleaming silver and bronze, shining mirrors and mahogany are everywhere," he wrote, "and the most fastidious person of the most refined taste can find here everything to his liking." Good wine and, in hot weather, ice cream added to the attractions of this waterborne, steam-driven palace for the people.

By the 1840's the nation was firmly binding its parts together with an abundance of such transportation routes. By then there were at least one hundred steamboats on the Hudson River, some with far more elaborate arrangements than the *Paragon* had displayed. (In 1827 Robert L. Stevens, the Hoboken engineer and entrepreneur, hired such eminent artists as Thomas Sully, John Vanderlyn, Samuel F. B. Morse, Thomas Doughty, and Thomas Cole to paint pictures for the steamboat *Albany*.) There were far more plying the western waterways. In one twelve-month period a few years later more than four thousand steamboats put in at Cincinnati on their way up or down the Ohio River. The railroads did not offer as much comfort and elegance as the river boats, but they went places the steamboats could not reach. By mid-century over nine thousand miles of track had been laid, piercing the East in all directions and finding their way to the West, peopling the country, and creating new markets wherever they went. As early as 1830 one French-born Philadelphia cabinetmaker advertised that he was prepared to execute orders "from any part of the Union." And in the years under discussion the New York firm of Tweed and Bonnell (the son of the first of those partners was later known, and has been remembered, as "Boss" Tweed) was in fact shipping chairs all over the country—as well as to Casablanca and Constantinople.

America in the 1840's was already a far different country from the one Calhoun had addressed in 1817. The population had swollen to more than seventeen million people and was almost doubling itself every twenty years. The center of population had moved westward across the Appalachians. Americans were still predominantly farmers, by a large measure, but cities played a much more important part in the life of the nation. And factory-made goods were inexorably replacing the work of handicraftsmen. During the three decades following the War of 1812 the character of American society and of American life was obviously becoming increasingly complex. The crosscurrents of world-wide trade, the spread of democratic ideals, new methods of production, and the steady growth of communications by all means and in all mediums generated new interests and tastes that quickly reached across the land.

It was under these circumstances and during this span of years that the classical revival style came to a climax and slowly started to ebb. Varied as the national scene was, the classical theme was constantly in evidence, most obviously in architecture. As early as 1798, shortly after his arrival in America, Latrobe provided a new accent in American architecture with his design for the Bank of Pennsylvania, the first structure in the New World to look to ancient Greece as a

Fulton's Paragon *steaming up the Hudson*

101

The Bank of Pennsylvania in Philadelphia, drawn by the architect Benjamin Latrobe

source of inspiration. "My *principles* of good taste are rigid in Grecian architecture," he wrote his friend, Thomas Jefferson. "I am a bigoted Greek." Later, in an address to a Philadelphia audience, he envisioned a future when "the days of Greece may be revived in the woods of America." In a sense that time came, but only after Latrobe's death in 1820. It was during the next generation that the breadth of the land, from Maine to the farthest western outposts, was dotted with buildings that in one way or another revived the vocabulary of Greek forms and ornaments. Farmhouses and city banks, wayside stores and state capitols, prisons, hospitals, and even saloons—buildings of every pretension and no pretension, including privies, according to one acerbic English critic—traced some aspect of their appearance to ancient Greek precedent. So it was in 1832 when Samuel F. Smith wrote "My Country, 'Tis of Thee" and referred to the "templed hills" that were by then already so characteristic of the American landscape. Buildings were now painted white—"the whitest of the white," wrote Charles Dickens—recalling the gleaming marble of ancient temples. Tocqueville was delighted by the sight of such "little palaces of white marble" until he learned they were of whitewashed brick and painted wood.

No other style, before or since, has so dominated the American architectural scene as did the Greek Revival during those years. Some part of that widespread popularity may have stemmed from Americans' deep sympathy for the contemporary Greeks, who were engaged in the 1820's in their own war of independence from Turkish domination—a war which Lord Byron dramatized by dying while actively helping to deliver the Greeks from their oppressors. Also, in this period of ascendant democracy, Americans were quick to identify their own civic and political virtues with those of the ancient Greeks: "*Greece was free*," as Latrobe had observed, "in Greece every citizen felt himself an important...part of his republic." And thus every white American liked to think of himself, including the southern planter in his porticoed mansion who saw the perfect democracy based on a system of slavery, as society in ancient Greece had been.

The American sculptor Hiram Powers modeled his *Greek Slave*, a marble statue of a nude young girl bound in chains, standing on view in a Turkish slave market, more than a full decade after the Greek war had ended. However, such was the prevailing and enduring sentiment that the work was an immediate and smashing popular success. In a day of prudery the statue was a lascivious state-

A design for a Greek Revival front doorway

ment but, as one clergyman maintained, it was "clothed all over with sentiment, sheltered, protected by it, from every profane eye." The spirit of those times is reflected by a bit of doggerel in which John Quincy Adams urged Powers to:

> Go forth, and rival Greece's art sublime;
> Return, and bid the statesmen of thy land
> Live in thy marble through all after-time!

Powers did in fact plan a series of marble portraits of all the Presidents of the United States to be placed in the Capitol. Appropriately, one of his finest works was a bust of that arch-democrat, President Andrew Jackson. Powers reported that when he asked the rugged old warrior if he wished the portrait to be idealized the President replied: "Make me as I am, Mr. Powers, and be true to nature always....I have no desire to *look* young as long as I *feel* old [he was sixty-eight years old at the time]: and then it seems to me, although I don't know much about sculpture, that the only object in making a bust is to get a representation of the man who sits, that it be as nearly as possible a perfect likeness." Nevertheless, true to the prevailing convention, the artist draped the President with a classical toga.

Jackson's bitter enemy in the controversy over the Second Bank of the United States, Nicholas Biddle of Philadelphia, was one of the foremost promoters of the Greek Revival style. Biddle—a traveler, dilettante, sometime ambassador, as well as banker—had visited Greece in 1806 and succumbed to the beauty of the land and its ancient structures. "The two great truths in the world," he confided to his diary, "are the Bible and Grecian architecture." And the enthusiasm that underlaid that statement endured throughout his lifetime.

However, the major factor in the growth and spread of the Greek Revival style in architecture was the flow of books and builders' manuals between about 1820 and 1845, which showed how Greek forms and motifs could be adapted to serve every purpose from the design of a façade to the ornamentation of a fireplace. Although English publications were the main sources for the handbooks produced in this country, the latter were prepared by American architects and builders who had in mind the conditions, needs, and the tastes of the American public. The seven guides published by Asher Benjamin of Greenfield, Massachusetts, for instance, which went through forty-five editions, were specifically intended to represent the economical use of native materials with practical plans and construction details. Local carpenters throughout the land, with a saw, hammer, and nails at one hand and such a guide as Benjamin's at the other, could work out their problems on the spot to their own or their client's taste. And this they did in towns named Athens, Sparta, Corinth, Syracuse, and so on. In all events, the Greek Revival became a ubiquitous and decidedly Americanized style that served as an accommodating background for the furniture and furnishings in what is commonly called the Empire style as it evolved during those same decades.

The "Grecian" or "modern" style, as it was known to its contemporaries, introduced the actual use of ancient furniture forms as they were represented in the pattern books of Napoleon Bonaparte's French Empire and the roughly parallel versions of the English Regency. One of the earliest suites of furniture made in this country following such archaeological models was designed by that "bigoted Greek," Latrobe, and ordered by him from the Baltimore cabinetmakers John and Hugh Findlay for the President's House. For eight years preceding

Hiram Powers' bust of Andrew Jackson, about 1835

the War of 1812 Latrobe had been responsible for the continuing work on the mansion, including its interior decoration. When James Madison succeeded Jefferson as President in 1809 Latrobe worked closely with Dolley Madison, a childhood friend of Mrs. Latrobe's, selecting the carpets, silverware, lighting fixtures, and draperies that would complete "the domestic arrangements of the house." Congress had thoughtfully provided fourteen thousand dollars for the purchase of such embellishments.

In designing the chairs and sofas for "Queen Dolley's" drawing room, Latrobe turned to the illustrations in Thomas Hope's *Household Furniture and Interior Decoration*—an English guide, published in 1807, that expressly acknowledged its debt to the earlier work of Charles Percier and Pierre Fontaine. In their *Recueil de Décorations Intérieures,* published in 1801, those two Frenchmen had illustrated for the first time anywhere examples in the new archaeological style. Three years later Napoleon made the pair his official court architects and decorators, from which eminent post they influenced the direction of furniture design throughout the western world. They by no means restricted themselves to reproductions of Greek forms but used whatever ancient sources—Roman, Etruscan, Egyptian, and Greek—they could adapt to satisfy the needs and vanities of Napoleon and his imperial family and court. Hope, a wealthy amateur architect and a friend of Percier's, was one of the first to publish an English equivalent of these archaic designs, and his book was apparently in Latrobe's hands shortly after it was issued.

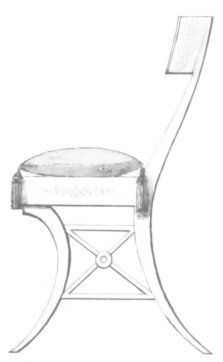

Design by Latrobe for the chairs in the Greek manner for the President's House

Through those interpreters Latrobe's design for the chairs, with incurved back rest, curved back rails, and saber-shaped legs, reaches back to the klismos form of ancient Greece, so often depicted in vase paintings of the fifth century B.C. Similarly, the sofa design closely resembles the ancient triclinium as it was illustrated by Hope. In any case, Latrobe's efforts resulted in what Washington Irving described in 1811 as a room of "blazing splendor," an unfortunately apt phrase, for all those appointments went up in flames just three years later. When the house was restored and refurbished in the Monroe administration after the war, the President temporarily installed the furniture and silver he had bought in France when he was minister to that country in the 1790's. To this was added cabinetwork made in Baltimore and Georgetown and, with the twenty thousand dollars appropriated by Congress, other furnishings in the latest style from Paris, the bills for which far exceeded the amount allotted.

The tendency to turn to European craftsmen for furnishing the President's House was sharply questioned in 1826 by an Act of Congress stipulating that "as far as practicable" domestic artisans should be patronized. However, the practice of buying abroad continued. In 1840 a member of Congress roundly criticized President Martin Van Buren for filling what was then becoming commonly known as the White House with "all imaginable luxuries and gaudy ornaments" and other "costly fripperies of Europe" to the point where it resembled "*a* PALACE *as splendid as that of the Caesars, and as richly adorned as the proudest Asiatic mansion.*"

In the years following the war, thanks partly to a proliferation of published sources, partly to the increased inventiveness of native talent, and partly to the continued immigration of French and other foreign artisans, the American Empire style assumed a richer and more varied character. As had occurred earlier in France and England, the repertory of antique forms that could be reconciled or adapted to current needs and habits was fully exploited. The klismos type of chair was and still is a perfectly comfortable and handsome seating form. Another variety of chair with "Grecian Cross" legs, based on the curule, or folding seat, of Roman magistrates, was also popular as were "Grecian" couches of the sort painted by Jacques Louis David in his famous portrait of Madame Récamier. Greco-Roman tripods suggested new shapes for tables and candlestands. Other supports took the form of the monopodium, an ancient design with an animal leg surmounted by an animal head in a single composition. Winged figures resembling sphinxes, sofa legs in the nature of a winged lion's paw, dolphins and swans, and all manner of inlaid, applied, painted, and stenciled ornament traced their designs to classical sources. Silversmiths, glassmakers, and craftsmen in other mediums adapted the style to their own ends. Even many of the machine-made products later in the period still reflected the classical style in their general outlines.

As time passed, forms in most mediums became progressively heavier and carved, and other detail became coarser in character. The slim and delicate nature of the designs that had introduced the classical revival was lost and forgotten. New style trends of nonclassical inspiration were competing for favor among the fashionable. As late as 1862 at least one English furniture book was still featuring classical designs exclusively, but by then the style had had its day. In 1854 Benjamin Silliman, Jr., the eminent Yale professor, could look back on what he considered the "ponderous and frigid monstrosities" of the classical style. "The solemn affectation of Greek and Roman forms was so ridiculous," he observed, "that only the inherent vitality and grand simplicity of the classic motives [sic] enabled them to survive 'the deep damnation of this *taking off.*'" All Silliman was really saying was that taste was changing, as it constantly does. The classical style had endured longer than any other style that was to follow.

Portrait of Juliette Récamier, by David

More Light from the Past

126. *Writing and sewing table by Allison*

The American naval victories early in the War of 1812 caused consternation in England, where marine insurance rates soared, and elation in America, where native artists proudly depicted each triumph. Such scenes sometimes appeared on the painted glass panels of so-called tabernacle mirrors (128), a Sheraton style form that retained its popularity through the second decade of the nineteenth century. In his *Cabinet Dictionary* (1803) Sheraton described, as a relatively new convenience, dining tables made up of sections that could be bolted together. The tops, he explained, were supported by columns resting on curved legs with claw feet and casters, as in this example (127), probably by Phyfe. *The Supplement to The London Chair-Makers' and Carvers' Book of Prices*, published in 1808 and no doubt soon after available in New York, described chairs with "Grecian Cross" legs, such as this one (129) from Phyfe's shop. Chairs of this type were modeled on the folding seats, or curule, used by ancient Roman magistrates. With its swan-neck lyres and eagle-head feet the work table and desk (126), labeled by Michael Allison, approaches a more advanced expression of the Empire style.

127. *Below: a sectional table, made 1810–20*

128. *Above: gilt mirror with a painted panel*

129. *Right: a chair with "Grecian Cross" legs*

130. *Above: detail from* The Tea Party, *possibly in the artist's home, painted by Henry Sargent*

131. *Below, left: lyre-back armchair from a group of furniture made by Lannuier for James Bosley*

132. *Below, right: design for a* fauteuil, *or open armchair, from Percier and Fontaine's* Receuil

Lannuier left France before Napoleon Bonaparte crowned himself emperor and before he appointed Percier and Fontaine official architects and designers to his court. However, in their *Recueil de Décorations Intérieures* (1801), those two talented men had already formulated the essentials of what would be known as the Empire style. The winged figures, saber-shaped legs, lion-paw feet, and other transcriptions of furniture forms of classical antiquity that they pictured sooner or later became part of the basic vocabulary of design in the western world, reiterated and developed in books by other designers, both French and English.

French influence, however direct or indirect, was clearly reflected in much of the furniture made in America in the several decades following 1815. The Boston interior shown here (130) was furnished completely in the Empire style.

Whether those pieces were made in France or America cannot easily be determined. However, they are allied in spirit to the carved and gilded forms (131, 133) by Lannuier and, in turn, to the inventions of Percier and Fontaine (132).

In the years following the War of 1812 numerous Frenchmen of different occupations and various ranks, cabinetmakers among them, and including Joseph Bonaparte, sometime king of Naples and of Spain, sailed for the New World in the aftermath of the Napoleonic Wars to find respite from the turmoil abroad. Looking back on the New York scene, one extravagantly reminiscent native of the city remarked: "Have we not jostled ex-kings and ex-empresses and ex-nobles in Broadway; trod on the toes of exotic naturalists, Waterloo marshals, and great foreign academicians...and seen more heroes all over town than would fill a new Iliad?"

133. A carved and gilded card table probably by Lannuier

134. *Above: a painted "Grecian" chair*

135. *Below: a detail from a Greek vase*

136. *Right: stenciled couch by Phyfe*

137. *Opposite: ormolu mount from a bed*

Although little furniture survived from antiquity, a variety of forms had been depicted on Greek pottery, on gravestones, and on Egyptian and Roman wall paintings, and Europe (and America) became increasingly familiar with these through book illustrations. The klismos, a type of chair developed by Greek designers in the fifth century B.C. and one of the most graceful furniture forms ever conceived, was frequently represented in Greek vase paintings (135). Percier and Fontaine illustrated such a chair in the first edition of their publication, and subsequently the shape was widely copied and adopted. A Philadelphia example (134) closely follows the Grecian pattern, although its back is caned in the "modern" fashion and its painted decorations are a mixture of Greek, Pompeian, and Egyptian motifs.

Jacques Louis David, court painter to both Louis XVI and to Napoleon, did much to lay the groundwork for the Empire style through his fashionable portraits and historical scenes with their representations of furniture in the ancient style. Couches with scrolled ends, like this one (136), were termed "Grecian" in the early nineteenth century; they are often called "Récamiers" today, recalling David's famous portraits of the lady of that name. The example shown here is painted and grained to simulate rosewood, with stenciled gilt decoration in imitation of ormolu.

138. *Above: easel in the Empire style*

139. *Right: secretary by Quervelle, 1827*

140. *Opposite, top: an ormolu appliqué*

141. *Opposite, below: a scroll-end couch*

The use of painted graining and gilding as a substitute for exotic woods, ormolu mounts, and other costly materials was widely practiced in America during the Empire period. This kind of economical but highly effective "fancy work" appears again at its best on the scroll-end stool, or couch, below (141).

Toward the middle years of the nineteenth century the zeal with which adult Americans sought to continue and further their education amounted almost to a crusade. For artisans, laborers, factory girls, and others, wrote an English visitor, going to lectures was "the next most important duty to going to church." The lyceum movement, dedicated to the "general diffusion of knowledge," was organized in 1826 and soon all but covered the nation with lecturers. Two years earlier The Franklin Institute of the State of Pennsylvania for the Promotion of the Mechanic Arts was chartered. At the public exhibition it staged in 1827 the judges awarded a silver medal to Anthony G. Quervelle, a Paris-born Philadelphian, for the secretary illustrated here (139)—a piece the maker proudly labeled five times. With its decorative carving, Baccarat glass drawer pulls, and ormolu mounts and fittings it was, the judges agreed, "A splendid piece of furniture" by an "excellent workman."

Another highly competent craftsman fashioned an artist's easel (138) with swan-head terminals and a delicately modeled ormolu appliqué, which may have been a part of the suite of Empire furniture represented in Henry Sargent's painting *The Tea Party* (see page 108).

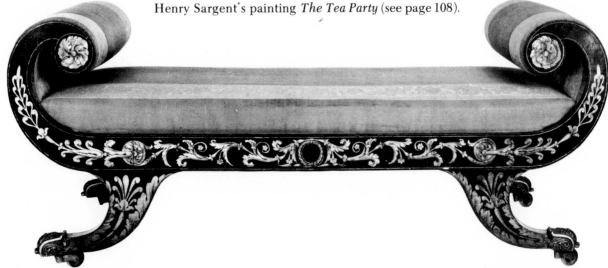

142. OVERLEAF: *Water color by Alexander J. Davis, 1845,
depicting an ideal interior in the Greek Revival style*

143. *Top: label used by Anthony Quervelle*

144. *Above: a guéridon made by Lannuier*

145. *Right: sofa with a drawer in each arm*

During the Presidency of Andrew Jackson, Quervelle was commissioned to supply a number of tables for the East Room in the White House. A few years earlier one visitor reported that the room was then furnished only with "13 old mahogany armed chairs (representing probably the old 13 states), most of which had bottoms, indicating that but few of the states would ever be found unsafe and useless; and all of them were destitute of any covering...." Jackson spent almost ten thousand dollars to decorate the room with, in addition to Quervelle's furniture, cutglass chandeliers, a Brussels carpet, new chairs and sofas, and twenty spittoons.

Before his untimely death in 1819 Lannuier finished (and labeled) a *guéridon* (144), or small, round table, which has since found its way to the Red Room of the White House. This table, with its inlaid marble top and gracefully curved legs capped by bronze female heads, is one of that French *émigré's* happiest creations.

In the federal period sofas, couches, and settees were relatively uncommon luxuries, conveniences enjoyed by only some of the well to do. As the century advanced such forms became familiar equipment in well-appointed American homes. They were to be found even on the frontier, according to Mrs. Basil Hall, who complained of the "miserable, nasty, narrow" wooden example she had to sit on in Illinois in 1828. About the time Mrs. Hall issued that complaint William Hancock, upholsterer at 39–41 Market Street, Boston, made and labeled an amply padded sofa (145), which would have provided that aristocratic lady with comfort she craved "at the end of a fagging day's work." For further convenience Hancock incorporated two drawers in the cylindrical ends of the piece.

146. *Right: a mahogany card table*

147. *Below: sideboard with tambour
shutters, made in Phyfe's workshop*

In 1805 David Longworth's *New-York
Register, and City Directory* proudly announced that the furniture made in that
city was quite as elegant as any that was
being imported from Europe, and that it
was "scarcely equalled in any other city
in America." That local pride was not un-
justified. At the time, Duncan Phyfe was
giving initial form to what would develop
over the ensuing years into a full-blown
American version of the Empire style.

Both the pieces illustrated on this page
were made in New York within ten or fifteen years after the conclusion of the War
of 1812, and both incorporate elements
typical of the more advanced local style
of cabinetwork of that period. The sideboard (147), with its engaged columns of
the Ionic order, its lion-paw feet, and
lion-head drawer pulls, is fairly attributed
to Duncan Phyfe's shop; the card table
(146), along with its massive paw feet and
its lyre with swan-head terminals, un-
expectedly displays a richly carved, brim-
ming basket of vegetables and leaves.

A succession of English books charted the changes in taste during the period of the Regency, changes which were in large part further variations on classical themes, which were related to developments of the Empire style in France, and which had their counterparts in American furniture and decoration. In England the search for novelty reached a point that led one reporter in 1820 to suggest that furniture designs, "like female fashions, should be published monthly." However, most Americans tended to resist the excesses of innovation that marked the English scene while they created their own variations of the current modes. An armchair (148), from a set of nine pieces, with ormolu mounts and painted red with gilt stripes, continues the tradition of Sheraton's earlier designs in its outlines and decoration. A mahogany side chair (149) with gilt stenciling follows the Greek klismos form, a form so basically satisfactory that it provided inspiration to chairmakers for years to come, even to the present time.

148. *Top: a painted armchair with ormolu ornaments*

149. *Above: a side chair with stenciled gilt designs*

French fashions, as they changed over the years, were widely publicized by Pierre de la Mésangère, a college professor and picturesque ecclesiastic whose periodical, *Collection des Meubles et Objets de Goût*, was published continuously in Paris from 1802 until 1835. Mésangère was to Percier and Fontaine what Hepplewhite and Sheraton had been to the brothers Adam, a popularizer who modified the most elegant designs of the day into something within range of the public's taste and purse. From the start he pictured designs for console, or pier, tables, which became one of the most characteristic forms in Empire furniture. An American example (152), with its marble top, ormolu fittings, and pillared supports, like examples shown by Mésangère, has a mirror panel which by its reflections creates the illusion that the table is twice as large as it actually is.

By the third and fourth decades of the century the delicate grace the classical revival had assumed in its first phases fifty years earlier had given way, in America as elsewhere, to a massive solidity that was a symptom of decline. Even so, there was what might be called a bourgeois opulence in the best work of this period which had its own distinctive attractions—and still does. The dressing bureau (150), an example of a highly popular form, has stout pillars terminating in huge lion-paw feet with sharply delineated claws. In place of the inlays so typical of furniture in the Federal style, designs neatly stenciled in gilt border the drawers. On a work, or sewing, table (151) the gilt stenciling decorating the four stocky pillars simulates ormolu. (The back of the piece has false drawer fronts so that it could be placed in the middle of a room and look well from either side.) The deeply carved, four-legged pedestal could support a case far heavier than the one it was called upon to do.

150. Opposite: bureau, mahogany veneer with carved and gilded decoration

151. Above: sewing table, on a four-footed pedestal, brass inlays on the top

152. Right: a French-style console table

153. *Top: a mahogany sofa in the Empire style with carved ornament*

154. *Above: chair with voluted arms and gilt and ebonized decoration*

155. *Opposite: a rosewood drum table with marble top and stenciling*

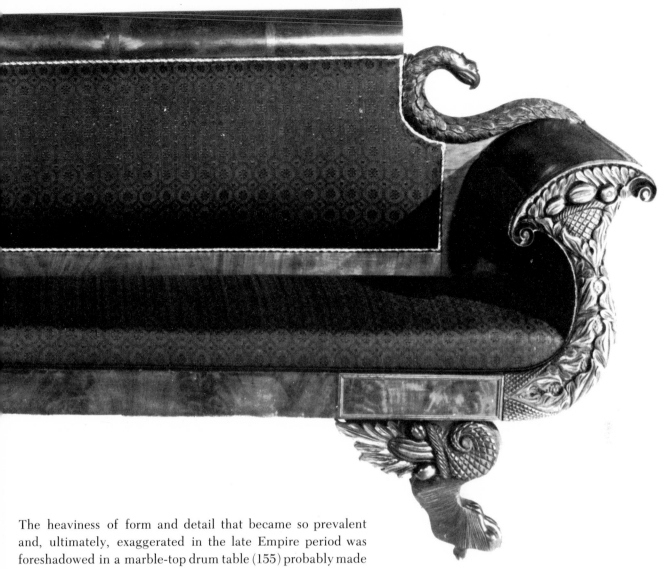

The heaviness of form and detail that became so prevalent and, ultimately, exaggerated in the late Empire period was foreshadowed in a marble-top drum table (155) probably made in the 1820's. However, some relief to the bulkiness of the piece is provided by the finely stenciled designs that border the pedestal base and the top apron. A chair (154) with arms ending in enormous volutes and standing (all but walking, apparently) on four boldly curved paw-footed legs, and a sofa (153) with a rich medley of carved ornament represent the style as it reached its climax in the 1830's. The "solemn affectation of Greek and Roman forms" that Professor Benjamin Silliman thought so ridiculous had now reached a point of overdevelopment where classical lines and proportions were barely discernible.

The wealth of the country was greater and more widely distributed than ever before. Among other indications of this, visitors found it increasingly difficult to distinguish the social position of Americans by their appearance. Critics at home, on the other hand, were beginning to complain that "the extravagance of all classes" was a matter for worry, as Lydia Maria Francis Child did in 1838 in her influential book, *The American Frugal Housewife*. That title had first been published in 1829, and it helped to launch a long series of other household manuals by different authors. All of them were issued to explain the proprieties and economies of housekeeping to those who were facing such problems for the first time.

Forms
of Antiquity

Between the time when the blowpipe was first used, probably in Syria about two thousand years ago, and the 1820's, when Americans perfected the mechanical pressing machine, there had been no significant development in the manufacture of glass. Almost every technique known to the early glasshouses of America was long ago familiar to the workmen at Alexandria, Sidon, and other centers of production, who supplied the ancient Roman world with bottles, pitchers, bowls, flasks, and other paraphernalia. Between times, itinerant glassblowers roamed from one region to another and from one country to the next, spreading styles and technical habits as they went. From Jamestown on, early American glasshouses depended heavily on craftsmen from Europe who brought with them the traditions of their various homelands.

By coincidence, in the first half of the nineteenth century when Americans were giving their cities such names as Rome, Carthage, and Alexandria, glasshouses in America were producing wares which often showed startling resemblances to the glass known and used in the ancient cities of those names during the first five centuries of our era. Roman glass, unlike Roman architecture, was practically unknown in America, so it could hardly have been copied. However, as the paired examples on this page make clear, by using similar molds, by applying much of the same kind of stringing and other overlaid decorations, and otherwise by the practice of various fundamental techniques in fashioning essential forms, the nineteenth-century American craftsman arrived at much the same end product as his Roman predecessor.

156, 157. An American pitcher (left) and a fragment of an ancient vase (right), both free-blown bulbous shapes with overlaid decoration in a "lily-pad" pattern

124

158, 159. Opposite, top: ancient Roman and 19th-century American (beneath) fish-shaped flasks; each one was blown in a two-part, full-size mold

160, 161. Pitcher (above) made in Midwest; blown in a small pattern mold and expanded and swirled, with glass stringing applied about the neck. A counterpart (right) was probably blown at Roman Alexandria and fashioned by the same techniques.

162, 163. American mug (left) blown in a full-size, three-part, hinged mold. An ancient example (right) with the name of its maker, ENNION, incorporated into the geometric design

Glass, East & West

Most American glasshouses of the early nineteenth century were established to produce bottles and windowpanes. From the same batches of glass, the workmen also made pitchers, bowls, mugs, and the like for local customers—pieces that show the same variety and uncertainty of hue as the basic product, ranging from the deep olive greens and ambers of bottles to the pale aquamarine of window glass.

Successive generations of itinerant glassmakers continued accustomed practices in making such individually designed objects, practices that stemmed from colonial experience. Much of the output of the New England and Middle Atlantic states followed traditions developed generations earlier in southern New Jersey, as in the case of the pitcher (165) and candlestick (164) shown here. Glass of this so-called South Jersey type is free blown, and is often decorated with overlaid patterns in loops or "waves." Glassblowers who carried on their work at factories in the Midwest, on the other hand, often made use of small pattern molds into which a gathering of glass was dipped, then withdrawn and expanded, a technique associated with "Baron" Stiegel's pre-Revolutionary operations in Pennsylvania. All three pieces shown on the opposite page were made in Ohio or near-by areas.

164. *Above: a South Jersey type glass candlestick*

165. *Right: a free-blown pitcher with applied so-called lily-pad decoration, made about 1840–50*

166. *Top: sugar bowl with pattern-molded design*

167. *Left: a flask with a twice-impressed pattern*

168. *Above: pattern-molded compote from Ohio*

The quest for a colorless, crystal-like glass was an expensive pursuit long discouraged by conditions in America. Throughout the colonial period and for decades following, glassmaking was a precarious business in this country. Even factories which produced the most immediate necessities, bottles and window glass, did not often long survive.

One early indication of the booming potential of the American Midwest came in 1808 with the establishment by Benjamin Bakewell of a glasshouse in Pittsburgh, which from the start produced clear, dense, brilliantly cut and engraved tablewares. The factory created a sensation of sorts. One English visitor remarked that Bakewell's cut glass equalled the best he had ever seen in England. Another traveler was astonished that Pittsburgh, "which a New Yorker supposes to be at the farther end of the world," found its principal market for glittering chandeliers and other luxuries in the western states. In 1817 President James Monroe visited Bakewell's and was so impressed that he ordered a large service engraved with the arms of the United States for the White House.

169. Opposite: glassmaking in Pittsburgh, 1887. Bakewell's glasshouse operated continuously for 74 years.

170. Above: cut-glass tumbler, made in Bakewell's glasshouse, about 1824

171. Right: goblet engraved with the arms of Pennsylvania; Pittsburgh area

Merchants
&
Mandarins

"On Sunday last sailed from New York, the ship *Empress of China*, Captain John Green of this port for Canton in China," ran a newspaper report in 1784. "The Captain and crew, with several young American adventurers, were all happy and cheerful, in good health and high spirits; and with a becoming decency, elated on being considered the first instruments, in the hands of Providence, who have undertaken to extend the commerce of the United States of America to that distant, and to us unexplored, country."

China had not, in fact, been extensively explored by any travelers from the western world. Marco Polo (in company with his father, Niccolo, and his uncle, Maffeo) had been a guest of the Mongol emperor, Kublai Khan, in the thirteenth century, and from the 1600's on returning Jesuits, mostly French, had been the chief sources of information. But the Celestial Empire had little use for foreign barbarians, thanks to the treacheries and cruelties of sixteenth-century Portuguese merchants. A policy of stern isolation was directed against the "Ho-lan devils" from Holland, the "red-haired devils" from England, and after the American Revolution the "flowery-flag devils" from the United States. Further, the Chinese did not deal with other governments on a basis of equality, but they received all envoys as humble bearers of homage—and imperiously dismissed them. "Our dynasty's majestic virtue has penetrated unto every country under Heaven, and Kings of all nations have offered their costly tribute by land and sea," wrote the emperor Ch'ien Lung at the close of the 1700's in a mandate dispatched to George III of England. "As your Ambassador can see for himself, we possess all things. I set no value on objects strange or ingenious, and have no use for your country's manufactures. This then is my answer to your request to appoint a representative at my Court."

Until the time of the Opium War (1839–42), when the British forces opened the ports of Amoy, Foochow, Ningpo, and Shanghai, trade with the sprawling empire was limited to the port of Canton. Here the *Co-hong*, a small group of Chinese merchants appointed by the emperor (often at a price), controlled foreign trade and in return for this lucrative monopoly was responsible for the credit and deportment of their clients. Canton itself was closed to foreign merchants, who were relegated to a narrow strip of land lying between the city wall and the Canton River, where factories (or warehouses), known as "hongs," were established for the exchange of goods. As a further token of isolation the Chinese were forbidden to teach their native tongue to foreigners, which resulted in a sing-song business language called pidgin English, pidgin being a corruption of the word "business." The presence of foreign women was also strictly prohibited, and in 1832 when two Boston ladies, Miss Harriette Low and her aunt, dared arrive in Canton in disguise all commerce stopped until they had left the forbidden ground.

But despite the annoyances of such minutely regulated trade, the hazards of attack and of slaughter in the pirate-infested China Sea, uncharted waters, and the perils of Cape Horn's lashing

storms and icebergs, the Orient beckoned, offering the golden lures of adventure and riches. American men in American ships entered the China trade with gusto and fervor and set sail for the Pacific Ocean, its "Milky-ways of coral isles, and low-lying, endless, unknown archipelagoes and impenetrable Japans." In contrast to the Dutch and British East India companies with their government backing American merchants entered the trade as individuals, at their own risk. In England if a gentleman went to sea he chose the navy. But in New England the social standing of the merchant service remained as high as in colonial days. (On Cape Cod it used to be said of a pretty, well-bred girl: "She's good enough to marry an East-India Cap'n!") Sons of prominent families sailed as supercargoes, the business agents of the voyage, and successive waves of intrepid teen-age boys, drawn by tradition and the prestige of the shipmaster's calling, served as seamen on American vessels. "We have an excellent crew," wrote the supercargo of the *George*, out of Salem, 1818. "They are all young & very smart, & noisy enough. It is always 'drive on boys!'" Often their captains were scarcely older than themselves. It was not uncommon for a ship to be in the command of a skipper nineteen, twenty, or twenty-one years old, who thought nothing of taking his crew of youngsters around the world, putting in at "every nook of barbarism which had a market and a shore."

Not every teen-age sailor, of course, became a captain and shipowner, but among those who did were the merchant princes to the next generation of boys who went to sea. Robert Bennet Forbes, for example, a merchant–shipowner of Boston, rose through the ranks in a maritime career that began at the age of thirteen when he shipped before the mast of the *Canton Packet* in 1817, with a capital consisting of a quadrant, a Bowditch's *Navigator,* a full outfit of sailor's clothes, a Testament, and "my mother's blessing."

In the early years America had little except specie to tempt the self-sufficient Chinese in return for the desired tea, silks, and porcelains. The *Empress of China*, however, and the ships that followed her were eminently successful with their cargoes of ginseng, a wild root of the eastern states and worth its weight in gold in the Orient, where ginseng was considered the "dose of immortality." But it was the fur of the sea otter, warmer than sable, more delicate and more durable than mink, that became the principal commodity in the China trade. "Next to a beautiful woman and a lovely infant," declared one Boston shipmaster, "a prime sea-otter skin...was the finest natural object in the world." And the pelts could be ob-

tained for a mere handful of trinkets from the Indians of the northwest coast. So profitable, in fact, was the sea otter trade that the hapless creatures were butchered to the brink of extinction. Seals, too, were clubbed and skinned by the millions on remote South Sea beaches. A deft hunter "would skin sixty in an hour." Sandalwood, tortoise shell, mother-of-pearl, sea slugs *(bêche-de-mer)*, and edible bird's nests were harvested from such perilous shores as the Fiji Islands, where hostile cannibals all too frequently killed and ate the crew of a Yankee ship bound for Canton. (In the 1850's an enterprising captain picked up a bizarre but profitable cargo in San Francisco, consisting of one hundred coffined Chinese being returned to their homeland for burial—at seventy-five dollars per "passenger.")

Trade with India, later carried on chiefly by Boston and Salem, began at the same time as the China trade and brought an amazingly diverse list of items to America: alum, arrowroot, shellac, twine, hides, carpeting, straw matting, feather tippets, elephants, and cheap textiles—with such exotic names as "frocketsay romals" and "gauzipore baftas," which dry-goods clerks simply referred to as "hum hums." The Dutch islands southeast of India bartered coffee and pepper, and Salem's trading vessels were so successful in these distant ports that the Dutch outposts were soon known as the "Salem East Indies."

Meantime, speed became the essence of the merchant service, spurred on by the prospects of higher and higher profits. America entered the great age of sail and developed the clipper ship, "strikingly beautiful with a dashy, man-of-war air," the towering spars reaching "up near Orion." Clippers, technically three-masted, square-rigged ships, had sharp hulls that cut through the waves, whereas the older bluff-bowed ships butted their way. In the hands of a master who was a driver, "a daredevil with a mania for speed," clipper runs to China in less than a hundred days were a common occurrence. The *Sea Witch*, under Captain Robert Waterman, was brought home in 1849 in a breathtaking seventy-four days and fourteen hours, a record never broken by any larger, later, or sharper clipper. In Canton these sleek American ships stole the tea trade from lumbering British merchantmen and carried their perishable cargo (at double and triple rates per ton) to London in record-breaking time. "Let our shipbuilders and employers take warning," cried *The Times* of London. "We want fast vessels for the long voyages which...fall into American hands."

But times were changing. The China trade was on the wane. Porcelains, silks, and nankeens were imitated by European and American industries. Only tea remained as an irreplaceable commodity. Too many clipper ships and packet boats had been built, and they became a glut on the market. New England boys no longer left the farm to go to sea. The West had fired their imagination as the path to adventure and wealth. Shipowners were hiring cheap foreign labor to man their vessels or were rounding up a motley gang of drunks and vagrants, many shanghaied aboard and beaten into shape as crewmen. "It was sometimes a toss-up," wrote the master of such a crew, "whether they or the captain and officers would have charge of the ship." Still, he said, "to see these fellows laying out on an eighty-foot main-yard in a whistling gale off Cape Horn, fisting hold of a big No. 1 Colt's cotton canvas mainsail, heavy and stiff with sleet and snow, bellying, slatting, and thundering in the gear...made it easy to forget their sins in admiration of their splendid courage."

The China Trade

During the heyday of the China trade the name of Houqua, senior hong merchant at Canton, often appeared in the records of Yankee traders. He was described in 1809 as a man of honor, "rather dear, loves flattery & can be coaxed." (Among his colleagues were others candidly appraised as "a great scoundrel" or as one who "cannot be depended upon.") Houqua's portrait (173) was painted about 1825 by George Chinnery, an Englishman who lived in the East for fifty years taking likenesses in India and China. Chinnery, clearly not a family man, fled to Canton when his wife threatened to join him in his travels. "What a kind providence is this Chinese government," he remarked, "that it forbids the softer sex from coming and bothering us here." The foreign quarter of the Canton River, open to western visitors but closed to their wives and daughters, is shown here (172) on an early nineteenth-century lacquered tray designed for the export trade. The foreign factories fly American, English, and Dutch flags. Among porcelains offered for export, these examples (174, 175, 176) were made expressly for the American market. The plate (174) is part of a set owned by Washington.

172. *Opposite: a view of the water front at Canton*

173. *Opposite, below: Cantonese merchant Houqua*

174. *Right: a plate with the Order of the Cincinnati*

175. *Below: urn with Declaration of Independence*

176. *Below, right: plate with the* Friendship, *Salem*

133

Export porcelain decorated to personal taste became such a flourishing enterprise that shipments from Chinese ceramic centers arrived in Canton unfinished, there to be painted by special order. (The finest porcelains never found their way to the export market, but they were reserved for imperial use.) In Canton an assembly line of painters completed the decorating process. "In one long gallery we found upwards of a hundred persons at work in sketching or finishing the various ornaments upon each particular piece of the ware, some parts being executed by men of a very advanced age, and others by children even so young as six or seven years." This initialed plate (179), an example of such special orders, displays the figure of an Indian with a bow and quiver of arrows to complete its Americanization. The urn (178) is decorated with the cipher of Mary Alexander Duane, wife of James Duane, mayor of New York, 1784–89. The porcelain tureen (180) and its mate were brought to Salem by Captain Ward Blackler and presented in 1803 to the East India Marine Society, whose membership was limited to Salem shipmasters or supercargoes, "Who shall have actually navigated the Seas near the Cape of Good Hope or Cape Horn." The painting (177), showing the lavish assortment of goods offered by a Chinese merchant, was originally meant to be used for a fan.

177. *Left: a Chinese painting showing a shop's interior*

178. *Opposite: porcelain pistol-handled urn with cipher*

179. *Above: plate with cipher circled by Latin motto*

180. *Below: a soup tureen, 22 inches long, one of a pair*

181. Above: picture of Chinese workmen making western-styled export furniture. 182. Below: lacquered export dressing stand

Despite imperial disapproval of "barbarian influences" the Chinese were quick to incorporate American and European furniture forms into their export trade. Typical of such foreign designs are this dressing stand (182), made about 1790, and the sewing table (183), made between 1820 and 1840. Both, however, are finished in a thoroughly Chinese manner with lacquered ornamentation and landscape vignettes; the interior of this table is also decorated and fitted with ivory sewing accessories. In the cabinetmaker's shop (181) are pictured such distinctly western forms as an armchair in the Greek mode, an Empire settee, a tilt-top table, and against the right wall, a pair of gate-leg tables. The traditional Chinese forms continued, of course, to fascinate, such as this stained and varnished bamboo and cane chair (184), one of a set of four shipped to the United States in the 1800's. One of the finest collections of artifacts gathered during the early years of the China trade was brought to America in 1795 by a former director of the Dutch East India Company in Canton, Andreas Everardus van Braam Houckgeest. Of Van Braam's villa, China Retreat, on the banks of the Delaware, Moreau de Saint-Méry wrote: "the furniture, ornaments, everything at Mr. Van Braam's reminds us of China. It was even impossible to avoid fancying ourselves in China, while surrounded at once by living Chinese [Van Braam's servants], and by representations of their manners, their usages, their monuments, and their arts."

183. Above: Chinese export sewing table, black and gold lacquer

184. Right: a bamboo and cane armchair made in a Chinese design

137

Reverend William Bentley of Salem noted in his diary in 1796 that Captain Gibaut "had private orders to execute in his ship at Canton amounting to $4000, for the little elegancies of life...so rapid are our strides to wealth and luxury." Both China and East India traders, in behalf of their land-bound families and friends, carried such private orders—for red carnelian necklaces, pots of preserved ginger, a Sanskrit Bible, pieces of cobweb muslin. A note pasted in the ledger of the brig *Caravan* of Salem, early in 1812, requested the purchase of two white Cashmere shawls with palm-leaf borders. And a feminine hand added the further shopping directions, "narrow Border round Edge avoid Red." (On the same voyage Captain Augustine Heard was also given varying sums of specie to invest in profitable goods for "private adventures"—two thousand silver dollars from his father, and from twenty to one hundred dollars from maiden aunts and retired sea captains.)

Illustrated here are a few of the "little elegancies of life" carried to America by returning ships. The plaster figurines belonged to Edward Carrington, American consul in Canton from 1802 to 1811, who founded a shipping firm in Providence and built a house from which he could scan the harbor when awaiting the arrival of one of his twenty-six merchantmen. The eighteenth-century Chinese wallpaper (188) delicately pictures the never-never land of the Orient. The same delicacy of landscape and figures was also achieved in the carvings on the rhinoceros horn (187) and its ebony stand. The ivory chessmen (186) again demonstrate western influences on eastern design; the king's crown in this set is topped by a cross.

185. *Above: Chinese plaster figurines*

186. *Below: chessmen of Indian ivory*

187. *Opposite: carved rhinoceros horn*

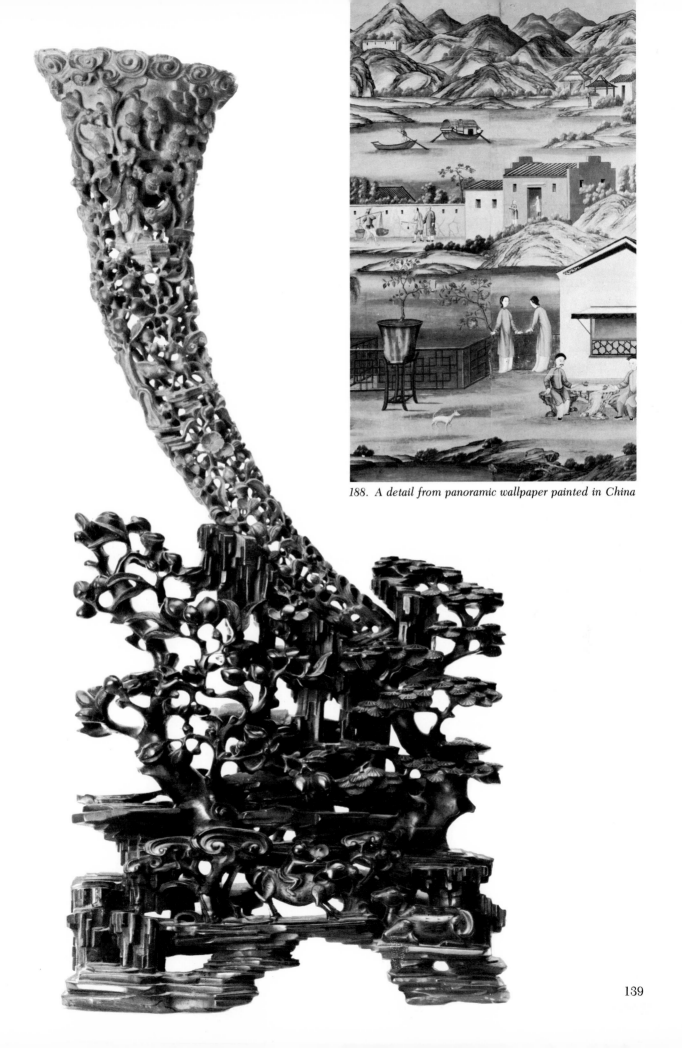

188. *A detail from panoramic wallpaper painted in China*

With the opening of Japan new ports of call offered Oriental goods and exotica to Yankee traders. And after centuries of isolation the Japanese, in turn, looked at the western visitors as exotica in themselves. One Japanese poet wrote:

What are those strangely-clad beings
Who move quickly from one spot of interest to another
Like butterflies flitting from flower to flower?
    These are Americans.

Japanese artists, both amazed and amused by the mysterious West, produced a flurry of prints depicting the fantastic strangers (191) and their fantastic homeland. In this imaginative view of America (190) the handsome building—in a tropic setting—is actually a picture of Frederiksborg castle in Denmark. In America, meanwhile, equally imaginative versions of the mysterious East were being produced. This carved wooden shop figure (189) might well have stood in front of an importer's showroom, as cigar-store Indians stood before tobacconists as an attractive advertisement.

189. *Opposite: American shop figure of a Chinese woman*

190. *Above: Japanese print showing "Prosperous America"*

191. *Below: a Japanese print depicting an American family*

Patterns from Abroad

192. *Pilgrims landing at Plymouth Rock*

As early as 1765 Josiah Wedgwood wrote that the principal market for Staffordshire pottery was "the Continent & Islands of North America." This export trade, in fact, was so extensive that when it stopped during the Revolution Staffordshire pottery centers were afflicted with impoverishment, starvation, and food riots. In the first days of peace, however, the export trade was quickly reclaimed. In following years America was inundated with inexpensive pottery bearing transfer-printed pictures of American landscapes, public buildings, heroes, and historic events (as shown here). Until around 1830 these scenes were printed in a rich, dark cobalt blue, often known as "Old Blue." After 1830 other colors were introduced: "pink Staffordshire," sepia, black, green, lavender. All told, about eight hundred subjects were offered during the phenomenal vogue for Staffordshire imports, at its height in America from the War of 1812 until the Civil War. "Gaudy Dutch" ware (197) was designed specifically (and successfully) for the Pennsylvania German market; and spatterware, with sponged color and painted designs, here in the "Schoolhouse" pattern (198), was designed for a generalized provincial American trade.

193. *A view of the City Hall in New York*

194. *Fairmount Waterworks, Philadelphia*

195. Center: a soup tureen depicting the arrival of the Marquis de Lafayette at Castle Garden in New York, on August 16, 1824, for his tour of the country upon the invitation of the Congress and President Monroe

196. Top: a pitcher showing a view of a decisive naval battle of the War of 1812, "Com Macdonoughs Victory on Lake Champlain"

197. Above: a "Gaudy Dutch" export plate

198. Left: spatterware for American market

American Porcelain

America's pottery industry remained in an infant state for many years after the Revolution; the output was principally red-clay earthenware and salt-glazed stoneware. Until the establishment of the Tucker China Factory in Philadelphia in 1825 all earlier attempts had failed to produce sufficient porcelain to compete commercially with imports from Europe and the Orient. The Tucker enterprise, which had begun with an experimental kiln run by William Ellis Tucker in the back yard of his father's china shop, ended after a scant thirteen years of precarious financial footing and a series of partners— John N. Bird, Thomas Hulme, and Judge Joseph Hemphill of Philadelphia. But during its brief existence the Tucker china works brought a high degree of perfection to "this valuable and difficult art...." A native kaolin, the pure china clay so essential to the production of fine translucent ware, came from isolated deposits found by William Tucker in Delaware. The porcelains fired from this substance and from a fine blue clay discovered in Pennsylvania and New Jersey were compared with the "best specimens of French China."

A younger brother, Thomas, joined the firm as an apprentice in 1828. After William's untimely death in 1832 Thomas ran the company until 1838. "I then discontinued the manufacture of porcelain and commenced ordering from Europe." It was Thomas who painted the exquisite bouquets on this gold-trimmed vase (200), with ormolu handles, made about 1835 during Judge Hemphill's partnership. The teapot (199) depicts a popular view, Philadelphia's Fairmount Waterworks. On the teapot's stand, containing a candle or a spirit lamp, is a rustic landscape. The patriotic motifs on the pitcher (201) reflect the Tuckers' Quaker persuasion; wherever the American eagle appeared on their china, it was never shown carrying arrows in its talons. Another popular historic view was Castle Garden, also used on this pitcher. Built as a fort in 1807 Castle Garden served successively as an auditorium (Jenny Lind made her New York debut there), as an immigration station prior to the opening of Ellis Island, and as New York's aquarium until it was demolished by the city early in the 1940's.

199. Opposite: a porcelain teapot with stand, decorated with painted scenes

200. Left: a porcelain vase, one of a pair

201. Above: porcelain pitcher by Tucker

The Grand Style in Silver

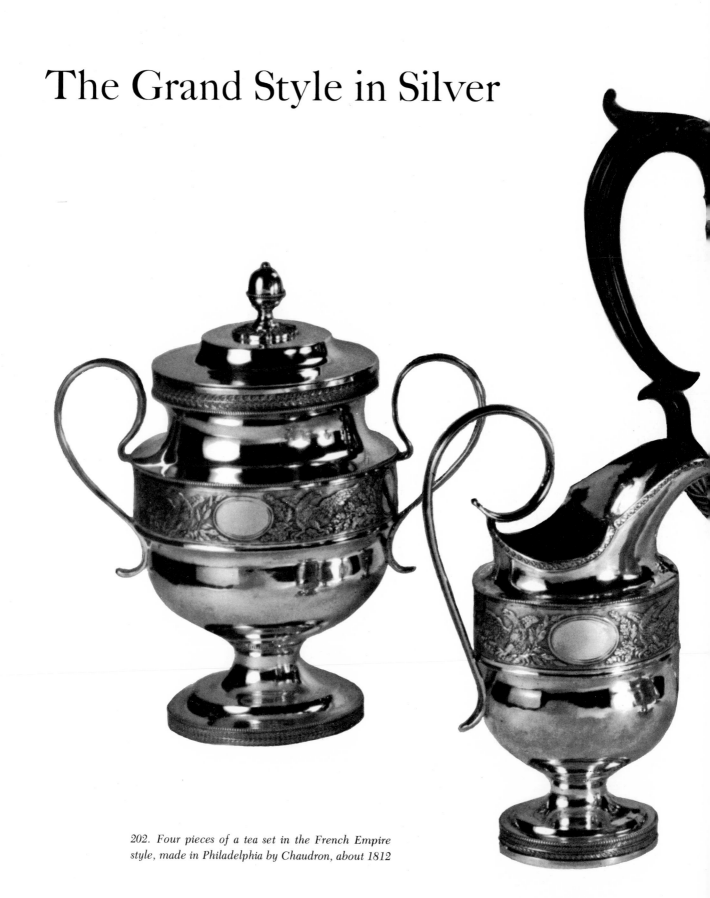

202. *Four pieces of a tea set in the French Empire style, made in Philadelphia by Chaudron, about 1812*

As the nineteenth century advanced, new methods of production and an ever-growing market of prospering people encouraged an unprecedented output of silverware. The smith could now purchase rolled sheets of metal, thin enough in section so that he could shape hollow ware without laboriously raising the forms on anvils. Ornamental bands, as on these elements of a tea and coffee set (202) by Simon Chaudron, were stamped from dies cut in various patterns by specialists in such practices. By using these devices the smith could dispense with the time-consuming work involved in engraving and embossing.

With the advent of the Empire style silverware, like furniture, tended to assume a bolder scale both in form and detail. Chaudron's set, which clearly reveals the influence of French fashions of the early nineteenth century, was given to Snowden Henry of Philadelphia by his friend the Marquis de Lafayette. Chaudron's talents were also called upon by the citizens of Philadelphia for two monumental presentation pieces to honor Captain James Lawrence and Jacob Jones for gallantry at sea in the War of 1812.

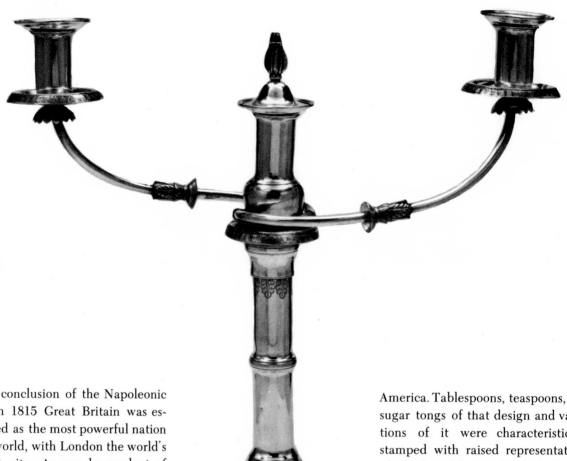

At the conclusion of the Napoleonic Wars in 1815 Great Britain was established as the most powerful nation in the world, with London the world's greatest city. As one by-product of those wars, England had secured a firm hold in India and in doing so abolished the monopoly the East India Company had long enjoyed in that area. The price of tea and sugar fell to the point where those once costly and exotic commodities were within the range of a much larger public than ever before. Americans were indirect beneficiaries of this state of affairs, as the proliferation of tea services made in this country bore witness. By the 1820's the capacious forms that made up such services had lost virtually all relationship to the classical urn and vase shapes that had inspired Paul Revere and his contemporaries in the decades following the Revolution. A sugar bowl (207) from one set, made about 1825 by George Baker of Providence, Rhode Island, with its heavily lobed body and somewhat squat over-all contour, is typical of the design of a large number of such pieces made at that time.

It was in the postwar years that the so-called fiddle-back pattern in flatware became widely popular in America. Tablespoons, teaspoons, and sugar tongs of that design and variations of it were characteristically stamped with raised representations of a basket of flowers (204) or a bound sheaf of wheat (205) with a scythe.

In spite of the development of new and brighter lamp illuminants over the second quarter of the century, and the gradual introduction of lighting with gas, the candle retained its useful and traditional place in the household. As in ages past the inadequacies of the light they provided were in some measure compensated for by the elegance of the devices fashioned to support the candles. (One highly ornamental pair of candelabras made in England of silver gilt in 1816 for presentation to the Duke of Wellington stood almost five feet high.) One of a pair of candelabras (203), probably made by John Owen of Philadelphia in the 1820's, represents the American Empire style in silver at its discreet best. Here, as in the case of a ewer (206), also one of a pair, made at about the same time by Baldwin Gardiner of Philadelphia and New York, the classical grace of the form itself is accented by the play of ornamental details against larger surfaces of plain silver.

203. Opposite: a two-armed candelabra

204. Above, left: shell-clasp sugar tongs

205. Above, right: fiddleback tablespoon

206. Above: one of a pair of tall ewers made by Baldwin Gardiner
207. Left: a silver sugar bowl with domed cover and flower finial

When Washington ordered a mirrored, silver plateau for Mount Vernon in 1789 (see page 82), he specified that "the mirrors will of course be in pieces that they may be adapted to the company, (the size of it I mean) the aggregate length of them may be ten feet, the breadth two feet." A generation or so later an elaborate example of such a centerpiece, of comparable generous and adjustable proportions (209), was made by John W. Forbes of New York. Aside from the cast eagles with outstretched wings atop each pedestal, the die-stamped ornament copies classical designs from some contemporary source. The figures on the paw-foot pedestals represent the Roman goddesses Flora (209a) and Pomona. A sugar bowl (208), from a tea set by Samuel Kirk of Baltimore, approximates the form of an ancient Greek kylix. In this case the pseudoclassical ornament of the bowl proper is *repoussé*, that is, raised by hammering the metal up from the inside. The kylix, a form of shallow, footed, and two-handled bowl often represented in Greek vase paintings, was originally used as a drinking vessel at banquets.

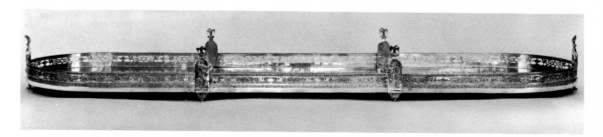

208. *Opposite, top: a sugar bowl in the Empire style by Kirk*

209. *Opposite: a three-section silver plateau by John W. Forbes*

209a. *Above: detail of plateau showing Flora, goddess of flowers*

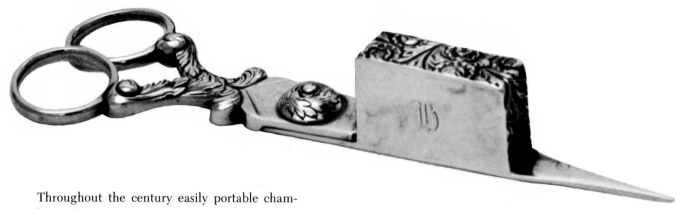

Throughout the century easily portable chambersticks (210), usually with accompanying snuffers and extinguishers, remained indispensable household conveniences. At the other end of the scale from such small forms were a considerable number of massive, extravagantly ornamented presentation pieces, given to heroes of the day in recognition of their outstanding deeds. In 1771 a monumental marble Roman vase (later acquired by the Earl of Warwick) was excavated from the ruins of Hadrian's villa, and both English and American silversmiths used this as a model for some of their most ambitious undertakings. In 1824–25, following a drawing (212) by Hugh Bridport based on the "Warwick vase," the prominent Philadelphia silversmiths Thomas Fletcher and Sidney Gardiner fashioned a pair of great urns which the grateful merchants of Pearl Street in New York gave to DeWitt Clinton upon the successful completion of the Erie Canal.

Some years later when he visited Fletcher's shop (Gardiner had since died), Philip Hone concluded that "nobody in this 'world' of ours hereabouts can compete with them in their kind of work." Actually, Sidney Gardiner's brother, Baldwin, turned out hardly less impressive pieces, including a great bowl made in 1829 for presentation to New York's distinguished district attorney, Hugh Maxwell. The two sculptured sphinx supports (211) of that great bowl presage the Egyptian influences that played a passing part in American art in the decades to come.

210. Portable candlestick (right) with its accessory trimmers (top) and its conical extinguisher (middle)

211. Above: detail from a punch bowl by Baldwin Gardiner
212. Below: drawing by Hugh Bridport of the urn presented to DeWitt Clinton, 1825

154

213. *Left: Pomona, carved by John and Simeon Skillin*

214. *Above: bust of Voltaire, made for William Bentley*

The Whittlers & Chiselers

During the colonial and federal periods a number of skilled woodworkers who specialized in ornamental carvings for ships, buildings, and furniture produced somewhat primitive but appealing figures in the round. In this branch of art, according to one contemporary, Samuel McIntire of Salem "had no rival in New England," a statement vindicated by his bust of Voltaire (214). His most apparent Yankee rivals were the Skillins of Boston, who for several generations cut ship figureheads and fashioned architectural and furniture decoration. It was John and Simeon Skillin who carved a figure of *Pomona* (213), goddess of plenty, for Elias Hasket Derby's splendid garden. For this and three other figures the Skillins charged just over twenty-nine pounds.

The most celebrated examples of such early Yankee statuary were the great company of personages (215) carved over a period of years by Joseph Wilson of Newburyport to ornament the house and property of the eccentric local merchant "Lord" Timothy Dexter. Of that august group, which included effigies of Washington, Jefferson, Adams, Bonaparte, Nelson, and others, only the figure of William Pitt (216) has survived. Dexter was renowned for his fabulous pronouncements and his imaginative ventures. According to his legend he managed to sell warming pans and woolen mittens in the West Indies, coal in Newcastle, and cats in Malta.

215. Top: Timothy Dexter's house

216. Above: figure of William Pitt

The most skilled of all those early American woodcarver-sculptors was William Rush of Philadelphia. His various creations were to be seen all about that city, and their variety suggests how firmly rooted his art was in the craft of the woodworker. Professors of anatomy used his oversize models of human organs to instruct their pupils. Churches displayed the crucifixes he carved for them and, in niches above the street level, the façade of the magnificent Chestnut Street Theatre (see page 21) sported his allegorical figures of *Tragedy* (220) and *Comedy*. He designed figureheads for the frigates authorized by Congress to subdue the Barbary pirates and sketched a Hercules for the ship *Constitution*, a heroic image he thought John Skillen of Boston capable of cutting. For other vessels he fashioned portrait busts of personages of the day. "Commerce has called for beauty in the forms and decorations of her ships," Latrobe wrote, "and where in Europe is there a Rush."

When Latrobe's pump house was installed in Center Square, Rush carved a figure for the grounds of a water nymph holding a bittern, from whose mouth water sprayed into a fountain (217). Not content to imagine an ideal form for the nymph, Rush persuaded a local young lady, under proper chaperonage, to pose as his model.

Jefferson felt that domestic talent was inadequate for cutting sculptures and ornament for the rising Capitol, and he imported Italian craftsmen. It was two of these immigrants who translated Latrobe's designs for two series of columns within the building. Jefferson had insisted that these be in the Corinthian order. Following the spirit rather than the letter of that instruction, Latrobe substituted for the acanthus leaves and scrolls of classical models ears of American corn in one instance (219) and the leaves and blossoms of the American tobacco plant in the other (218). These original, all-American variations on an ancient theme pleased Jefferson, the members of Congress, and even Mrs. Trollope, who opined that they were "peculiarly beautiful." Jefferson used Latrobe's model of the corn-capital column as the support for a sundial at Monticello.

217. *Opposite: detail of painting by John Lewis Krimmel,* Fourth of July in Center Square, *shows Rush's carved figure beside Latrobe's pump house*

218. *Top: drawing for the tobacco plant columns*

219. *Above: drawing for the Indian corn columns*

220. *Right: figure of* Tragedy *by William Rush*

American sculpture in stone was born and nourished in the graveyard. The first stone-cut images were the grim designs of early colonial tombstones (222). By the second quarter of the last century, concerned by the menace to the communities' health from overcrowded urban burial grounds, the major cities established new, land-scaped cemeteries in the neighboring countrysides—cemeteries that combined grave-yard and botanical garden ("grave gardens," as one contemporary called them). These rural retreats for the dead soon became popular retreats for the quick as well, quiet sanctuaries from urban congestion and noise. With their more elaborately carved memorials (223, 224) they also constituted outdoor sculpture galleries of a sort, and influenced the conception of public parks in years shortly to come.

There were no art academies in America where sculpture was taught with any degree of competence or enthusiasm, and no native tradition of any consequence in the working of stone in the grand manner. Almost the only practical training the budding sculptor could gain was in the marble yard (221) where tombstones were made.

221. *Opposite, top: Fisher & Bird's Marble Yard, about 1837*

222. *Opposite, bottom: detail of a gravestone, Boston, 1743*

223. *Above: the memorial to Nathaniel Bowditch at Mount Auburn, Boston, Mass., the first rural cemetery in America*

224. *Right: model of the Bowditch statue, by Robert Hughes*

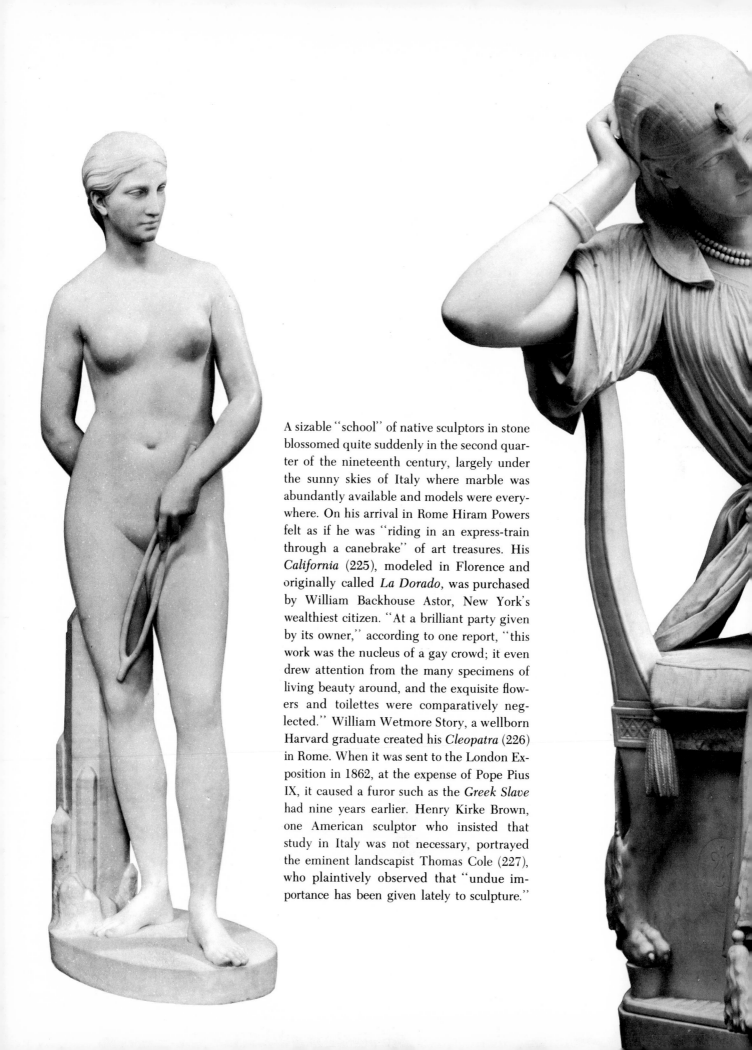

A sizable "school" of native sculptors in stone blossomed quite suddenly in the second quarter of the nineteenth century, largely under the sunny skies of Italy where marble was abundantly available and models were everywhere. On his arrival in Rome Hiram Powers felt as if he was "riding in an express-train through a canebrake" of art treasures. His *California* (225), modeled in Florence and originally called *La Dorado*, was purchased by William Backhouse Astor, New York's wealthiest citizen. "At a brilliant party given by its owner," according to one report, "this work was the nucleus of a gay crowd; it even drew attention from the many specimens of living beauty around, and the exquisite flowers and toilettes were comparatively neglected." William Wetmore Story, a wellborn Harvard graduate created his *Cleopatra* (226) in Rome. When it was sent to the London Exposition in 1862, at the expense of Pope Pius IX, it caused a furor such as the *Greek Slave* had nine years earlier. Henry Kirke Brown, one American sculptor who insisted that study in Italy was not necessary, portrayed the eminent landscapist Thomas Cole (227), who plaintively observed that "undue importance has been given lately to sculpture."

225. *Opposite:* California, *by Hiram Powers*

226. *Left: a version of Story's* Cleopatra

227. *Above: Brown's bust of Thomas Cole*

161

Hiram Powers, Yankee Stonecutter

Around the middle of the last century the most celebrated living American artist was unquestionably the sculptor Hiram Powers. His fame, which was all but world-wide, rested in good measure on his *Greek Slave*. When that nude marble figure was exhibited in New York and Cincinnati in 1847, under the direction of a very astute business agent and with the blessings of guardians of public morals, one female art critic reported that "shrieks of admiration" rang through the newspapers. The same lady admitted that she herself sat for five hours before the *Slave*, stupefied with rapture. Thousands of others paid for the privilege of watching the figure revolving on its pedestal in the National Academy of Design. A Boston artist labeled the piece as simply lascivious, of no artistic merit, but his voice did not carry far amid the general public excitement and the fanfare of the press.

Four years later when the statue was shown in London (for the second time) at the Crystal Palace Great Exhibition, Powers became an international celebrity. That such a "sublime" vision could have been realized by a virtually unheralded artist from the cultural wasteland of America caught European audiences by surprise. Elizabeth Barrett Browning was moved to write a sonnet in praise of the *Slave*. Queen Victoria and Prince Albert gave it their royal approbation. Clergymen sermonized on its moral message. And a duke of the realm bought it. Powers went on to make six replicas, all of which he succeeded in selling at an average price of about four thousand dollars, a handsome sum for a work of modern art in the 1850's. Even so, popular interest in the subject was far from exhausted. Henry James later recalled that for years parlors across the American continent displayed miniature copies of the *Slave*, "so undressed, yet so refined, even so pensive, in sugar-white alabaster, exposed under little domed glass covers in such...homes as could bring themselves to think such things right." (Prudery in America was never carried quite so far as it was in Mannheim, Germany, where in 1853 a cast of the *Venus de Milo* was tried, convicted, and condemned in a court of law on a charge of nakedness.)

At the height of his fame Powers was compared, favorably and extravagantly, with Praxiteles and Michelangelo. The curator of the Grand Ducal Gallery in Florence called the American "the first sculptor of the age." Whatever his dubious claim to such distinction, Powers enjoyed the patronage not only of his wealthy countrymen but of Russian princes and British nobles. He was a shrewd negotiator and he prospered. (The well-managed American tour of the *Greek Slave* alone grossed $23,500.) Appropriately, Powers was born among the marble hills of Vermont, and although he lived the last thirty-six years of his life in Florence he retained his "New England homeliness" all his days. The Yankee twang in his speech was just one of his personal characteristics that intrigued his listeners—and that reassured the hardheaded businessmen who came to his studio that they were dealing with a down-to-earth type, artist though he might be. Powers could indeed be as

hardheaded as any of his customers. When one of them fell behind in his payment, the sculptor prominently displayed a bust of the man in his studio and labeled it "Delinquent." He referred to the shelf on which he placed these subjects as his "pillory."

Powers rose to fame and fortune by a strange and unlikely route. His family had moved to Cincinnati when he was a youth, and there he exercised his considerable mechanical skill by working in a clock factory. During the time Mrs. Trollope made her visit to that western city, from 1828 to 1830, Powers moved on to the local museum where he was employed in producing wax effigies and automata to entertain the public. Thanks largely to his ingenuity and imagination the exhibits attracted visitors from miles around, and the show was a decided financial success. The main feature was a model of hell filled, as Mrs. Trollope discovered to her great amusement, with "all the images of horror that his fertile fancy could devise; dwarfs that by machinery grow into giants before the eyes of the spectator; imps of ebony with eyes of flame; monstrous reptiles devouring youth and beauty; lakes of fire, and mountains of ice; in short, wax, paint and springs have done wonders." To make the performance even more exciting, an electrical apparatus gave off sparks and shocked those whose curiosity brought them too close to the display.

As he turned thirty Powers quit his museum post and headed for Italy by way of Washington, where he made the likeness of Andrew Jackson shown on page 103. However grotesque his waxwork exhibits had been, they had trained Powers in creating an illusion of reality, a knack he easily carried over to portraits he modeled so faithfully to life in years to come. Here, too, his mechanical ingenuity served his best purpose. For, as one reporter observed in 1857, Powers had invented "almost an entire new set of tools, far superior to those used in sculpture from time immemorial. One of these instruments imparts to the surface of the marble a delicate 'roughness,' which so perfectly counterfeits the porosities and wrinkles of the skin as to produce the impression of excessive...labor."

Indeed, the eminent expatriate sculptor remained ever the "ingenious Yankee mechanic." In Florence he diverted himself by inventing a jew's-harp with two tongues, a machine for punching holes through iron, and other devices. "I have devoted many an evening...to mechanical contrivances...," he wrote one of his patrons, "which I think would pay well if *exploited*." He talked to Nathaniel Hawthorne about plans for laying the transatlantic cable that were far better than those that had been unsuccessfully tried. He prophesied that flying machines would soon be feasible, although "not till the moral condition of mankind is so improved as to obviate the bad uses to which the power might be applied." He had cures for burns and remedies for complaints of the chest. He had opinions on virtually everything from life on distant planets to the sound of the bells of Florence. And he was a superb conversationalist.

In Florence, Powers became a close and favorite friend of the Brownings. He was, wrote Mrs. Browning, "a most charming, simple, straightforward, genuine American" with eyes "like a wild Indian's, so black and full of light.

You would scarcely wonder if they clave the marble without the help of his hands." And in Florence he remained until his death in 1873, partly because there he could hire trained marble cutters to translate his clay images into stone at inexpensive rates, saving himself the time and bother, and partly because had he returned to America he would have faced a lawsuit for not having repaid his agent for past loans and expenses. To the end he exercised his native shrewdness in what he referred to as "this lucrative business" of making portrait busts. He never did surpass his early likeness of Jackson, one of the few of his works that he chiseled in the marble with his own hands. When he was laid to rest in the Protestant cemetery in Florence his genius was still widely acclaimed. But then, and very quickly, his reputation went into the decline from which it has never recovered. As some of his intimate contemporaries suggested, had Powers never discovered an artistic bent, and rather developed his very apparent mechanical genius, he might today be remembered as one of the world's great inventors.

228. *The Santa Manuela Rancho, California, drawn by William Rich Hutton in 1851; an example of Spanish colonial architecture*

Meetings of Cultures

When the English settled Jamestown in 1607, the Spanish ambassador in London sent a purloined plan of the James Fort to his king, Philip III, with the message: "I hope that you will give orders to have these insolent people quickly annihilated." To the Spaniards, whose American claims began with Columbus, their domination of the New World seemed a God-given inevitability. But the last of their North American territory was taken in 1821 by the newly formed republic of Mexico, which formally ceded about a million square miles of land north of the Gila River and the Rio Grande to the United States in 1848. A feudal, largely illiterate, pastoral society, loosely joined by a string of forts and missions, had drowsed for centuries in the far-flung, untapped, western wilderness. Local artisans were largely mission-trained Indians working with the materials at hand—sacred paintings done in earth and vegetable pigments, buildings made of adobe (mud bricks)—and a primitive interpretation of Spanish traditions developed, as illustrated here with the chip-carved chair (229), the window grille (230), used in lieu of glass, and the vesting table (231). Derivative versions of old Spanish forms persisted; similar rectangular patterns were mass produced in the early 1900's as "mission furniture." Spanish colonial design (228), with a patio and a long veranda, left a lasting imprint on American architecture.

229. *Pine side chair, 1750–1800*

230. Above: pine window grille in the Spanish colonial tradition

231. Below: New Mexican vesting table for ecclesiastical robes

"France once possessed in America a vast empire that extended from Labrador to the Floridas, and from the shores of the Atlantic to the most distant lakes of upper Canada." Thus begins a romantic novel by Chateaubriand, written in 1801 and set in the Indian wilds of New France. With the sale of the Louisiana territory in 1803, Napoleon ceded the last of this "vast empire" to the United States. The Louisiana territory (ultimately divided into thirteen states), like the French holdings in Canada and the East, had been governed in a feudal rule comparable to that of the Spaniards in the West. Again, a chain of forts, trading posts, and missionary outposts were strung out across the countryside. Extensive colonization had been thwarted by royal ineptitude, but there were self-sustaining French settlements strung along the western waterways from Detroit to New Orleans, where the traditions and skills of the homeland were firmly rooted. Although Detroit became British in 1760 and then American in 1796, the French flavor of the town persisted for years. Silversmiths were producing typically French forms (234) into the third decade of the nineteenth century. Early buildings in the French style still stand in small villages in Illinois and Missouri. Amusingly, *Bois Brûlé* (burnt wood), the name of an old French village, has been Anglicized as Bob Ruly (Missouri); among other similar examples, *Chemin Couvert* (covered bridge) has become Smackover (Arkansas). In the French section of St. Louis, Dickens described "quaint and picturesque" wooden houses, whose outside galleries were approached by a flight of steps, and the "abundance of crazy old tenements with blinking casements, such as may be seen in Flanders." This armoire, or cupboard (232), carved with fleurs-de-lis, belonged to Pierre Chouteau, a member of the founding family of St. Louis; an armoire was "the pride of every provincial housewife and a visible sign of her prosperity."

And in New Orleans, in 1828, Mrs. Basil Hall wrote with delighted approval about the city's Creole gaiety and "old Continental aspect...[a] lively, French tone heard in the streets...houses with queerly-shaped, high roofs and iron balconies" built around Spanish patios, and looking "deliciously cool for summer use."

232. *Opposite: walnut armoire, St. Louis, about 1780*

233. *Above: a water color of a St. Louis belle, 1818*

234. *Right: chalice made in 1819 by silversmith Victor Rouquette for the Church of Sainte Anne, Detroit*

Short Cuts to Style

Craftsmen & Machines

Years before Professor Silliman damned the "monstrosities" that had been created in the classical style, other critics were calling for less imitation and more inventiveness in American design. The architects, now solidly assured of their professional status, as they had not been in earlier times, were especially outspoken. As man progressed in goodness and in wisdom, one member of the profession observed in 1841, so must the structures that he built manifest the changes that were taking place in society. "Let us all try and see," he added, "which of us will first produce something in the art peculiar—characteristic—suited to the age—national." That was as much an expression of American ego as it was of a desire for more effective living arrangements and a growing disenchantment with the Grecian formulas. The same year, in an address before the Franklin Institute in Philadelphia, another architect advised his colleagues that if they were to achieve originality in their work they must "*think* as the Greeks thought," rather than "*do* as the Greeks did." The Greeks, after all, were originators of a way of life and of an art; they were not mere copyists.

A decade later Horatio Greenough, a prominent American sculptor, was more pointed in his remarks. "What imitation of the Greeks," he asked, ever produced such a "marvel of construction" as a sailing ship? (The *America* had recently beaten the English contender in the first of the challenge races.) And, he went on, "the men who have reduced locomotion to its simplest elements, in the trotting wagon and the yacht America, are nearer to Athens at this moment than they who would bend the Greek temple to every use. I contend for Greek principles, not Greek things." Greenough was an early apostle of functionalism in the arts. "By beauty," he wrote in his essay, *The Stonecutter's Creed*, "I mean the promise of function. By action I mean the presence of function. By character I mean the record of function."

Yet even this professed "modernist" could not escape the set conventions of his own craft. When he was commissioned by the government in 1832 to produce a statue of George Washington for the Capitol rotunda (Greenough was the first American artist to be given an important assignment by the United States government), he turned for inspiration to a late Roman copy of the great seated figure of Zeus carved by Phidias, the fifth-century B.C. Greek sculptor, for Olympia. Even in its own day Greenough's finished work was a subject of some ridicule. "It looks like a great herculean Warrior-like *Venus of the bath*," wrote

Opposite: enlarged detail of the lacy pressed-glass plate shown above in its entirety

the witty and urbane onetime mayor of New York, Philip Hone, "a grand Martial Magog—undraped, with a huge napkin lying on his lap and covering his lower extremities, and he preparing to perform his ablutions is in the act of consigning his sword to the care of the attendant." Furthermore, Hone suggested, Washington had been too careful of his health and too fastidious ever to have exposed his naked frame like that, especially considering the uncertainties of the American climate.

Nevertheless, the changes that were taking place in American society did result in developments in the arts and crafts that were in fact "peculiar—characteristic—suited to the age—national." Although the rate of those changes and developments increased dramatically in the second quarter of the nineteenth century, the circumstances that underlaid them were deeply rooted in earlier American experience. From the beginnings of colonization, time and man power were precious commodities in the New World; the point was made abundantly clear by frequent and meticulous legislation against the "misspending" of time in the Massachusetts Bay colony. In the *Lawes and Libertyes* promulgated in 1648, for example, it was specifically decreed that "no person, Houshoulder or other, shall spend his time, idlely or unprofitably" under pain of punishment by the General Court. If a New Zion were to be built in the wilderness both time and labor had to be carefully and zealously husbanded to provide for the essential needs of the community. Unremitting labor was indeed a condition of survival in the raw New World. That tireless, but rarely tiresome, Puritan diarist Samuel Sewall even condemned the April Fools' Day pranks of Boston children not because they were naughty or a nuisance, but because they were "an abuse of precious time...a profanation!" It was God's time they wasted, a gift from heaven that should be improved upon on earth and not frittered away. Benjamin Franklin reduced the matter to the simplest and most worldly terms when he pointed out to his fellow colonists in a homely maxim that time was money.

Those attitudes, which were shaped by the daily conditions of life, were reflected in colonial craftsmanship. Before the start of the Revolution the colonists had, to be sure, developed a variety of forms in furniture and other household furnishings that served their purpose so well they have not since been improved upon. Today we still use chairs, tables, teapots, and other eighteenth-century forms, in originals or reproductions, finding that they both please the eye and satisfy our modern notions of comfort and convenience.

However, for practical and economic reasons colonial furniture and silverware remained relatively modest in design and decoration. The conditions of life in America did not encourage the time-consuming, highly specialized craftsmanship that provided the courts and capitals of Europe with their very precious and extravagant examples of cabinetwork and metalwork. The most elaborate Philadelphia Chippendale highboy, the most ambitious silverwork by such master smiths as John Coney and Paul Revere were comparatively simple pieces by the standards of style set at Versailles, Hampton Court Palace, and other European centers. In a society where everyone worked, where there was no idle class of any consequence, rich or otherwise, there was no time to waste on such ultimate refinements of workmanship, or any demand to do so. As Alexis de Tocqueville remarked of the American people shortly after the Revolution: "They will habitually prefer the useful to the beautiful." And, he added, they will also "require that the beautiful should be useful."

As one response to the continuing compulsion to increase essential production

George Washington by Horatio Greenough

170

in the late eighteenth century the traditional term of apprenticeship tended to become shorter, helping in some measure to increase the work force of certified craftsmen. Even more important, as it seemed to one French visitor who reviewed the scene in the 1830's, the American had developed "a mechanic in his soul," a peculiar ingenuity in contriving ways of getting things done quickly and with the least expenditure of man power. That native bent was impressively demonstrated in 1793 when the Connecticut Yankee Eli Whitney invented the cotton gin, a remarkably simple substitute for manual labor that drastically affected the history of the United States—indeed, of the world. A few years later, during the undeclared naval war with France, Whitney contracted to supply the government with ten thousand muskets—an unheard-of quantity. This he did in fact do by devising a system of manufacturing interchangeable mechanical parts, one of the earliest successful applications of that principle in industrial history. As Thomas Jefferson wrote James Monroe in 1801, Whitney had "invented molds and machines for making all the pieces of his locks so exactly equal, that take 100 locks to pieces and mingle their parts and the hundred locks may be put together as well by taking the first pieces which come to hand."

Even earlier, in the 1780's, an ingenious Philadelphian, Oliver Evans, had designed a water-driven mechanical gristmill that in surviving engravings of its plan resembles one of the most fanciful contraptions of the cartoonist Rube Goldberg. Nevertheless, raw grain fed into the mill from the farmers' wagons at one end of the apparatus was carried from one operation to another by a series of belt, screw, and endless-chain bucket conveyers to emerge at the other end, "untouched by human hands," as processed flour ready to be packed in barrels. Evans' machine anticipated almost all the mechanical handling procedures common to modern mass production. Early in the present century Henry Ford combined Evans' system of mechanical conveyers and Whitney's system of producing interchangeable parts and created a modern method of power-driven assembly-line manufacture to cover the nation with his Model T automobiles; but the individual techniques were more than a century old when he did it.

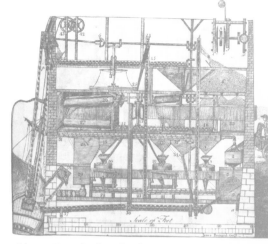

Oliver Evans' plan for his mechanical gristmill

The "Colossus" Bridge over the Schuylkill River

When the young Russian diplomat Paul Svinin visited America in 1811–13 he was astonished by the fact that almost every task from sawing rocks and making bricks to milling flour, forging nails, and cobbling shoes was done by machine. This was a rather extravagant estimate of the situation, but it calls attention to the early development of American technology. Svinin was a highly competent but very favorably prejudiced witness. He was one Russian who liked almost everything he saw in and learned about America as he toured the country from Maine to Virginia. He was struck by the remarkable growth of public works—canals, roads, and, particularly, handsome bridges—some of them were "truly worthy of the glorious age of the Roman Empire"—that were being financed and constructed for the most part by private enterprise without government aid. He was also impressed by the speculations of "Ivan" Astor, who had sent an overland expedition to the Pacific Northwest for a harvest of furs and, at the same time, a ship around the Horn to join the land Astorians at an appointed rendezvous. "This expedition will cost him 250,000 rubles," Svinin reported. "What an enterprise for a private citizen! May it be crowned with success." In 1815 Svinin published at St. Petersburg a report of his experiences in the United States in which he cautioned his readers that conditions were changing too rapidly in the new nation for any valid analysis.

In the homespun economy of our colonial ancestors the rate of production had been largely geared to human endurance. At the time the colonists won their independence the material conditions of life in America were more like those of Caesar's day than like those of the present. For the most part, the average American exercised no greater control over his natural surroundings than man had done for ages past. His tools were largely handmade to old, familiar patterns. His major sources of prime-moving power, aside from his own muscles, were the ox, the horse, and the water wheel.

Because of the abundance of rivers and streams that coursed through the countryside American industry relied largely upon water power for years after England had converted to steam. At the end of the eighteenth century there were fewer than a half-dozen steam engines of any considerable power in this land. In the first decades of the next century, as already noted, steamboats proliferated on the inland waterways of America with dramatic results. "There isn't any one," wrote Alexis de Tocqueville referring to these growing fleets of vessels, as well as to the railroads, "who does not recognize that the discovery of steam has added unbelievably to the strength and prosperity of the Union, and has done so by facilitating rapid communications between the diverse parts of this vast body." However, along the riverbanks water power continued to turn most of the wheels of industry until the century was further advanced.

The most prominent and attractive early exception was the white marble pumping station at Center (now Penn) Square in Philadelphia, built by Latrobe in the classical style to house the steam pumps which distributed water from the Schuylkill River throughout the city. Although Latrobe's plan was considered hopelessly visionary at the time it was proposed, the public rejoiced the day clear water started to flow from the city hydrants in January, 1801. Philadelphia had become the first major American city with an adequate system for supplying water to its inhabitants. Now every householder could, at modest cost, have fresh water carried "even to the attic story." Years later Charles Dickens remarked with surprise at the fresh water, which was "showered and jerked about, and turned on, and poured off everywhere" in Philadelphia.

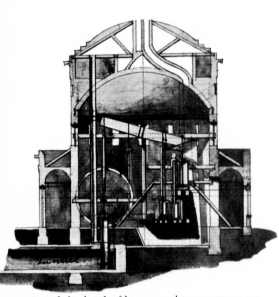

Latrobe's sketch of his steam-driven water pump

By the time Dickens made his first tour of America, steam was gradually being adopted for manufacturing of various sorts, including furniture making. In 1848 the Cincinnati Chamber of Commerce boasted that "every description of furniture, almost from the common bedstead to the most costly articles" were made in the steam-powered factories of which there were at least seven in that city.

Whether steam-driven or not, American woodworking machinery made spectacular advances in the second quarter of the nineteenth century. The seemingly inexhaustible forests of America tempted both the artisan and manufacturer to use wood for all sorts of objects that might otherwise have been made of metal. As a consequence of this concentration on wood a whole new system of laborsaving machines was developed for sawing, planing, boring, mortising, tenoning, and other operations useful to the furniture and other trades. "Invention," as Thorstein Veblen has pointed out, "is the mother of necessity"; as the rate of production soared, the general American public was made aware of a need for more and more kinds of household effects than had ever before entered their minds to own. Chairs, for instance, which in the first years of the colonial settlements had been important and highly prized possessions, were now turned out in prodigious numbers at increasingly low cost. The mass-produced, painted Hitchcock chairs—a type then known to the trade as "fancy chairs," and cherished by today's collectors—sold for $1.50 retail and were a stock in trade of many a wandering Yankee peddler. Chairs were peddled much farther from the factories than even that ingenious and imaginative salesman could reach. In a single day's sailings from Baltimore in 1827 twelve thousand chairs of all descriptions were dispatched to points beyond the Horn.

Until the early years of the nineteenth century, at least, good clocks cost more than the average person could afford to pay. The price of a case for a tall clock was prohibitive for those with modest purses, and so long as the brass mechanism had to be laboriously cast, hammered, and finished by hand no clock could be really inexpensive. When, however, early in the 1800's Eli Terry first manufactured clocks with wooden works by machinery, then adopted the idea of interchangeable parts, and finally reduced his product to the size of his famous pillar and scroll shelf clock, the Yankee peddler—with his legendary powers of persuasion and unique trading techniques—had another item he could hawk without difficulty throughout the land. At the same time veneer and mortising mills and circular saws, operated first by water power and later by steam, reduced the cost of the smaller cases needed for those newly contrived movements far below former costs. (By the mid-nineteenth century common shelf-clock cases could be manufactured for less than fifty cents apiece.) When another Connecticut Yankee, Chauncey Jerome, adapted the simplified mechanism to the rolled brass that became commercially available in the 1830's, cheap American clocks won markets around the world. "For the last three years," read one report from Hartford, Connecticut, in 1841, "we have been gradually pushing our *notes of time* into foreign countries; and such has been our success that within a few hours' ride of this city one thousand clocks are finished daily, and it is a fair estimate to put down five hundred thousand clocks as being manufactured in this State last year. This year the number will be still increased, as John Bull is so slow in his movements that there is no hope of reform until he has plenty of Yankee monitors....India, too, is looked to as a mart for these wares. Several lots have been forwarded to the ports of China."

The progressive democratization of American society over the first half of the

A painted and stenciled Hitchcock chair

Advertisement for mass-produced clocks

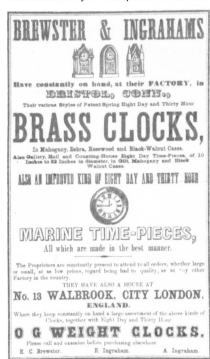

173

nineteenth century raised confident hopes throughout the population, at every level, that the material conditions of life would constantly improve. When education and freedom were widely diffused and where hereditary distinction neither guaranteed the comforts of life nor denied the expectation of them, the promise of more and better things for everyone was real and immediate. In relation to the unexploited resources of the continent man power remained in short supply for decades to come, in spite of the swelling population. So, as the nation expanded and the immense wealth of those resources became ever more apparent, the need for short cuts in production became increasingly urgent if American society were to realize its dreams of a better and more plentiful life in the days and years to come. Any device that would save the time and the cost of a day's work or that would quicken the rate of an individual's output was welcomed and put into service.

Glass and metal, as well as wood, were turned over to the machine for more rapid and inexpensive processing. Sometime in the 1820's a method was developed for mechanically pressing glass into patterned molds to produce various forms with more or less intricate designs. It seems quite probable that this process was invented in America. In any event, the method was rapidly refined and quickly put to use in a number of American glasshouses, both east and west of the Allegheny Mountains, among them the Boston and Sandwich Glass Company on Cape Cod. By 1839 that company alone employed 225 workmen and manufactured $300,000 worth of glassware a year. The mechanically pressed forms, with their various attractive designs, offered immediate and serious competition to the more expensive cut glass. By the 1840's complete sets of matched dinnerware were being produced, some of it for export. Even earlier, in 1836, one Bohemian glassmaking firm complained that the importation of cheap pressed glass from America, and from France, threatened "to eclipse our glass manufacture." Such automatic pressing today remains one of the principal means of producing glassware efficiently and inexpensively.

The pewterers of the first half of the nineteenth century were increasingly hard put to meet the competition presented by inexpensive glassware and pottery, the latter largely imported from the earthenware manufactories in Staffordshire, England. However, borrowing basic formulas developed by the trade in England, they resorted to a new alloy consisting largely of tin with some copper and antimony added. This so-called britannia ware, according to a report issued in 1845, "takes a high polish, and does not readily tarnish: when kept perfectly bright it has great beauty, far excelling pewter, and approaching in lustre to silver." Moreover, it was a tougher alloy than that earlier used by pewterers and could be cast and rolled into thin sheets without cracking under the pressure. And beyond that, it could be stamped into shape by heavy dies, or forms could be spun on wooden lathes, thus dispensing with the costly bronze molds traditionally used by pewterers, which opened the way to relatively quick mass production. As a replacement for pewter and a passable substitute for silver, and priced within reach of virtually everyone, britannia ware enjoyed a popularity throughout the nation for about half a century.

When, in the 1840's, it was learned that the britannia metal could be electroplated, this process was rapidly adopted and a new, important industry developed. The difference in cost between the silver-plated ware and solid silver was, of course, considerable, and the new ware was eagerly acquired by a large public with a growing taste for "elegant" accessories. "An American artisan," exulted

One of a pair of pressed-glass candlesticks

174

Drawing of the Fair of the American Institute of New York, held at Niblo's Garden, about 1845

one enthusiastic historian of the times, "can now command exact copies of the choicest plate in the repertory of kings."

Machine-made furnishings may have lacked the individual refinements of handmade products. However, they were nonetheless serviceable and, since they were cheaper, they introduced to the average citizen a variety of domestic comforts and conveniences that had previously been restricted to people of considerable means. As the variety of such novel, quantity-produced articles increased from year to year the public had to be advised about what was new and available and why it was desirable. With the double purpose of whetting the people's appetite for those new commodities and of spurring industry to ever greater performances, in 1828 the American Institute inaugurated a series of annual fairs in New York City whose displays were actively supported and promoted by prominent men in all walks of life. Advertising began to assume a greater importance than it had ever had before, and as the nomadic American people moved westward the producers of goods—and their salesmen—followed them across the mountains to supply their wants. Even as early as 1831, when he visited the United States, Tocqueville remarked on the almost universal disposition among the citizens of the young democracy to acquire the good and useful things that were being offered to them. "To enlarge a dwelling," he reflected when he returned to France, "to be always making life more comfortable and convenient,...to satisfy the smallest wants without effort and almost without cost" were aspirations common to Americans at large.

Amid all these developments the individual self-employed craftsman tended to disappear from the scene. The celebrated furniture-making establishment of Duncan Phyfe in New York, for example, is said to have employed more than a hundred workmen at times. The cabinetmaking, glassmaking, and other crafts became businesses. Ready-made articles offered for sale in warehouses or stores became the rule rather than the exception. And, inevitably, the journeymen who worked for the producers were more and more inclined to organize into incipient labor unions in order to protect their separate interests. However, so long as the demand for skilled labor remained high and urgent the situation of such workmen was rarely serious. When Miss Harriet Martineau visited America in the 1830's she observed that "the wages of labour [in this country] are so good that there is less cause for discontent on the part of the workmen than elsewhere." On one occasion she noted with astonishment a procession of "gentlemen... with sleek coats, glossy hats, gay watch-guards, and doe-skin gloves!" marching down Broadway in New York "with an easy air of gentility." These, she learned, were the journeymen mechanics of the city—"such dandy mechanics" as she had never seen before.

The years following 1825 saw an unprecedented flowering of periodicals. "The whole tendency of the age is Magazine-ward," wrote one reporter in 1845. Prominent among such publications were those designed especially for women readers. Through their pages, carrying household hints, fashion plates, and other features appealing to homemakers, news of current styles and domestic equipment quickly reached every corner of the land. "From Maine to the Rocky Mountains," wrote the jubilant publisher of *Godey's Lady's Book*, the woman's magazine par excellence, in 1841, "there is scarcely a hamlet, however inconsiderable, where it is not received and read; and in the larger towns and cities, it is universally distributed." For its time *Godey's* did in fact enjoy a large circulation, and it provided for the "fair Ladies" to whom it was addressed a wide variety of fare ranging from essays by Edgar Allan Poe to recipes and illustrated reports on up-to-date furniture styles. Sarah Josepha Hale, for years *Godey's* distinguished editor, was a leader in causes. She was, it has been said, "an imposing spectacle, rather like a duchess of fiction"—and she was persuasive. It was largely because of her agitation that in 1864 Abraham Lincoln proclaimed Thanksgiving Day a national holiday. And it was Mrs. Hale who wrote the poem:

> Mary had a little lamb;
> Its fleece was white as snow;
> And everywhere that Mary went
> The lamb was sure to go.

The rapid spread of new ideas and fashions throughout the nation in the second quarter of the last century was also furthered by the widespread distribution of lithographs, as individual prints as well as in book and magazine illustrations. Both types of reproductions were far superior to the line engravings of colonial times, and they served as persuasive visual aids in reporting and promoting the changing trends of the times. Lithography, a technique based on the mutual antipathy of oil and water, not only quickened the production of printed pictures but also made possible a range of tone from deep black to light gray that enhanced the appeal of the illustration (as Goya and Daumier so brilliantly demonstrated in Europe). Until the 1850's and 1860's all lithographs were colored by hand, if they were colored at all. By that time the well-known firm of Currier & Ives was deluging the country with inexpensive prints picturing an enormous variety of subjects.

By that time, also, reproduction by photography had become a firmly rooted and widely practiced craft in the United States, a craft that gradually but inexorably affected the art of painting. Some of the most convincing likenesses we have of famous men in the 1850's—and other persons not so famous—are daguerreotypes from that period, rather than painted portraits of those subjects. Daguerreotype portrait studios had opened up in all the large cities, and carts fitted up as studios roamed the land in quest of customers in smaller towns.

The visual record left by those printmakers and daguerreotypists reveals a country vastly different from the America of the eighteenth century. In America of the 1850's the common man enjoyed a greater degree and variety of material comfort than his like had known in any other society. And the application of the machine and the development of new sources of power were bringing about changes at a progressively faster rate. The day was coming, it seemed, when furniture and other accessories of daily life, like clothes, that had once embodied the slowly evolving taste of an age, would reflect instead the passing fashion of a season; the "period style" would become the current year's mass-produced novelty. The time was coming, too, when one London reporter could remark, "the American mechanizes as an old Greek sculptured"—an observation that would probably have made Horatio Greenough happy in his grave.

A daguerreotype portrait of John Quincy Adams

235. *Above: a girandole clock with painted glass panel*
236. *Right: painted Hepplewhite oval-back side chair*

Patterns in Paint

Ornamental painting on furniture, a revival initiated by Adam, was enthusiastically taken up in America at the close of the Revolution. Every type of furniture imaginable was decorated with glowing designs, applied both freehand and by stenciling. The examples here stand as works of art in themselves. The chair (236), with splats in a pattern of "Prince of Wales' feathers," is one of a set of twenty-four ordered from Philadelphia in 1796 by Elias Hasket Derby of Salem. The clock (235), made about 1815 by Lemuel Curtis of Concord, Massachusetts, has a glass panel painted with an unidentified street scene, believed to have been executed by his brother Benjamin. The painted convex panel and gilt moldings with gilt balls suggest the popular girandole mirrors; hence the term "girandole" in designating this type of clock.

Hepplewhite's *Guide* had recommended that furniture panels be painted with subjects taken from "Raphael, Italian engravings, and also some French works," and Sheraton had offered "a variety of ornaments," for amateurs and professionals, with detailed instructions for decorative brushwork. American craftsmen often adapted these designs and techniques as an economy measure and painted pieces of furniture with simulations of such expensive materials and methods as ormolu mounts, inlays, rare woods, marble, and fine carving. These ornamental touches were an ancient device. Egyptian furniture, for example, was often painted in imitation of similar luxuries.

237. *Left: a bentwood chair trimmed with striping, leaves, and a peacock feather, and branded with the mark "S. Gragg/Boston/Patent," around 1808–15*

238. *Above: New York "landscape chair," with a view of the Hudson River and valley, one of a set of six*

239. *Opposite, above: painted glass panel from gilt looking glass, possibly made in Albany or New York*

240. *Opposite: bird's-eye maple sewing table painted with foliage, the top with draped figures, about 1800*

241, 242. *Carving on a New York chair (left) contrasted with stenciling on the turned Pennsylvania chair (right)*

243, 244. *Ormolu mountings and brass inlays, as seen on this mahogany silver chest (left), were simulated by such stenciled designs as those on the commode (right).*

245, 246. A tilt-top table (right), the top inlaid with satinwood, the fluted vase section with bone, exemplifies the
elaborate cabinetwork imitated with a brush, as on this
table (left) with painted simulation of grain and inlay.

247. *A water color by Joseph H. Davis of New Hampshire, 1837, shows the Tilton family and their brightly painted parlor furniture.*

248. *Above: painted drop-leaf table*

249. *Opposite: painted woodwork as shown in a child's portrait by Mark*

The delicate harmonies of painted woodwork and painted furniture, as conceived by Adam, blossomed in America into a wholehearted burst of color. A versatile country craftsman, such as George Washington Mark of Massachusetts, turned his brush to portraits (249), landscapes, and "Coach, Sign and House Painting." The painting and stenciling of chairs became a particularly extensive industry. Early copies of London fashions, commonly known as "fancy chairs" (250, 251), were soon being mass produced throughout the United States in sturdier, simplified forms. Lambert Hitchcock (1795–1852), whose name is popularly given to *all* chairs of this type, opened his famous factory in what is now Riverton, Connecticut, in 1820, employing over a hundred workers at the peak of his success—including women and children who painted and stenciled on the assembly line. A Hitchcock chair (253) retailed for $1.50.

250, 251. *The water color portrait (above) of a little girl with her toys and her dog shows a miniature version of the painted and stenciled chair (left) with canted arm posts and a pierced eagle-shaped splat.*

252. *Opposite: painted, grained, and stenciled rocker, about 1835, known as a Boston rocker, though produced throughout the country*

253. *Opposite, above: maple and hickory stenciled chair, the rush seat painted gray, bearing the Hitchcock mark used between the years 1825 and 1828, "L. Hitchcock, Hitchcocksville, Conn. Warrented."*

In the early 1800's the craze for wallpapers, both patterned and scenic, domestic and imported, was an indulgence only the well to do could afford. In rural areas, particularly throughout New England and New York State, colorful wall decorations were achieved in the comparatively inexpensive medium of paint. Both plaster and wood walls were richly ornamented with stenciled patterns (254) or with freehand, charmingly primitive landscapes. Such decorations were usually done by journeymen painters, who traveled from door to door with their work kits packed across their saddles. The room shown here (255), the hall of a house originally in Sherburne, New York, was probably stenciled about 1820 by Moses Eaton (1753–1833), an itinerant artist whose designs have been identified as far west as Ohio and Indiana. Paint was also used to create brilliantly stenciled floors, geometrically patterned in the manner of expensive carpets.

254. *Left: pattern for stencilin*

255. *Opposite: a stenciled wa*

S. F. B. Morse
Art
&
Invention

Among the American exhibits at the Great Exhibition at London's Crystal Palace in 1851 the only display that won acclaim for artistic merit, by European standards, was Hiram Powers' *Greek Slave,* which the sculptor modeled in Italy. The official catalogue of the exhibition felt obliged to explain that, for the rest, "the expenditure of months or years of labour upon a single article, not to increase its intrinsic value, but solely to augment its cost or its estimation as an object of *virtù,* is not common in the United States. On the contrary, both manual and mechanical labour are applied with direct reference to increasing the number or the quantity of articles suited to the wants of a whole people, and adapted to promote the enjoyment of that moderate competency which prevails among them."

The progressive mechanization of life in America as the nineteenth century advanced challenged the traditional, painstaking practices of art and craftsmanship at almost every turn. In 1841 a young artist found himself in a studio at the University of the City of New York where he saw sculpture models covered with dust and cobwebs, dirty canvases with their faces to the wall, and evidence everywhere of disuse and neglect. To his utter dismay he learned that these had been the quarters of Samuel Finley Breese Morse, president of the National Academy of Design, the most exalted position the youth could conceive. Morse was still president of the Academy, but he had put aside his easel and his brushes for more practical pursuits. Several years later Morse confided that he had not abandoned art but that art had abandoned him. Painting may have been a smiling mistress to some, he wrote his old friend James Fenimore Cooper, but to Morse she had been "a cruel jilt." His change of heart was in a real sense symptomatic of the changes taking place in American society.

As a youth Morse had approached his art with religious zeal. He had a "calling" and he followed it in a spirit of total consecration, spurred on by his parents' pious hope that he would indeed "consecrate his acquisitions to the glory of God and the best good of his fellow man." His father, the Reverend Jedidiah Morse, was the author of the first

American geography and a fifth-generation Yankee Puritan. To have sired an artist was at first a disconcerting shock to the elder Morse. However, he was reassured by Washington Allston, a brother-in-law of William Ellery Channing's and, although an artist, a man of unquestionable spiritual qualities and of oracular authority. Under Allston's guardian wing young Samuel (left) was sent abroad for a few years to perfect his burgeoning talents.

From London Morse wrote his parents that he intended "to rival the genius of a Raphael, a Michael Angelo, or a Titian; my ambition is to be enlisted in the constellation of genius now rising in this country; I wish to shine, not by a light borrowed from them, but to strive to shine the brightest." Allston thought that with proper encouragement Morse would indeed become a great painter; but in the end he did not. He was a good painter; some of his portraits are as fine as any by his American contem-

poraries. But, although most of the paintings he produced were portraits, Morse never thought of them as a true measure of his art. He yearned to create large historical and allegorical compositions that would fully exercise the talents which Heaven had given him "for the higher branches of art." And in these the American public was simply not interested.

Even so, determined to do "something for the Arts in our country," in 1826 he helped organize the National

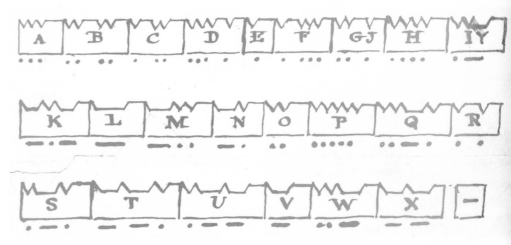

Academy of the Arts of Design. This group of working artists would, he hoped, by presenting exhibits of "modern" American art, by offering instruction and awards, and by setting standards of excellence elevate the public taste and win for the artists the dignity and prestige that was rightly theirs.

The influential *North American Review* challenged some of Morse's statements about the place of the artist in American society. "Painting and sculpture are not among the necessaries of life," wrote the editors. "Much as they improve and adorn society, a taste for them is not even the necessary accompaniment of a high degree of civilization." And again, "the forms and occupations of society are growing every day less favorable to the highest efforts of the imagination. We live in an age of utility....Eloquence, poetry, painting, and sculpture, do not belong to such an age; they are already declining, and they must give way before the progress of popular education, science, and the useful arts." All of which Morse refuted with dignified and eloquent rhetoric. Yet, ironically, the observations in the *Review* were a summary commentary on Morse's own career.

A few years later, in 1829, Morse made a second trip to Europe to rekindle his own former ardor and to renew his recollection "of excellence in the art." Actually, it was the beginning of the end of his career as a painter. Following his return to America he continued to produce canvases of high merit, and joined the faculty of the newly formed University of the City of New York (now New York University) as the first professor of fine arts in any American college. He needed the money from both those sources, little as it was. But to the consternation of his students and colleagues his studio was now cluttered with mysterious wires and batteries and magnets. He had become obsessed with the notion of transmitting human intelligence by wire over vast distances. For the rest of his life, until he won final success with the telegraph, Morse was almost completely preoccupied with the solution to this problem. Once he had mastered his "thunder and lightning 'Jim crack,'" he believed he might return to the pursuit of the muse

and overtake her with the speed of electricity itself. But this he did not do. He soon put aside his brushes forever.

When he needed money to continue his experiments with the wonder-working wires he now turned to a mechanical contrivance, the camera, rather than the easel. In 1839 Morse had met and talked with Daguerre, the inventor, in Paris, and he much admired this new method of "drawing," as he referred to it. Here was a device, Morse pointed out to members of the National Academy, that would put an end to the "sketchy, slovenly daubs" of artists who had neither the intelligence nor the skill to master details in their renderings; here was "Rembrandt perfected."

Morse became a highly proficient daguerreotypist in his own right. He is, indeed, still respectfully referred to as the father of American photography. Like some other artists, he planned to use the images quickly taken with a camera as models for paintings. But his reference to this new medium as a kind of "instant art" provoked a controversy that was long in subsiding, if indeed it ever has. The celebrated contemporary landscapist, Thomas Cole, wrote to a friend in 1840 that if you listened to that sort of nonsense "you would be led to suppose that the poor craft of painting was knocked in the head by this new machinery for making Nature take her own likeness, and we [artists] nothing to do but to give up the ghost....The art of painting is a creative, as well as an imitative art, and is in no danger of being superseded by any mechanical contrivance." (In spite of those remarks, over the years to come the art of painting was profoundly affected by develop-

ments in photography, albeit in ways that could not have been foreseen.)

By then Morse was completely absorbed in his experiments with telegraphy. He remembered his painting, but only with sadness; the passion was spent—or rather transferred to a new dream that for him held greater magic. At times he went hungry as he pursued that dream, until he secured substantial help from others and, finally, a government appropriation that saw him through to the successful conclusion of his enterprise. With that, in his own case, Morse had justified those remarks in the *North American Review* to which he had once taken such strong exception. Art, for him, had given way to science. Actually, his activity in rapid communication soon mushroomed into a vast commercial operation; he had become rich as well as famous through his "talking sparks." In the end, Morse explained, he was but an instrument of Providence, and Providence had dictated that he sacrifice his art to serve humanity in another way. It was an "age of utility," indeed, and with his telegraph he had opened an electrifying new phase in history.

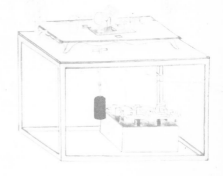

Mirror with a Memory

"If this thing were at all possible," observed a German publication shortly before Louis Jacques Daguerre's photographic process was made public in 1839, "then something similar would have been done a long time ago in antiquity by men like Archimedes or Moses. But if these wise men knew nothing of mirror pictures made permanent, then one can straightway call the Frenchman Daguerre, who boasts of such unheard of things, the fool of fools." Even Madame Daguerre is said to have questioned her husband's sanity for attempting to capture "evanescent reflections" with a man-made machine. The rest, of course, is history. The daguerreotype was the first practicable method of photography, and it swept America like wildfire. By 1853 the *New-York Daily Tribune* estimated that three million daguerreotypes were being made annually, with at least two thousand persons practicing this new trade, which in turn created supporting industries that manufactured apparatus, chemicals, plates, and cases. Traveling photographers in horse-drawn vans journeyed to rural and frontier areas, and flatboat studios, fitted out with "sitting rooms" and "chemical rooms," put in at river ports. One such flatboat daguerreotypist logged a fourteen-hundred-mile trip down the Mississippi, took over a thousand likenesses, and further enjoyed fishing and hunting in idle moments, "as the rivers are thronged with ducks and wild geese." Galleries in the cities, meanwhile, outdid themselves in the lavishness of their *décor*. "They are palaces," exclaimed one European visitor, agog at the profusion of marbled halls and statuary, rich carpeting and draperies, singing birds in gilded cages, and "exotic plants whose flowers perfume the air."

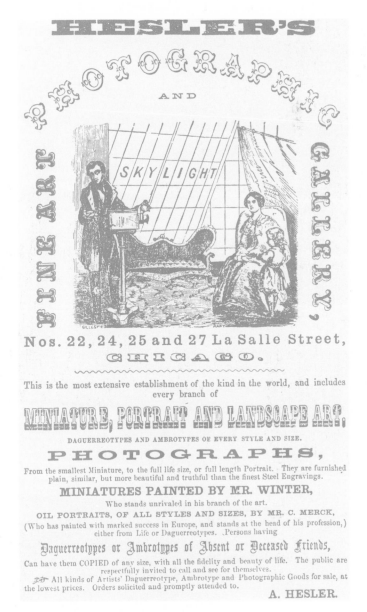

256. *Opposite: a daguerreotypist with camera typical of the 1850's*

257. *Above: advertisement of a photographer's gallery, about 1854*

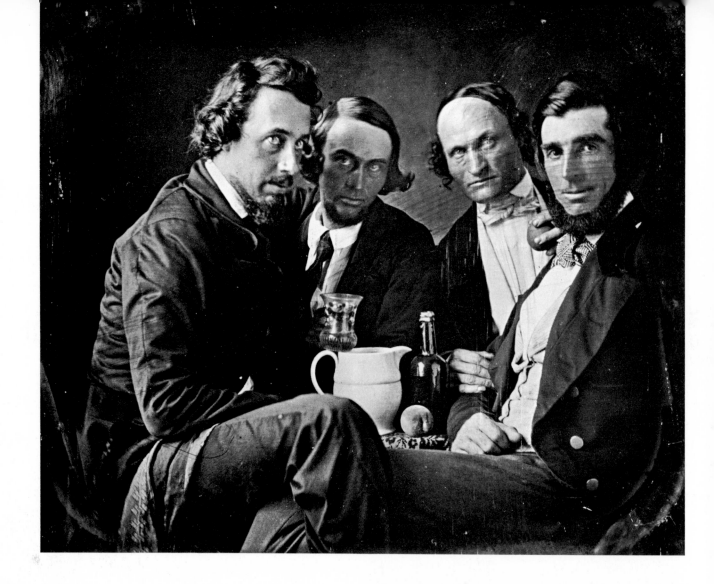

In 1839 an enthusiast of the daguerreotype wrote that "their exquisite perfection almost transcends the bounds of sober belief." A year later Edgar Allan Poe noted that "the daguerreotyped plate is infinitely more accurate in its presentation than any painting by human hands." This acclaimed perfection and accuracy was achieved by an exacting process. A silvered copper plate, burnished until mirror-bright, was treated with iodine vapor to render it sensitive to light. The exposed plate was developed over heated mercury, fixed in hyposulphite of soda, rinsed in distilled water, dried, and mounted under glass to protect the perishable film of mercury which "held" the image. American daguerreotypes were extravagantly praised at the Great Exhibition in London, 1851, and Horace Greeley explained that the brilliance and clarity of these entries was due to the pure air in American cities, which were "free from smoke, at least upon the Atlantic coasts." In the late 1850's, however, the daguerreotype was superseded by the refinement of collodion-coated plates, which led to such simplified and inexpensive photographic techniques as ambrotypes on glass, tintypes on thin sheets of iron, and pictures printed on paper.

258. *Opposite, top: four veterans of the "California Battalion," which recaptured Los Angeles in 1847 during the Mexican War. The daguerreotype is inscribed to their officer, Colonel John Charles Frémont, the Pathfinder.*

259. *Opposite: daguerreotype of Andrew Jackson, shortly before his death. Public figures were often invited to sit for the camera, and Mathew Brady's photographic career began with his daguerreotypes of great and famous people.*

260. *Above: a daguerreotype of gold miners in California*

Handsomely decorated daguerreotype cases were made from a variety of materials: morocco leather with gold clasps, papier-mâché, tortoise shell inlaid with pearl and silver, or wood covered with a paper-thin skin of leather or velvet. This case (261), with its scene of Sir Roger de Coverley stopping to have his palm read by a shawled, barefooted fortune-teller, is made from a thermoplastic compound of gum, shellac, and fibers, which was heated and then pressed with the desired pattern. Lockets and brooches were also designed to hold small daguerreotypes. In the 1840's, when photographs of the departed became an important part of daguerrean art, a firm that made cases designed for "sepulchral daguerreotypes" advertised their wares as "appropriate—rich without being gaudy." But most importantly, whoever the model and whatever the mounting of the picture, the portrait had been brought within reach of the average citizen. The daguerreotype was, in fact, "the poor man's portrait."

261. *Above: daguerreotype case made of a pressed compound*

262. *Below: an example of early photography, 1859. Rembrandt Peale and his wife posed with one of his Washington portraits.*

263. *Opposite: a Morse daguerreotype of his wife and daughter*

Britannia Rules

Horace Greeley, commenting on American industry, wrote that the various utensils "produced in such quantities by the leading manufacturers of Britannia ware, and at such low rates...place them within the reach of every one." Britannia ware, in effect, a fine grade of pewter containing no lead, was at the height of its popularity from the 1830's to the 1860's. The formula for this silver-white alloy had been perfected earlier by English pewterers, and as a general rule of thumb consisted of one hundred and fifty parts of tin, three parts of copper, to give the metal hardness and resonance, and ten parts of antimony, to add to the hardness of the metal and to contribute a bright sheen. The patriotic name, britannia ware, bestowed upon it by English pewterers about 1750, appears to have been selected as an advertising device.

One of the first accounts of britannia ware in America was written by Thomas Danforth Boardman of Hartford, who described his experiments with tin, copper, and antimony. The resultant teapots were deemed "equal to English" and orders poured in for "50 Dos at a time." In 1814 the Reverend William Bentley noted in his diary a visit in Beverly, Massachusetts, to the britannia ware shop of Israel Trask, "who introduced the manufacture into that place. He was a goldsmith & jeweller, & employs about a dozen hands, & sells his work in Boston. Just above his [shop] works a Mr. Smith, formerly a cabinet maker, who has gone to the same extent of the same business & the persons he employs are seamen & fishermen. They seem to be pleased with the present success." A teapot by Smith is shown here (264).

264. *Opposite: teapot stamped with mark of Eben Smith, Beverly, Mass., before 1830*   199

265. *Above: an 1850's daguerreotype shows a metalworker, apparently of britannia ware*

Traditional pewter forms, such as mugs, plates, tankards, and porringers, which had been cast in brass molds by past generations of pewterers, were gradually outmoded with the advent of britannia metal. Because it was a tough alloy that could be rolled into thin sheets, then spun into the desired shape on a lathe, or stamped into the needed component parts by a press, britannia ware lent itself to a host of diversified objects. Teapots were manufactured by the thousands to meet the popular demand. In William Sidney Mount's painting, *Dregs in the Cup, or Fortune Telling* (269), just such a britannia teapot shines here on the tea table. A report on Meriden, Connecticut, in 1833, noted: "One company employed two hundred and fifty hands in the manufacture of Britannia wares, such as coffee pots and mills, spoons, waffle irons, signal lanterns, etc., to the value of $200,-000 per annum." Whale-oil lamps were another highly successful item throughout the country, as was church plate, particularly for parishes that could not afford silver. In 1834 Sellew & Company, Cincinnati, which made the coffeepot and teapot shown here (267, 268), advertised "Communion Furniture...Britannia Metal Flagons, Goblets, Beakers, Plates and Baptismal Founts." Spoons, candlesticks, and cake baskets of "unsurpassed elegance" were also made, as well as picture frames, earpieces for hearing trumpets, faucets, candle molds, snuffboxes, "fancy bar tobacco boxes," and cuspidors.

266. Opposite: a britannia caster by Homan & Co., Cincinnati

267, 268. Left: coffeepot and teapot, by Sellew & Co., Cincinnati

269. Above: Mount's painting, 1838, shows a britannia teapot.

270. Left: a detail of a hexagonal coffeepot

271. Above, right: Rufus Dunham's advertisement, in The Portland Directory, Maine, 1844

272. Right: an engraved teapot by Israel Trask

273. Opposite, above: sugar box with hinged lid

274. Opposite: whale-oil lamp by Rufus Dunham

A variety of popular britannia forms are illustrated here. The lamp (274) was cast by Rufus Dunham, who worked in Westbrook and Portland, Maine, between 1837 and 1882. The sugar box (273) was made by a contemporary, English-born George Richardson, who produced britannia ware both in Boston and Providence. Israel Trask's early training as a silversmith is evident in the teapot (272) with engraved decoration rarely found on britannia ware; the Reverend William Bentley noted that in Trask's factory "the engraving was done with great facility by tools Mr. Traske made." The body of this teapot was shaped by an early process called "seaming," that is, a sheet of metal rolled into a tubular shape and soldered at the seam, in this instance down the front where the spout joins the pot. Rising mechanization, which spurred the britannia ware industry in the 1830's, is exemplified by the coffeepot (270), one of a set, its panels stamped in a press and soldered into their hexagonal pattern. The set was made by Roswell Gleason, whose factory in Dorchester, Massachusetts, flourished from 1822 to 1871 and was one of the largest of its kind. A similar factory was admiringly described as having "every modern improvement in machinery that can facilitate the manufacture, embracing rolls of great size and exquisite finish... heavy drop-hammers for fluting, &c., with steam to heat the building as well as drive the machinery, and many conveniences for the employees."

275. Left: cut-glass sugar bowl
276. Above: blown, molded bowl
277. Right: a blown, molded dish
278. Opposite: a cut-glass pitcher

Cut, Pressed, or Molded

Cutting decorative patterns into the surface of glass is a technique thousands of years old. At Warrington, England, some years ago, the excavation of an ancient Roman glass furnace revealed a stone cutting-wheel and fragments that had been cut with it in designs similar to those used by Irish glass cutters early in the nineteenth century. During those years roughly corresponding to the Regency period English and Irish glasshouses were producing luxurious tableware of heavy, clear glass deeply incised with patterns derived from classical sources; ware that found an appreciative market in America among those who could afford it. The efforts of American factories to reach and share that market with domestic cut glass "as good as any imported" (and often cut from imported patterns by immigrant craftsmen) won increasing success in the decades following the War of 1812. The sugar bowl (275) and pitcher (278) are representative of work produced at glasshouses in various parts of this country during the third and fourth decades of the nineteenth century.

To reach a still larger market throughout the nation, during those same decades many American glasshouses reverted to another ancient practice, although the craftsmen did not know of the precedent, so far as one can tell (see page 124). By blowing a gathering of glass into patterned, full-size, hinged molds in several sections, they produced relatively inexpensive tableware with impressed designs approximating those of cut glass. A covered sugar bowl (276) probably made at the New England Glass Company and a preserve dish (277) probably from the Boston and Sandwich Glass Company were obviously inspired by cut-glass models. The method could not, however, duplicate the sharp facets of cut glass.

279. *Above: clear, mechanically pressed, lacy-glass plate with a portrait of George Washington surrounded by sprays of acorns*
280. *Opposite, left: boat-shaped salt in leaf and scroll design.* 281. *Opposite, right: oval salt in strawberry-diamond pattern*
282. *Opposite, center: covered and footed sugar bowl with a design of anthemia and flowers against a stippled background*

In 1829 an English tourist, who called himself a "Citizen of the World," remarked on the "cut and beautifully moulded glass" he had seen that year in New York at the Fair of the American Institute. He probably referred to types such as are shown on the preceding pages. He was more impressed, however, by the mechanically pressed glassware also displayed at the fair. This, he wrote, "was far superior, both in design and execution, to anything of the kind I had ever seen either in London or elsewhere. The merit of this invention is due to the Americans; and it is likely to prove one of great national importance."

Although at the start such pressed glass may have been considered a cheap substitute for cut glass, and although early pressed designs resembled those of cut ware, the new process quickly developed patterns of its own. Iron or brass molds into which the glass was forced under pressure could be modeled with more precise and intricate details than a glass cutter's wheel could achieve. The various forms of so-called "lacy" glass shown here, with their backgrounds of delicate stippling that caught, reflected, and refracted any light that played against them, constituted a novel and distinctive product; one that could be mass manufactured in exact duplicates quickly and at moderate cost. Creative artistry was by no means eliminated by the intrusion of the machine and the standardization of the product. The new technique shifted the emphasis from the craftsmen in glass to the mold designers and cutters, but the latter were craftsmen in their own right who for several decades gave their work the spirited, careful attention of the traditional bench artisans.

The development of lacy glass was actually a by-product of technical problems. In its contact with the metal mold during pressing, glass lost its brilliance and crystal-like clarity, although the glass itself was of good quality. Allover stippling effectively hid that defect and, with those myriad small facets, provided scintillating backgrounds for the principal designs. Although lacy glass is popularly associated with the factory at Sandwich, Massachusetts, it was made at numerous glasshouses. It lent itself to all manner of purposes, from miscellaneous tableware to "panes for steamboats" (285), as one midwestern house advertised in 1836, in clear glass and pure colors. With the "beautiful Ohio" flowing past their doors to markets throughout the vast midwestern hinterland, and with abundant supplies of coal available for fuel, the glasshouses of Pittsburgh, Wheeling, and other cities in western Pennsylvania, present-day West Virginia, and Ohio enjoyed distinct advantages. However, by the late 1820's a number of eastern factories were firmly established and operating successfully. As early as 1819 the New England Glass Company was producing cut glass that rivaled the Pittsburgh output (see page 129). The best-remembered of all these early operations, the Boston and Sandwich Glass Company on Cape Cod, was founded in 1825. Shortly thereafter it was producing large quantities of cut, molded, and pressed glass. Long after the factory closed in 1888, the purity of colors in fragments of glass found at the site reminded one craftsman of the windows of twelfth-century French cathedrals; from those fragments he composed comparably brilliant "stained glass" panels.

283. Above: blown, pressed, and cut lamp

284. Top: engraving from a billhead, 1815

285. Opposite: lacy-glass steamboat panel

It's About Time

Following the Revolution American clockmaking took a new and vital turn. Not only were smaller, cheaper clocks being made (as opposed to the costly European imports and tall case clocks), but English patterns were gradually replaced by types and styles of clocks that were distinctly American. In the attempt to provide a moderately priced product, one of the earliest variations was the Massachusetts wall clock. The light-weight thirty-hour brass movement could be contained in a comparatively small space. This one (286) was made by Aaron Willard, a member of the notable family of clockmakers from eastern Massachusetts. (In earlier wag-on-the-wall clocks comparable movements were left unhoused.) The case containing Willard's mechanism was presumably designed to simulate a small clock standing on a matching bracket.

Until 1830, when machine-made clocks swept the market, the Massachusetts shelf clock was extremely popular. The example illustrated (287) was made by David Wood of Newburyport, who "Set up a shop in Market Square, near Rev. Andrews' Meeting House" in 1792. Such shelf clocks were often set in simple pine boxes. Wood's clock, however, in its inlaid mahogany case topped by a fretwork of gilded pewter, was mounted in the elegant tradition of tall case clocks, as were similar examples made by the Willards.

The rotund gentleman with his top hat in hand (288) is one John Doggett of Roxbury, Massachusetts, a carver, gilder, cabinetmaker, and a looking-glass maker. Among the accounts meticulously listed in his ledgers was that of Simon Willard, the most renowned of this clockmaking family: "Clock case woodwork and Gilding complete," at seventy dollars, and "piece of Looking glass for timepiece," at thirty-seven cents. The ledger also shows that Aaron Willard, as a young man, often turned his hand to painting, enameling, and lettering glass panels in Doggett's shop.

286. *Opposite: a Massachusetts wall clock, a type made from 1775 to 1795*

287. *Left: Massachusetts shelf clock*

288. *Above: silhouette of J. Doggett*

289. *Left: banjo clock made by Simon Willard*

290. *Above: a lighthouse clock by Simon Willard*

291. *Opposite: an acorn clock by Jonathan Brown*

291a. *Opposite, above: detail from Brown's clock*

The triumph of Simon Willard's career was the eight-day banjo clock. This "Improved Patent Time piece," as Willard always referred to it, was most likely a refinement of the Massachusetts wall clock and won immediate success for its precise workmanship and fine proportions. Despite Willard's patent of 1802 the design was widely copied; indeed, the banjo shape is still reproduced to this day. On the banjo clock shown here (289), with gilt case and bracket base, a glass panel pictures the 1812 sea victory of Isaac Hull, commander of the *Constitution*. Willard also designed the "Eddystone Lighthouse Alarm Time piece" (290), but it did not prove as popular as the banjo clock. The glass dome of the lighthouse clock is removable for the weekly winding, the "alarm set" is at the center of the face, and the silvered alarm bell is suspended above. The case is grained mahogany with brass mounts. This design was derived from the famous lighthouse built upon the Eddystone Rocks, a reef "obnoxious to navigation," that lay fourteen miles south-southwest off the coast of Plymouth, England.

Around 1845 clockcase designs underwent a radical change. The coiled spring was now being manufactured in New England and selling for seventy-five cents or less. Among the new forms that no longer needed to accommodate weight-driven works was the acorn clock (291) made by Jonathan Clark Brown at his factory in Forestville, Connecticut. The detail (291a), a view sometimes used on Brown's clockcases, shows his house, built in 1832 in the Greek Revival manner, in nearby Bristol.

The manufacture of wooden works with standardized, interchangeable parts was an American innovation. Clocks with wooden works had been perfected by Eli Terry, of Connecticut, who amazed his colleagues in 1806 by accepting an order for four thousand clocks, an unheard-of production quota in the days of hand-crafted brass works. Terry filled the order in an assembly-line factory, the interchangeable wooden components cut by waterpower-driven machines. He sold his interest in this successful enterprise to Seth Thomas and Silas Hoadley and concentrated on improving his own designs, an effort which culminated in the pillar and scroll clock (292) about 1816. To fill the rising demand for low-priced clocks, dozens of small factories in Connecticut now turned out wooden works set in inexpensive wooden cases. Following the introduction of coiled springs and strip-rolled brass works, Connecticut factories continued to fill the need for low-priced clocks.

292. *Top: Eli Terry's pillar and scroll clock.* 293. *Above: Yankee peddler, with a clock among his wares, painted by J. W. Ehninger*

294. *Opposite: wooden works from a patented Terry clock (pictured above), as manufactured by Seth Thomas of Connecticut*

Pate... ocks,
Made and Sold by
Seth Thomas;
And warrante...

DIREC...
For setting up and Regula... Clocks.

Let the clock be set in a perpendicular position: this is necessary, in order to its having an equal beat; and if it fails to

History on Flasks

Despite the evangelical zeal of the temperance societies the consumption of "ardent spirits" continued and the distilling industry kept pace with America's growing population. From the 1820's to the 1870's pictorial whiskey flasks were a steady source of profit for glasshouses from New England to Ohio. They were produced in a profusion of colors—ambers, greens, aquas, blues, and purples—and designed to catch the political and historical fancy of the buyer. Bottle patterns included Masonic emblems, patriotic motifs (stars, eagles, flags), agricultural symbols (sheaves of grain, ears of corn, bunches of grapes), and commercial themes, such as a ship with the legend: FREE TRADE AND SAILORS' RIGHTS. Presidential portraits were used—of Washington, Adams, Jackson, Harrison, and Taylor—while Jenny Lind, the "Swedish Nightingale," became the only woman known to have been immortalized on a flask. (Her adoring public could also purchase Jenny Lind gloves, bonnets, pianos, and even Jenny Lind ironing boards.) With a nod to temperance several patterns wreathed a sheaf of rye with the inscription: USE ME BUT DO NOT ABUSE ME. Cabins were also a popular form. The example here (295) was made for E.G. Booz, a Philadelphia dealer whose name is often taken as the origin of the slang term "booze." However, booze derives from an old English verb, bouse, "to drink sottishly," as an 1844 dictionary defined it.

295. *Opposite: Old Cabin Whiskey bottle, dark brown*

Clockwise: 296. *Colorless flask commemorating the 1824 protective tariff.* 297. *Flask,* FOR PIKE'S PEAK. 298. *Aqua calabash bottle with popular Jenny Lind motif.* 299. *Light green calabash bottle in honor of the 1851 visit of Louis Kossuth, the Hungarian patriot.* 300. *An amber flask with* SUCCESS TO THE RAILROAD

Styled for Scrolls

In the broadside of 1833 illustrated opposite (302), Joseph Meeks & Sons claimed to be one of the oldest and the largest furniture-making establishments in America. That statement can be substantiated from contemporary evidence. When Joseph died in 1868, at the age of ninety-seven, an obituary reported that he had been in business for "nearly eighty years" and that for much of that period he had supplied the markets from Boston to New Orleans with "the most expensive, elegant and durable cabinet work" made in this country. Members of his family acted as sales agents in numerous cities, possibly in some as far away as Argentina, Bolivia, and Brazil. His faith in New York, the obituary added, had caused him to prosper. In the course of his long career, he had been the peer and competitor of Duncan Phyfe; he had supplied furniture for the White House; and he died rich enough to own a vault with "eighty separate apartments" in Brooklyn's Greenwood Cemetery.

For the most part the broadside illustrates a style of furniture widely popular in the 1830's and 1840's. It was, in effect, the last phase of the classical revival. The rich carving and gilded decoration of the late Empire style were replaced by flat, often veneered, surfaces of mahogany and rosewood. Forms assumed an almost geometric simplicity. The ubiquitous symbol of this new fashion, which remained in vogue for decades, was the bold scroll support (301) made in square section and used in various combinations on sofas, tables, and case pieces.

301. *Left: scroll support from a mahogany bookcase*

302. *Opposite: detail from an advertisement of 1833*

303. *Left: armchair made by the émigré furniture maker Michel Bouvier, an ancestor of Mrs. John F. Kennedy's*

304. *Top: wall clock from Forestville, Conn., about 1845*

305. *Right: mahogany-veneered sofa with scroll supports*

As Professor Silliman explained in 1854, "the inherent vitality and grand simplicity" of classical designs enabled them to survive for years after other styles had won public favor. Even as late as 1850, Andrew Jackson Downing observed that "the furniture most generally used in private houses is some modification of the classical style." Such modifications, he pointed out, had "the merit of being simple, easily made, and very modest in cost." The progressive simplification of the Empire style is demonstrated by the three pieces here illustrated. In the case of a chair (303) by Michel Bouvier, French *menuisier ébéniste*, who came to America after the banishment of Napoleon, a trace of the grand style remains in the carved details of the arms. (Among Bouvier's patrons was Napoleon Bonaparte's brother, Joseph, who when he settled in America adopted the title of Comte de Survilliers.) In the sofa (305) such carved detail is eliminated in favor of broad, uncomplicated contours. The design of the lyre-shaped wall clock (304), with its painted panel, is reduced to a sawed profile that is both simply executed and attractive.

This culminating stage of the classical revival was influenced by styles that had been introduced in France with the restoration of the Bourbon monarchy, following the defeat of Napoleon at Waterloo. A number of the designs shown in the Meeks circular were derived more or less directly from English books that illustrated adaptations of French originals. At one point, in 1835, the importation of furniture directly from France so disturbed the New York journeymen, who felt it interfered with their trade, that they descended on a salesroom and scratched the offerings of those imports "in such a diabolical manner that the injury exceeds a thousand dollars."

In 1837 Duncan Phyfe produced a suite of parlor furniture, consisting of fourteen pieces, for the prominent New York lawyer, Samuel A. Foot, that clearly reflected the post-Empire French taste, or Restauration style. Three pieces from that set—a *méridienne* (306), a day bed or couch, a *chaise gondole* (307), or gondola chair, similar to number 12 in the Meeks advertisement, and an oblong bench (308)—are shown here. Foot was more fortunate than some of his fellow New Yorkers. It was a depression year. "One of the signs of the times," wrote Philip Hone in April, "is to be seen in the sales of rich furniture. Men who a year ago thought themselves rich, and such expenditures justifiable, are now bankrupt."

306. *Upper left: one of a pair of* méridiennes *made by Phyfe*

307. *Upper right: one of the side chairs from the same set*

308. *Above: one of two benches from the set, made in 1837*

309. Left: pier table of mahogany veneer in the style of Meeks and Hall

310. Above: detail from the Meeks advertisement, showing a similar table

311. Above: a card table with folding top, as illustrated in Meeks's circular

312. Right: a table closely related to designs both by Meeks and by Hall

313. *Portrait of Jane Rebecca Griffith of Baltimore, about 1844. The furniture closely resembles the designs of Hall.*

For a mahogany pier table such as the one shown opposite (309), with a white marble top, Meeks charged ninety dollars (with an Egyptian marble top the price was one hundred ten dollars). A mahogany card table (312) resembles an example offered in the Meeks circular priced at fifty dollars. At a time when carpenters were being paid only one dollar and a quarter and masons one dollar and three-quarters for a ten-hour working day, such furniture was by no means cheap. However, progressive simplifications of those designs in following years and the introduction of steam-driven band saws, which could cut out scrolls and other carved elements from wood of any thickness, brought prices down to a more popular level. It

was in 1840 that John Hall, an English immigrant working in Baltimore, published an illustrated guide in which he asserted that "novelty, simplicity and practicability, are blended with the present designs, in which originality mostly prevails....As far as possible, the style of the United States is blended with European taste, and a graceful outline and simplicity of parts are depicted in all the objects." By this time the classical ancestry of these forms was almost completely lost in the "blend" of influences and the "simplicity of parts" that were contrived in the interests of utmost practicality. However, in scale and design such pieces admirably complemented the fashionable Greek Revival interiors (313).

Heir
to the
Ages

———— ◆ ————

Victorian
Eclecticism
(1840-1860)

During the score of years that preceded the Civil War, America seemed to be in a constant ferment. The nation was growing in every sense—in size, in numbers, in wealth, and in strength—at a formidable rate. Within that relatively short span of years, as a result of war, annexation, and negotiation, great chunks of territory were added to and consolidated within the national domain; Texas, California, New Mexico, and Oregon were each as large as a good-sized European country. The nation had quickly taken on continental dimensions. During the same period the population almost doubled. Beyond the normal increase of native Americans, wave after wave of emigrants from Europe washed over the eastern coast and spread out over the land. Following the revolutionary disturbances of 1848 in Europe discontented Germans by the scores of thousands found their way to the New World. Most came in response to reports, some of them highly misleading prospectuses, that hailed the blessings of life in America. Whole villages packed up and headed for the nearest, and usually heavily congested, port of departure. "It is a lamentable sight," wrote one witness to that exodus, "...to see the long files of carts...carrying the whole property of these poor wretches who are about to cross the Atlantic on the faith of a lying prospectus." However, such eminent and learned men as Goethe and Hegel also extolled the satisfactions of life in the New World, and what they wrote was not forgotten by those who looked for additional persuasion to seek a new future overseas. Carl Schurz, the revolutionary, was only one of the more prominent Germans who joined the "poor wretches" in their overseas adventure, and who contributed importantly to the culture of America. In his adopted country he became a friend of and a campaigner for Abraham Lincoln, an influential journalist, author, and lecturer, and a general in the Union Army, among other things. A flood tide of that vast emigration came in 1854 when almost a quarter of a million Germans poured into this country. (It was about this time that Abraham Lincoln started to study German as a political expedient.)

The Irish came in similar numbers. A potato famine in that unhappy land brought 163,000 Irishmen to the port of New York alone in 1851. And the English, Scots, and Welsh continued to come. "Since the period when the Gothic tribes, under their hereditary kings, strode down the banks of the Borysthenes, and overwhelmed Greece and Germany and the whole empire of Rome," it was reported in *The Democratic Review* in 1852, "no migration of men has occurred in the world at all similar to that which is now pouring itself upon the shores of the United States....In a single week we have again and again received into the bosom of our society, numbers as great as a Gothic army." Compared with the

Opposite: detail of the carved rosewood chair, about 1850, shown above in its entirety

Irish emigrant outward bound for New York

epic surge of humanity that was heralded by these hordes of newcomers, the barbarian invasions of ancient Rome were indeed, numerically, a minor affair and hardly of greater consequence in the history of western man.

As Europe's demand for American products increased, immigrants actually became a leading article of commerce; that is, they constituted a large and important part of the "back freight" on ships making the return westward voyage across the Atlantic. Such human cargo was sought after by rival shippers eager to return to America with a full load. With every passing decade such transatlantic shuttles became swifter. American packet boats, which were inaugurated in 1818 and which sailed punctually in foul season or fair, almost incredibly kept to their tight schedules in spite of the caprices of wind and weather. They soon reduced the average westward crossing from more than seven weeks to barely more than five. On two occasions, as a result of a freakish reversal of the winds, such ships made the crossing in sixteen days. During his passage on one of those record-breaking packets Ralph Waldo Emerson complained that his sides were sore from rolling in his berth, because to keep on schedule the ship's captain refused to take in sail in a heavy storm that tossed the vessel unmercifully. In the 1850's when the Collins Line of super-steamships went into operation, subsidized by the United States government to compete with England's Cunarders, the time for the run was reduced to less than ten days. But these were luxury liners which made the crossing "a mere pleasure trip." Most immigrants were so tightly packed in common sailing ships that the death rate from disease en route was pathetically high. However, enough of them survived to add substantially to each successive census.

In the eighteenth century Benjamin Franklin, America's major prophet and foremost apostle of expansion, miscalculated that it would take ages to people the American continent. At that time, to be sure, no one knew much about the world that lay beyond the Appalachians. But even years later, after Lewis and Clark had reported on their epic journey across the uncharted wilderness to the shores of the Pacific, Thomas Jefferson concluded there was in this vast expanse of land "room enough for our descendants to the hundredth and thousandth generation." Yet, before Jefferson died in 1826, the immigrant John James Audubon foresaw the day soon to come when the American wilderness, as he knew it, would vanish before the plundering advance of civilization. Less than one generation later even the westernmost borderlands of the nation were attracting growing swarms of emigrants.

A Black Ball liner entering New York Harbor

"How beautiful," Thomas Carlyle wrote to Emerson in 1849, "to think of lean tough Yankee settlers, tough as gutta-percha, with most *occult* unsubduable fire in their belly, steering over the Western Mountains, to annihilate the jungle, and bring bacon and corn out of it for the Posterity of Adam!... There is no *Myth* of Athens or Herakles equal to this *fact*." But they were not all Yankees by any means. The discovery of gold in California, for example, brought contingents of hopeful emigrants from France, Germany, Italy, Japan, China, Australia, Peru, Chile, Mexico, as well as from every settled corner of eastern America. In a remarkably short time San Francisco

The bay and city of San Francisco about 1851

could fairly be described as "far more cosmopolitan than any other American city except New York." In the Midwest shortly after 1848 Milwaukee was for a while virtually a German town. And across the continent, from East to West, people who came from all points of the compass were finding their way to other towns and cities. Indeed, during those years when all America seemed to be moving to the West, more people were actually moving into the cities of the land. "We cannot all live in cities," exclaimed Horace Greeley as he observed the crowded scene in New York, "yet nearly all seem determined to do so." The urban movement, with all its growing list of problems, had commenced in earnest; it would soon become the greatest of all migrations.

In the 1840's and 1850's it seemed clear that the nation had a "manifest destiny," a destiny to expand and to progress in all areas of human endeavor. "We are all a little wild here with numberless projects of social reform," Emerson wrote Carlyle in 1840. He was referring to those various groups of all descriptions and of both native and foreign conception—Transcendentalists, Shakers, Fourierists, Harmonists, Millennialists, and the rest—each of which was intent on building a perfect community according to its lights. One of the best remembered of these communitarian experiments, Brook Farm, near West Roxbury, Massachusetts, described in Nathaniel Hawthorne's *Blithedale Romance*, was undertaken the next year, in 1841. Among its members were Hawthorne himself and Charles A. Dana, and among its visitors, Emerson, Sarah Margaret Fuller, and other highly distinguished New Englanders.

Like most of the others, the Brook Farm group disbanded after a few years. In America the promise of reward for individual enterprise sooner or later diverted all but the most dedicated from such socialistic and collectivist undertakings. But the air remained electric with a crusading spirit of reform and improvement. As Emerson also wrote: "there was an indefinite hope, and there was an assurance that all particular mischiefs were speedily coming to an end....What a fertility of projects for the salvation of the world!" Before it came to an end the particular "mischief" of slavery ultimately involved the entire nation in a tragic and bloody trial at arms. But until that great issue was joined on the battlefield, innumerable other evils called for correction. Timothy Shay Arthur's *Ten Nights in a Bar-Room, And What I Saw There*, written in 1854, was but one of hun-

A sacred dance of the Shakers, Mount Lebanon, N.Y.

dreds of tracts that kept the cause of temperance brightly blazing. Largely because of Richard Henry Dana, Jr.'s *Two Years Before the Mast*, flogging was abolished in the American Navy. Plans were developed to help the blind, the insane, impoverished immigrants, and other unfortunates. The Mormons, the most viable and most highly organized of the sectarian communities, discovered the promised land in Utah, where they hoped neither the United States government nor the devil could interfere with their special way of life, and won converts who came from far places to share their bliss. One appealing eccentric, the phrenologist Orson Squire Fowler, urged his countrymen to forsake the traditional square house and adopt, instead, an octagonal structure, and he persuaded a large number of people to do just that. America was, it seemed, a vast laboratory where, in all their diversity, the hopes of man could be tested with a fair trial and without fear of suppression. America remained, as Hegel had earlier claimed in the introduction to his *Philosophy of History*, "the land of the future...a land of desire for all those who are weary of the historical lumber-room of old Europe." For poet and peasant alike this was a land of new beginnings.

By the 1840's James Fenimore Cooper remarked, America was passing "from the gristle into the bone" in its national development. The country had reached a point of self-realization from which it could regard its achievements with reasonable satisfaction. Among other advances American democracy had grown out of its raw beginnings into an impressive state of political maturity. After two generations of successful self-government and rising prosperity, it was prepared to tell the world it held the key to the future. "We are pioneers of the world," Herman Melville declared in a moment of unrestrained optimism. "God has predestined, mankind expects, great things from our race; and great things we feel in our souls. The most of the nations must soon be in our rear. We are...the advance guard, sent on through the wilderness of untried things, to break a path in the New World that is ours."

Even visiting Englishmen, who in earlier decades had often been harshly critical of what they saw and heard in America, were now generally assuming more respectful attitudes. In 1855 one of them, William E. Baxter, sometime member of Parliament and Privy Councilor, went so far as to suggest that "the rise and progress of the United States appears to me the greatest and most important political fact of this century." Like many others, Baxter was strongly impressed by the general material well-being that characterized American society, and by the relative absence of poverty and want. Another observer, the Swedish author, Frederika Bremer, noted that even the humble cart driver and small farmer lived comfortably and enjoyed an abundance at table.

One of the first persons to greet Miss Bremer when she arrived at New York in 1849 was Andrew Jackson Downing, America's leading landscape architect and one of its most discerning critics. The Swedish spinster was deeply impressed by Downing's "noble and acutely discriminating mind." Beyond that, she wrote her sister, he had "dark eyes and dark hair, of a beautiful brown, and softly curling...quite a poetical appearance!" Downing also had a love of natural landscape and an unshakable belief, "above all things under heaven, in the power and virtue of the individual home," placed in the right setting, to preserve and support the dignity of man. He became one of the most influential tastemakers of his time. His books on horticulture, landscape architecture, and architectural and furniture design won him an international reputation. (The Queen of Denmark sent him a "magnificent ring" in appreciation of his writings.) And his principles and preachments were taken up and repeated by a host of other writers of books on domestic architecture. "The Greek temple disease had passed its crisis," he exulted in 1846. "The people have survived it." James Fenimore Cooper, when he returned from Europe in 1833, complained of the "mushroom temples" that lined the banks of the Hudson River and scarred the landscape with their whiteness. He had his own ancestral home in Cooperstown, Otsego Hall, remodeled in the Gothic style. Downing agreed with Cooper; white was a

"Father, Come Home!" Illustration from Ten Nights in a Bar-Room, And What I Saw There

The north front of Strawberry Hill, Horace Walpole's Gothic castle near Twickenham

Sir Walter Scott by Sir William Allan, 1832

"vulgar" color for a house and he urged his readers and clients to use the colors of grass, stone, and moss that would blend into the natural background. From his own Gothic cottage on the shores of the Hudson, through his writings, he spread that gospel from one end of the country to the other.

In the asymmetrical, uninhibited designs of the Gothic Revival the canons of the classical style were completely rejected. The balanced order and formal restraint that earlier had given the classical revival its essential character disappeared in picturesque arrangements that reflected the widespread contemporary mood of romantic nostalgia for the medieval past. Actually, the authority of classicism, strong as it remained over the years, had never been absolute or unquestioned; a "Gothic" strain in furniture and decoration and architecture had lingered through the centuries since the Middle Ages—especially in England. When the Adam versions of classicism were enjoying their greatest acclaim, Horace Walpole disparaged them as being all "gingerbread" and "filigraine." Walpole had an uncontrollable enthusiasm for the Gothic style, as he conceived it and as he revived it in the fantastic "castle," Strawberry Hill, at Twickenham near London, which he made his home and over which he labored so long and so lovingly. Like virtually all of his contemporaries, he knew next to nothing of medieval planning or craftsmanship. But, as he said, his curious edifice was "a very proper habitation" for the author of *The Castle of Otranto*—his own romantic Gothic novel. As the whimsical concoction of a prominent eccentric, Strawberry Hill was a tourist attraction while Walpole lived there and, after his death, it remained a curious historic monument over the years to come. But when, around the turn of the century, England's most fashionable and successful professional architect, James Wyatt—successor to Robert Adam in these distinctions—applied his talents to the Gothic Revival, the style could no longer be regarded as a mere caprice. Later in the nineteenth century, indeed, it was to become almost a national style in England, a style vividly recalled by the Houses of Parliament, designed by Sir Charles Barry and built in the middle years of the century and to this day one of Britain's most picturesque and beloved monuments.

America had neither medieval survivals nor medieval ruins to remind it of the Gothic past. That was a point that concerned Nathaniel Hawthorne in his writing. "No author, without a trial," he observed in the preface to *The Marble Faun,* "can conceive of the difficulty of writing a romance about a country where there is no shadow, no antiquity, no mystery, no picturesque and gloomy wrong, nor anything but a commonplace prosperity, in broad and simple daylight, as is happily the case with my dear native land." But Americans were as susceptible as the English to the romantic spirit that pervaded the nineteenth century. Everything remote in time or place, everything strange and picturesque, everything that pleasantly disturbed the emotions with its mystery or sublimity, or that excited fantasy, appealed to the romantic taste—a susceptibility fully exploited by Sir Walter Scott in his long series of novels. Scott's medieval romances were widely read and admired in America; the author himself was all but venerated. When Audubon visited Edinburgh in 1826 to launch the publication of his *Birds of America,* he wrote that, if necessary, he would "crawl on all fours for a mile" to win an audience with the great man. The actual meeting was something of an anticlimax, for Scott was not especially impressed by Audubon's drawings. Washington Irving had better luck; he spent four exhilarating days at Abbotsford, Scott's home near Melrose on the Tweed, walking and talking with the older man from breakfast until bedtime. Encouraged by Scott, Irving returned to America to devote himself to writing.

Somewhat paradoxically, the first Gothic Revival house to be built in America was designed by the "bigotted Greek," Benjamin Henry Latrobe. Sedgeley, the country retreat he constructed in 1799 for the Philadelphia merchant William Crammond, was, like Strawberry Hill, a sort of architectural "folly." Early in the nineteenth century it was followed by occasional other buildings in the Gothic manner. But it was Downing, a generation later, who gave the movement its first great impetus in America. Before his untimely, heroic death in a steamboat explosion in 1852, the American landscape was dotted with "castles" and cottages that by an extreme stretch of imagination could be associated with the spirit of the Middle Ages.

To most homeowners the specific architectural quality of such structures was less important than those associations evoked by their assorted crockets and cusps, their towers, turrets, and trellises, their pointed archways, and their oriel windows. Idlewild, the country home of the American editor and author, Nathaniel P. Willis, was planned for just such a spot on the Hudson River, his architect counseled him, "as a medieval knight would have selected for his stronghold...a little imagination may easily transmute the simple domestic cottage into the turreted and battlemented castle." In the variety of their functions as in their appearance the furniture—the chairs, tables, whatnots, and divers other forms—designed in the Gothic style would have bewildered people of the Middle Ages, who were largely unaware of such kinds of convenience, or of any need for them. However, the romance for the past transcended such considerations.

A number of Downing's books were illustrated by Alexander Jackson Davis, the most prolific and influential architect of the time. Davis was a versatile genius who worked in most of the popular contemporary styles. It was an eclectic age, and every past style known to man was revived for consideration and for

Washington Irving's home near Tarrytown, N.Y.

possible application to the needs and fancies of the day. That spirit of revivalism was theatrically pictured in 1840 by the American landscapist Thomas Cole in *The Architect's Dream* (see pages 270–71), a painting William Cullen Bryant described as "an assemblage of structures, Egyptian, Grecian, Gothic, Moorish, such as might present itself to the imagination of one who had fallen asleep after reading a work on the different styles of architecture." Buildings in all those styles, by Davis and others, were in fact to be seen here and there about the country. At one point Davis noted in his diary that he had designed buildings in fourteen different styles, including French suburban, Lombard Italian, ancient Etruscan, Oriental, and others. As Downing observed, America was "in the midst of what might be called the experimental stage of architectural taste. With the passion for novelty, and the feeling of independence that belong to this country, our people seem determined to *try everything.*"

In 1850, shortly before he died, Downing noted that *the* most popular and fashionable style of the moment in furniture followed "modern" French designs. He referred to those revivals of Louis XIV and eighteenth-century rococo patterns that had somewhat earlier won favor abroad and that were currently being "pushed" in *Godey's Magazine and Lady's Book.* The editors felt obliged to acquaint their large audience with the latest and most fashionable furniture "in all its variety of graceful forms, beauty of execution, and delicacy of finish," even though "honest country folk" might decry such emphasis on modishness and novelty. "If we stop a moment to examine details [of such furniture]," the magazine reported of the Rococo style, "we will be especially struck...with the varied, in fact ever changing, curves of artistic carving of some beautiful wreath, with the boldness, depth, and sharpness of a *bouquet* or cluster; in another, with the hanging foliage, budding flowers, and waving scrolls, many of which are triumphs of the chisel." (Actually, the application of new mechanical techniques and of steam power made relatively light work of many of those intricately contrived decorative features.) They were describing a piece, which we today very broadly characterize as "early Victorian," such as the one represented in the opening illustration to this chapter, and such as those shown later in this chapter. As a further service to their readers, the editors gave the common English equivalents of the French terms for furniture that were often met with in the best shops and warehouses. To end confusion on these points, they explained that a *toilettinette* was a lady's toilet table, an *étagère* was a whatnot, a *tête-à-tête* was a sofa, and so on.

A few years earlier one English traveler on the Continent had reported that the largest and most extravagant orders for household furnishings received at the French city of Lyons were from New York. At the same time, there were numerous French-born cabinetmakers, among others, working in this "modern" style in America during the 1840's and 1850's; such men as François Seignouret, Charles A. Baudouine, Alexander Roux, Augustus Eliaers, and Prudent Mallard. Among the others, the German-born John Henry Belter of New York is the best remembered, although a number of contemporaries, both native- and foreign-born, were working with comparable skills and on an equally large scale. For the guidance of those who needed it or wanted it, several French, English, and American pattern books pictured designs that gave various interpretations of the Rococo Revival. During the 1850's the Rococo remained the most popular of the several historic styles that were revived, with more or less elaborations, as the years passed. The resemblance of these revived styles to the actual produc-

Advertisement from Godey's Lady's Book

tions of the past was usually vague at best, and elements were blended one with another until even those who published the designs were confused by their own terminology in their efforts to caption their illustrations.

While *Godey's* sang the praises of the newest styles, the magazine spared room for occasional words of caution. In 1850 the editors ran a piece by Lydia Maria Francis Child in which that author and reformer suggested that people of "moderate fortunes" were putting altogether too much money into their home furnishings. Extravagance in these and other matters, she once again reminded her readers, was becoming a national vice. However, Ralph Waldo Emerson who spoke with unique authority, once remarked that he had never known a man as rich as all men should be. In 1853, when New York opened the first great American world's fair at the Crystal Palace, the prospect of all people enjoying benefits that in the past had been reserved for the opulent seemed bright and imminent. Democracy, the exhibits at the fair implied to all the world, held the promise of better things for everyone.

At what point raising the standards of living was becoming confused with exciting a taste for novelty and superfluity, was a point that already bothered some of Emerson's contemporaries. But, as Tocqueville had written years before, the Americans' love of comforts and conveniences, and the confusion of contraptions with civilization, was characteristic of a new democracy. The future would take care of itself.

The Crystal Palace

In 1853 the United States staged its first world's fair at its own Crystal Palace (315) in New York. Here, it was hoped, the European exhibits would broaden the American's outlook and the domestic displays would prove to the world at large that America had come of age both industrially and culturally. "If we effect our object," stated the Board of Directors of the fair, "...we shall have raised higher the standard of taste." Among the American exhibits one critic was "agreeably surprised to find a number of pieces of ornamental furniture of large size, which, in design and elaborate and excellent workmanship," were as good as any of the foreign products; proof enough, it seemed, that the taste of Americans was already rising with their increasing wealth. A rosewood *étagère* (314), or stand with open shelves (in effect, a French term for a whatnot), made in Brooklyn and singled out for praise was, for reasons not altogether clear, described as being in the Renaissance style. As one commentary explained, the styles of the day were actually "borrowed without judgment from every age and nation." Throughout the two decades on either side of 1850 such styles—the Grecian, Modern, Gothic, Elizabethan, Louis XIV, Rococo, Renaissance, and so on—flourished concurrently. The labels by which they were known were at best loosely defined, and at times were interchangeable according to personal preference.

314. *A carved* étagère *exhibited at the Crystal Palace by Thomas Brooks*

315. OVERLEAF: *The Crystal Palace in New York City; painting on glass*

237

The most elaborate furniture shown at the fair was not typical of the period, but doubtlessly was intended for "show." It did, however, accent the revival of historical styles which dominated the fashions of the time. To rationalize the extravagant nature of many of the exhibits, one contemporary observer explained "the tendency of civilisation is always from plainness to ornament. The articles of convenience of one age become objects of luxury in the next, and human ingenuity is taxed to decorate the common necessaries of life." If taste were to be improved and excesses to be avoided, acquaintance with the best works of art in all categories was essential. And that was what the fair hoped to make possible. This was no "vast curiosity-shop or raree-show," wrote Horace Greeley, but "the grandest and most instructive University ever opened...on this continent." It was hoped that such exhibitions might remain a permanent program.

The building was the first native large-scale experiment in construction with modern materials. Although in size it was much smaller than the Crystal Palace at London, it was a proud achievement. Made of ore and sand that had been scraped from the earth, melted, cast, and wrought into girders of iron and panels of glass, and then daringly flung in a soaring dome and arcades far above the stalls beneath (in size, the dome was second only to that of St. Peters in Rome), the Palace was a symbol of the control man was assuming over the natural materials.

In the end, however, the "mighty Exhibition" was not a success. People managed to stay away in sufficient numbers for the enterprise to go bankrupt. Even P. T. Barnum could do nothing to revive interest, and the building was leased for miscellaneous purposes in seasons to come. Then, on October 5, 1858, the building went up in flames, ironically attracting the biggest crowd since the opening. The great dome collapsed and fell with a roar on a calliope that had just played "Pop! Goes the Weasel."

316. *Above: porcelain and pottery from Vermont, at the Crystal Palace*
317. *Opposite: a detail from a lithograph showing the Palace in flames*

Some Cusps & Crockets

The declining authority of classical styles opened the way for experimentation with a variety of other historical styles. For a time, during the middle years of the nineteenth century, it seemed that the Gothic Revival might change the face of America, as it was already altering the appearance of the English countryside. At the Crystal Palace the architectural exhibits of Alexander Jackson Davis, foremost exponent of the growing vogue, won him diplomas and medals, and Gothic houses and cottages of his design could be seen throughout the land from Maine to the Bluegrass. In 1845 he created for the wealthy millowner William J. Rotch a "Pointed Cottage" (318), which fortunately still stands in New Bedford, Massachusetts. "The character expressed by...this design," explained A. J. Downing, "is that of a man or family of domestic tastes, but with strong aspirations after something higher than social pleasures." In New Bedford building was more expensive than in New York; Mr. Rotch's house cost about six thousand dollars.

318. A rendering of the Rotch house, by A. J. Davis

319. Left: a carved Gothic Revival bed

320. Above: a mahogany corner whatnot

As far back as the eighteenth century Thomas Jefferson had toyed with the idea of placing a Gothic temple in his garden at Monticello. And even the arch-classicist Nicholas Biddle had a Gothic dependency to his great, columned mansion, Andalusia—a dependency in which a Gothic bed (319), given to him by Joseph Bonaparte, was used. But the fashion for Gothic reached its broadest popularity in the middle years of the last century. "The ambition of almost every person building in the country," Downing wrote in 1850, was to put up a Gothic cottage. "Those who love shadow, and the sentiment of antiquity and repose," he claimed, "will find most pleasure in the quiet tone which prevails in the Gothic style." He also provided descriptions and illustrations of beds, chairs, tables, and other furniture forms which he recommended as "the most correct" and satisfactory examples in that style. The whatnot, a form mentioned in print as early as 1808, by mid-century became an almost indispensable convenience as a corner stand within the Gothic home.

321. Left: a dresser by Richard Byrnes

322. Above: upholstered chair by Jelliff

323. Opposite: detail of a carved chair

A contemporary critic of the Gothic style, remarking on chairs and other furniture forms to be seen in medieval manuscript illuminations, observed that it was so painful to see saints sitting on such uncomfortable "instruments of torture," he wondered that a belief in purgatory could have obtained "at a time in which even those who lived and died in the odor of sanctity were obliged to undergo such daily suffering." Generally speaking, the revival furniture bore little relation to any forms known in the Middle Ages; it was a style that by its nature called for inventiveness, especially for dressers (321), whatnots, bookcases and other strictly modern appurtenances. Downing's major objection to much of the furniture being marketed as Gothic was that it was "too elaborately Gothic—with the same high pointed arches, crockets, and carving usually seen in the front of some cathedral," a point convincingly demonstrated by the chair (323) shown here. In another chair (322) John Jelliff, for decades one of Newark's most accomplished and important furniture makers, provided an upholstered seat and back as a form of comfort unheard of in medieval times, but a feature fast assuming commanding importance in the 1850's as cheap textiles became abundant.

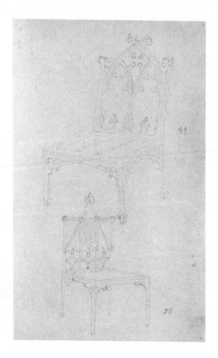

In 1838 Davis undertook to create a summer retreat (324) near Tarry-town, New York, for William Paulding and his son, Philip. Three years later, before work on the house was finished, Philip Hone visited the site and noted his impressions in his diary. They were not generous. "It is an immense edifice of white or gray marble," he wrote, "resem-bling a baronial castle, or rather a Gothic monastery, with towers, tur-rets, and trellises; minarets, mosaics, and mouse-holes; archways, armories, and air-holes; peaked windows and pinnacled roofs, and many other fantastics too tedious to enumerate, the whole constitut-ing an edifice of gigantic size, with no room in it; great cost and little comfort, which, if I mistake not, will one of these days be designated as 'Pauldings's Folly.'" Actually this was one of Davis' most impres-sive works. Asking Davis to approve the mantels chosen for the house, Paulding wrote: "If you see anything offensive to your gothick eye...put your veto upon it....I wish them to be correct specimens of the style. How the ladies will *dote* on them."

The house was enlarged by Davis in 1864–66 for George Merritt, who named it Lyndhurst. Davis also designed chairs (325) for the house, which were made by his cabinetmaker Richard H. Byrnes.

324. Opposite, top: the Pauldings'
Gothic villa, as drawn by A. J. Davis

325. Opposite: chair designs drawn
by Davis for the Pauldings' residence

326, 327. Gothic style chairs made by
Richard Byrnes for the Paulding home

249

Probably very few homes were furnished in a single style. Indeed, both English and American published guides in such matters suggested that certain different styles were most appropriately used in the separate rooms of a household. Although Gothic furniture was obviously made for every purpose, from steeple clocks (328) to dining tables (329), it was considered by some singularly fitting for the library—especially for bookcases (330)—and the hall. Downing proposed to his readers that busts of distinguished authors be placed along the tops of bookcases to designate the nature of the volumes below, a plan he followed in his own home according to Miss Fredrika Bremer.

Not all the furniture made in these years served out their time of normal use. The western routes to the California gold mines were quickly littered with all sorts of household furnishings, abandoned for want of strength and means to carry them farther. In one dump heap a group of forty-niners found "a very handsome and new Gothic bookcase! It was soon dismembered to boil our coffee kettles."

328. *Opposite, top: a Gothic steeple clock*

329. *Opposite: a Gothic dining table*

330. *Right: one of a set of five bookcases designed by the architect Richard Upjohn*

From the Old World to the New

"Being born in the City of Hamburg in Germany on September 8, 1830, we came to New York June 22, 1844, after a passage of 47 days in a small German sailing vessel. A year later, 1845, father indentured me to a party of German cabinet makers....With the incoming of the large German imigration about 1849–50, all those old residents moved away and a Colony of German mechanics took their place. There were cabinet makers shops, saw mills and marble mills everywhere...in the time from about 1840 to about 1865 a great deal of furniture was made there which is now sold for Antique to such as don't Know any better."

Thus begin the recollections of a cabinetmaker named Ernest Hagen, who recorded (at the age of seventy-eight) his impressions of that period of furniture fashions now designated as early Victorian. Hagen's descriptive phrase, "a Colony of German mechanics," was not ill-founded. During the years 1854 and 1855, for example, *Trow's New York City Directory* listed one hundred ninety-three cabinetmakers and furniture dealers in New York, of whom one hundred thirty-one had German names. In the allied trade of piano making, such immigrants as Henry Steinway in New York, Valentine Knabe in Baltimore, and Rudolph Wurlitzer in Cincinnati would soon found their respective piano companies.

In short, the field of cabinetmaking was dominated throughout America by foreign-born craftsmen, "Germans and Frenchmen being in the majority," as Professor Silliman pointed out again and again in his critique of the furniture shown at the Crystal Palace exhibition in 1853. Silliman, however, was quick to add that these craftsmen were "citizens by adoption" and the United States could "partly claim the talent which is naturalised among us." He lavished unbounded enthusiasm on an oak buffet designed by Gustave Herter of New York—a towering edifice carved from top to toe with cupids, fruits of the harvest, wild game, dolphins, a ship at sea, scrolls, strappings, and floral motifs, with a central group (opposite) entitled "Death of the Stag," and the entire extravaganza crowned with a loosely draped goddess wreathed in laurel leaves. Silliman took this occasion to declare: "While our native mechanics exhibit an unequalled constructive skill and versatility, they are not often gifted by nature with artistic cleverness," whereas many European workmen had received "an artistic education."

For some Americans, imbued with intense feelings of nationalism, foreign influences were a sore point. In 1840 Congressman Charles Ogle of Pennsylvania had lambasted Martin Van Buren for crowding the White House with dazzling foreign ornaments rather than buying furnishings produced by American artisans. The presidential purchase of Brussels carpets, Italian marble mantels, French bedsteads, and French gilt-bronze lamps was wrathfully itemized from the floor of the House of Representatives. Later, *Harper's New Monthly Magazine* would agree with Professor Silliman that the European exhibits at the Crystal Palace offered "our untraveled countrymen" the opportunity to study the "graceful and ornamental," as opposed to the "*merely useful.*" But, *Harper's* concluded in a burst of chauvinism: "The time is not far off, we feel sure, when we shall have no need of foreign designers of our plate and jewelry; and when our most admired furniture will not, as now, date from Paris." France, nonetheless, continued to set the style in America (as it did in Europe), not only in furniture but in such prized amenities as French dancing masters, French chefs, and French *couture.* (For example, Empress Eugénie's hoop skirts were instantly copied.)

Meanwhile, the leading exponent of "the old French taste," as the Rococo Revival was then described, was a German immigrant—John Henry Belter. Born in 1804, Belter served his apprenticeship in Württemberg during the years when the French Rococo Revival

was coming into flower in Germany. He is first listed in a New York directory in 1844 with a shop at Chatham Square. In 1858 he opened a large factory on Third Avenue near 76th Street where, it was said, he employed forty apprentices. Apparently it was a thoroughly German enterprise. His wife was Louisa Springmeyer, whose four brothers became business partners; his foreman was a Mr. Heintz, whom Belter brought from the old country; and many of the shop's carvers were from Alsace-Lorraine and

the Black Forest. Belter's laminating process, for which he applied for a patent in 1856, consisted of several thin layers of wood glued together, the grain of alternate layers set at right angles, with an average of six to eight layers, and the total thickness usually measuring about an inch. The layers were then pressed and steamed into the required curves. As Ernest Hagen described the process in his recollections: "[this] made a very strong and not heavy chair back...all the ornamental carved work glued on after the perforated part of the thin back was sawed out and prepared." Despite Belter's meticulous craftsmanship and enormous popularity, the firm was undermined by mass production, changing styles, and infringements on his patented process of laminating wood. In 1864, as Hagen phrased it, Belter "died a very poor man."

Although French immigration was comparatively moderate, a number of French cabinetmakers were successful in America. In New Orleans there were François Seignouret and Prudent Mallard. Seignouret, who fought under Andrew Jackson in the Battle of New Orleans, is known for his monumental

armoires, which were often ten feet tall, and designed for the vast, high-ceilinged rooms typical of New Orleans architecture at this time. Mallard, in turn, is known for his equally monumental and heavily carved bedsteads, with silk-lined canopies suitably constructed to carry the mosquito netting so necessary on a Louisiana night. French-born Augustus Eliaers, who worked in Boston, received praise from Professor Silliman for two Crystal Palace entries—a rosewood sideboard (again with the popular carvings of fruit, game, and cupids), and a pier table, "with a richly carved rosewood frame and white marble top."

In New York there was Charles A. Baudouine, whom Hagen recalled in his memoirs as the leading cabinetmaker in town. "He was a self made man, beginning in a small shop on Pearl Street on a capital of 300 Dollars, which he got from his wife....He was born in this city of French descend and spoke French fluently. He was a tall gentlemanly appearance and looked more like an army officer. He went to France every year and imported a great deal of French furniture and upholstery coverings, French hardware, trimmings, and other material used in his shop." After his retirement, Baudouine moved to Fifth Avenue in 1876, drove a four-in-hand coach, and left "a fortune between 4 and 5 Millions," as well as bequeathing his son-in-law "all my diamonds."

The handiwork of Alexander Roux, another French craftsman in New York, was acclaimed by Andrew Jackson

Downing for: "The most tasteful designs of Louis Quatorze, Renaissance, Gothic, etc., to be found in the country." Silliman commended Roux for a black walnut sideboard that was "not too large for the use and style of moderately wealthy families." A third French artisan, also living in New York, was Léon Marcotte, who arrived in 1854 followed by boatloads of "showy furniture." He quickly established himself as one of the city's most fashionable decorators and cabinetmakers. Marquetry, butterfly motifs in shaded woods, and inlaid mother-of-pearl stars were Marcotte's forte. As Hagen recalled his shop: "They worked principally in the pure Louis XVI style and done the very best work. This style is really the best of all and will never go out of fashion, and, if not overdone...is simply grand."

In White Plains, New York, lived another outstanding craftsman of the period, an Irishman named Richard H. Byrnes, who immigrated around 1835 from County Limerick where he had learned his trade. For thirty years Byrnes executed the furniture designs of the architectural firm of Town and Davis, particularly in the Gothic mode "for which he had a peculiar talent."

But the day of the individual cabinetmaker with the distinctive imprint of his tastes and skills was soon to be over. Hagen expressed it succinctly: "The factory work, and especially the Western factory work drove everything else out of the market. All the smaller cabinet makers were simply wiped out."

French, Modern & Rococo

While the Greek Revival style lingered and the Gothic Revival flourished, other styles recalling times past competed for public favor in the early years of the Victorian period. Most successful in that running "battle of styles" were those designs variously called Louis XIV, Louis XV, Rococo, and "antique" or "modern" French. Obviously, such designations were imprecise at best, but they all referred in some degree to the revival of eighteenth-century patterns that came about in France during the reign of Louis Philippe. In 1845 one visitor noted that styles in the most elegant American homes were Parisian rather than English. A few years later a New York parlor (331), furnished by "the French house of Bembe & Kimbel," was described as presenting "a true and classic idea of the beautiful in decorative art." Mr. Kimbel's "unique styles," it was reported, appeared to be "American modifications of those now in vogue abroad."

331. Opposite: parlor in the "modern" French taste, 1854
332. Above: a detail from a table used by Lincoln   255

In technical accomplishment American furniture making reached a peak of excellence in those forms with curvilinear outlines and richly carved ornament featuring S- and C-scrolls and intricate combinations of fruit and flowers, such as the center table (333) and the love seat (334) shown here. (This type of love seat, also called tête-à-tête or conversational, was a popular novelty of the time. With such an arrangement, Downing wrote, a wife could sit toward the light of a lamp, sewing, while her husband sat before the fire with his book to the light.) They owe an apparent debt to rococo designs of the previous century, but these have been modified, elaborated, and synthesized in novel arrangements that constitute an altogether separate style—and one that very clearly expressed the romantic spirit of the mid-nineteenth century. While John H. Belter was only one of numerous craftsmen who furthered the American Rococo Revival, he was also one of the best known; for this among other reasons chairs, tables, and other forms of this general nature are often referred to as "Belter furniture."

333. *Opposite: a rosewood table signed by Belter*

334. *Above: a love seat of laminated rosewood*

Belter and his contemporaries also interpreted the Rococo style in more restrained fashion, as indicated by the accompanying illustrations. In 1860, during the course of a general refurbishing of the White House, President James Buchanan bought from Gottlieb Vollmer of Philadelphia a Rococo Revival suite for the Blue Room, which included an ottoman (336) among other pieces. The ottoman, Downing had explained to his readers a decade earlier, was a form borrowed from Oriental countries, which had become "quite popular among us of late." It afforded, he added, "a more agreeable lounge than any other seat whatever." (Much earlier, Sheraton had described the form as a fashionable novelty in "imitation of Turkish mode of sitting.") During the next administration, to keep the White House stylish, Mrs. Lincoln constantly petitioned Congress for money for new furnishings. A chair (335), still in the White House and resembling the one represented in George P. A. Healy's portrait of Lincoln (337), may have been one of her acquisitions.

335. *Left: Rococo chair in the White House*
336. *Right: carved, gilded ottoman by Vollmer*
337. *Opposite: Lincoln in a Rococo chair*

258

338. *Right: gilt hanging mirror*

339. *Below: gilt rosewood sofa*

In 1854, commenting on the exhibits of American furniture at New York's Crystal Palace, Professor Benjamin Silliman repeatedly referred to the eclectic spirit of the times. Nevertheless, he pointed out, whatever designs and motifs were borrowed from the past and from distant places, were modified in the direction of increased comfort and convenience. "In fact," he wrote, "we have a furniture style of our own, which, though not original, bears yet the marks of our utilitarian age. It is a modification and a moderation of the style of Louis XIV; and while it assumes the graceful motives [sic] of that style, it also reduces them to greater simplicity, and moulds them into forms more consistent with comfort and constructive truth." He illustrated his point with an engraving of a sofa by a French-born contemporary of Belter's; a piece that was somewhat less elaborate than the gilded example (339) shown here. But the carving even on that piece he selected for illustration, he thought, formed surfaces "very uninviting to human shoulders." Nevertheless, he conceded, "we are no longer contented with the plainness that was once satisfactory. A demand for decoration has arisen in every branch of manufactures; and although ornament has sometimes been used to excess, and inappropriately, it is still a movement in the right direction." Here he spoke as a man of his times.

Before the vogue of the Rococo Revival waned during the 1860's, the style had invaded virtually every corner of the well-to-do American home. Cast-iron hatstands (342), stoves, and garden furniture; silver teapots (341); marble fireplaces, bronze lamps, chandeliers; and virtually all other household appurtenances flaunted the exuberant, curved outlines and S- and C-scroll ornament that gave the style its essential character; in those homes, that is, that did not favor one or another of the different styles that were also being advertised during the score of years preceding the Civil War. For that period witnessed not so much a progression of styles as a medley of styles that coexisted without significant internal developments in any one of them. As earlier indicated, in America and in England, certain styles were deemed singularly appropriate to certain rooms. If the Gothic, according to Downing, was especially suited to halls and libraries, furniture in the French taste was most properly used in drawing rooms or parlors and bedrooms. By 1860, the so-called balloon-back chair (343), a Rococo form that had gradually evolved from the klismos, was a very common type of seating furniture.

340. *Opposite, top: a fashionable parlor, around 1860*

341. *Opposite, below: a silver teapot, made about 1845*

342. *Left: a cast-iron hat and umbrella stand believed to have belonged to Washington Irving; made about 1840*

343. *Above: balloon-back side chair with cabriole legs*

344. *Left: a dressing table by Prudent Mallard*

345. *Right: rosewood bed made by John H. Belter*

In spite of the fact that the term "Belter furniture" has long been used to denote a whole category of chairs, sofas, tables, and other forms, pieces known with certainty to have been made by him are relatively few. The massive bed here illustrated (345) is stamped with his name and the date of his patent for the process of laminating thin layers of wood and molding them under steam heat to required shapes. That process is magnificently demonstrated in the "wrap-around" footboard and headboard of the bed, with their broad, unbroken expanses of figured rosewood veneer crested with luxuriantly carved ornament. Because of its attractive, strong color and its variegated figures, as well as its dense, durable character, tropical rosewood, veneered or solid, was a favorite of the early Victorian period. A dressing table (344) of solid rosewood was made by Prudent Mallard, French-trained cabinetmaker of New Orleans. Along with other craftsmen of that city, Mallard had to compete with products from the North. One New York cabinetmaker, who had a large shop on Essex Street and who sent most of his output to New Orleans, died a rich man, "leaving about 4 Millions."

Past & Present Diversified

While various and disparate historical styles coexisted amicably enough in the same house, sometimes in the same room, and occasionally as separate elements in a single suite of furniture, they also often mingled in an individual piece. The tripod base of a table (346), with its lion-paw feet and scroll extensions, is essentially classical in design; the pedestal supporting the top is composed of a pointed-arch, Gothic arcade; and the top (346a) is painted with pseudo-Oriental scenes. A painted cast-iron mantel clock (348) was made with Gothic crockets and cusped arches surmounting an arrangement of classical figures, urns and columns, and a romantic landscape. There was nothing novel about such combinations of stylistic elements. More than a century earlier, japanned furniture made in the American colonies had combined imitation-Oriental lacquer with classical and baroque details. Some fifty years later, Thomas Chippendale and his contemporaries worked Gothic and Chinese, along with "modern" French and classical motifs into their designs. But, through the proliferation of inexpensive prints and of illustrated books and periodicals, and through the agencies of international exhibitions and ever more elaborate advertising, more people were confronted with a wider variety of suggestions in matters of style and fashion in the early Victorian period than in any previous time in history. And the increasingly affluent and influential middle class created an unprecedented demand for house furnishings of every kind and in all styles. A rosewood and mahogany side chair (347), in what was known as the Elizabethan style, is actually composed of a very freely handled combination of motifs borrowed rather vaguely from various baroque and seventeenth-century sources. The spiral-twist turnings recall the roughly similar ornament of the reign of Charles II, generations after the death of Queen Elizabeth.

346. *Opposite: center table, the top (346a) with pseudo-Oriental motifs*

347. *Left: an Elizabethan style chair*

348. *Above: a cast-iron mantel clock*

In September, 1850, with P. T. Barnum as her impresario, the Swedish singer Jenny Lind arrived in New York to undertake her American concert tour. Her success began before she sang a phrase. As Philip Hone punned in his diary: "The good people of New York are anxious to part with their money *for a song*, and the 'nightingale' will make a profitable exchange of her *notes* for specie." From her first concert she netted more than twelve thousand dollars, which she donated to local charitable and benevolent institutions. Three thousand dollars went to the Widow and Orphan's Fund of the local fire department. In gratitude, the fire laddies presented Miss Lind with "the largest gold box ever made in America," enclosing their thanks, and a rosewood bookcase (350) containing a specially bound set of the octavo edition of Audubon's *Birds of America*. This was, she acknowledged, her "most beautiful souvenir of America." For the bookcase, the firemen called upon Thomas Brooks, the Brooklyn cabinetmaker (see pages 236-37), who produced what was virtually a sampler of mid-nineteenth-century design, combining in one piece Gothic, baroque, rococo, Elizabethan, and, for all one can say, "Renaissance" elements.

349. *Opposite: T. Brooks's shop*

350. *Left: Jenny Lind's bookcase*

351. *Above: an occasional table; ball- or spool-turned furniture is often associated with Jenny Lind*

352. OVERLEAF: The Architect's Dream, *painted by Thomas Cole*

269

PAINTED BY T. COLE
FOR I. TOWN ARCH^t
1840.

353. *Right: walnut table, sienna marble top, by Kingman and Murphy, New York, about 1860*

354. *Below: rosewood piano, by Nunns and Clark, New York, with mother-of-pearl keys*

355. *Opposite: rosewood bureau, made in Cincinnati about 1860 in the "Renaissance" style*

With its representation of mingled Greek, Roman, Egyptian, Gothic, and hybrid structures, Thomas Cole's painting (352) suggests only a few of the sources of design that fired the dreams of contemporary architects. "All we can do," conceded one well-known practitioner, "is to combine, using bits here and there, as our education affords more or less acquaintance with the models from which we steal our material." His observation applied equally to cabinetmakers. No design was presented without an attribution to one or another historical style—or to several styles—and titles of styles were devised with confusing abandon for this purpose. Those revivals of the past, variously interpreted, separately and in combination, produced forms unlike anything known to history.

273

Ruby Coatings
& Silver Linings

"We were repeatedly struck by the fact, new to us," wrote a visitor to the New England Glass Company factory, Cambridge, Massachusetts, in 1852, "that most of the exquisite, highly colored and decorated glassware, which is so much admired under the name of Bohemian glass, is manufactured at these works." He referred to cut and engraved, overlay-colored pieces of the sort shown here. At the London Crystal Palace the year before, the exhibits of the different nations, which included true Bohemian glass and English versions of it, led an American visitor to observe that "the character of our [American] articles was such as to show the world that we worked for the great masses, not for the luxurious and privileged few." However, the constantly expanding market for all manner of consumer goods was increasing the demand for an ever larger variety of glassware, as of other merchandise.

Bohemian-type glass was no doubt imported from abroad before it was made in America. And, as always, foreign glassworkers with special skills were also being recruited to man our expanding factories. By 1861 Bohemian-type ware was being produced here in such quantity that specific imposts on imported versions were incorporated into the tariff act of that year to protect the domestic product. When it was used for railroad lanterns and similar devices ruby glass was made in solid color so that if the piece was chipped it would still be red. But the tableware and other decorative forms, so popular in the 1850's, were customarily made by superimposing a relatively thin overlay of colored glass (by one of several methods) over the main body of clear glass. When a piece had been blown and tooled to its final shape, a glass cutter removed the coating to leave a pattern in the clear glass beneath.

356. *Opposite: ruby-glass compote, New England*

357. *Above: Sandwich overlaid glass string-holder*

358. *Right: covered vase, New England Glass Co.*

The emphatic and pleasing contrast of designs in clear glass against colored backgrounds encouraged engraving and cutting to a new degree of elaboration (359). In 1855 the New England Glass Company had ninety men in their cutting room. The next year they recruited Louis Vaupel, an expert engraver from Germany, whose infinitely detailed naturalistic scenes reflected the essence of mid-nineteenth-century taste. A wide range of colors was developed. Ruby was expensive to produce, since it was achieved by adding gold to a mix of glass. At the New England Glass Company twenty-dollar gold pieces from the local bank served this purpose. Silvered glassware (360, 361) was shown at the Crystal Palace at New York in 1853. "The glass vessels are double," it was reported of the company's exhibit there, "and between the layers the silver solution is poured in, and a solution of grape-sugar added. The latter reduces the silver in contact with it, and it is thrown down with a bright metallic surface on the glass." The liquid was then poured out and the aperture sealed.

359. *Opposite: elaborately engraved overlaid urn*

360. *Left: silvered glass goblet from New England*

361. *Above: a silvered and engraved glass pitcher*

362. *Above: a ceramic lion, 1849–58, was originally an English design.*

363. *Opposite: the stag was part of the Crystal Palace exhibit in 1853.*

From the Kilns of Vermont

"The neighborhood of Bennington, Vermont, is one well adapted for the establishment of a pottery manufacture, as there is a considerable deposit of plastic clay...of great purity." This contemporary comment accompanied an engraving (see page 240) of Christopher Webber Fenton's ceramic exhibit at the Crystal Palace in New York. During its brief existence, 1844–58, Fenton's pottery in Bennington produced a greater variety of wares than any other American pottery of the time—from slip-covered redwares to fine porcelains. Earthenware, mottled or streaked with a lustrous brown glaze, such as that associated with the Bennington output, was also made in countless factories throughout America from about 1835 on. Furthermore, so-called Bennington ware is properly called Rockingham because pottery so glazed was first made in England in the eighteenth century at the pottery on the Marquis of Rockingham's estate. Fenton, considered one of the greatest potters of his day, is particularly remembered for his improvement in applying colors and a flint glaze to the Rockingham ware. His new product, known as flint enamel ware, was patented in 1849 as "Fenton's Enamel." The pottery lion (362) and the stag (363) are flint enamel ware, as were numerous Fenton products—pitchers and bowls, Toby jugs, vases and "book flasks."

364. *Above: inkstand of the type advertised in 1841*

365. *Opposite, above: crock with popular deer motif*

366. *Opposite: water cooler used in a Vermont hotel*

The first pottery in Bennington had been founded in 1793 by Captain John Norton, a Revolutionary patriot, a substantial farmer, and large-scale distiller, who began the firm with a single kiln on his farm. The principal output of Norton's pottery, which would continue as a family enterprise for one hundred and one years, was domestic utensils—milk pans, flower pots, churns, butter tubs, and other such generalized kitchen crockery, as well as the inevitable spittoons, or cuspidors. (The word *cuspidor,* incidentally, is Portuguese, meaning "one who spits," and in eighteenth-century France, cuspidors were often de luxe objects made of faïence or porcelain.) The Norton pottery produced some Rockingham ware, but stoneware was the leading product. Stoneware's thin, hard, salt glaze, achieved by firing at extremely high temperatures, was resistant to acids, hence its wide use for cider, vinegar, pickles, preserves, and so forth. Cobalt was often used to create fanciful decorations, as it was on the water cooler (366) and the crock (365), marked with the number "2" to indicate its capacity in gallons. The inkstand (364), with the reclining duck-billed dog, is also of stoneware and colored with cobalt blue.

In the 1840's a white, waxy porcelain, named Parian ware because of its resemblance to Parian marble from the Aegean island of Paros, was developed at the Copeland works in England. Norton potteries brought a Copeland modeler to Bennington, where he and Christopher Fenton (then a partner of the Norton firm and married to Captain Norton's granddaughter) experimented with the new porcelain formula. Because of his keen interest in design and finer types of ware, Fenton left the manufacture of everyday utensils to the Nortons and began his own firm. Here he would perfect his flint enamel ware. And, "at the sacrifice of time and health," as the *New York Tribune* phrased it, Fenton also "succeeded in introducing the manufacture of Parian ware in this country;...and is engaged in the extension of porcelain manufacture." The porcelain vase (368), similar to English Staffordshire patterns, was made at this time. The Parian ewer (369) illustrates the limitless varieties possible in applying ornaments to Parian ware—vases, trinket boxes, cologne bottles, statuary. Color was often used, the white design in relief against a field of blue, pink, buff, or green; this water lily detail (367) is from a blue and white Parian pitcher. Unless marked, American Parian ware often cannot be distinguished from that produced in England.

367. Below: detail, Parian porcelain

368. Opposite, above: vase, 1850–58

369. Opposite: Parian ewer, 1847–58

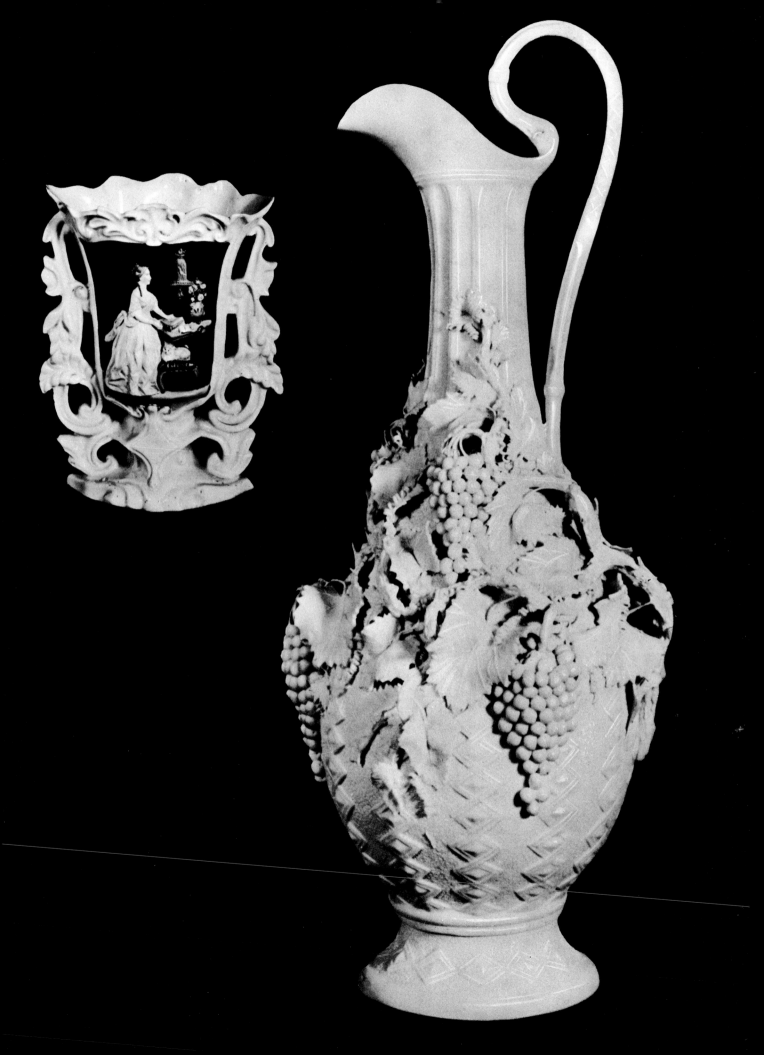

370. *Above: cast-iron bench in the Gothic mode*

371. *Right: a patented centripetal-spring chair*

372. *Opposite: rocking chair with a metal frame*

Innovated Seats

Metal furniture, which dates from antiquity, was revived in the nineteenth century in new shapes made possible by the advancements in iron founding and milling techniques. Cast-iron garden furniture was an immediate success. This example (370), one of a pair, originated in a rough sketch sent by Washington Irving to George Harvey, the miniature and landscape painter, who worked with the author in the remodeling of Sunnyside, Irving's "little nookery" near Tarrytown, New York. Harvey refined the initial sketch. When cast in iron in 1836, the "two gothic seats" were used on the porch. The sling rocking chair (372), similar to models made in England in the 1830's and France in the 1840's, is believed to be the design (about 1860) of Peter Cooper, manufacturer, inventor, and philanthropist. Another example (371), its metal frame upholstered in flowered carpeting, used the principle of the coiled spring (which revolutionized clockworks).

Worlds of Entertainment

Despite the number of fiery denunciations from pulpit and press, commercial entertainment blossomed in nineteenth-century America. In New York, for example, Barnum's museum with its pageant of dwarfs, giants, acrobats, fortunetellers, and waxworks was an instant success. At the theatre, vaudeville, minstrel shows, melodrama, and farce played to full houses, as did living models in such a *tableau vivant* as "Psyche Going to the Bath." Three thousand spectators (of whom only thirty were women) attended the debut of the scandalous Lola Montez (373), ex-mistress of Ludwig I of Bavaria—"a good-looking bold woman, with fine bad eyes." Shakespearean productions were often interlarded with popular skits, such as trained-animal shows; and Mrs. Trollope commented on the disorderly behavior of American audiences (374), the men in shirt sleeves, the "incessant spitting," and the "mixed smell of onions and whiskey." Prize fighting, bare-knuckled matches sometimes fought to the death, was outlawed. But boxing fans followed the champions to remote rural spots, beyond the arm of the law. When Yankee Sullivan and Tom Hyer (375) fought in 1849, the bout was held in the backwoods of Maryland.

373. Opposite: Lola Montez, dancer and adventuress, 1851

374. Above: lithograph of a rowdy audience, "Young Democracy at the Theater. The Stage in 1852 From the Pit."

375. Left: the bout between Tom Hyer and Yankee Sullivan

376. *Above: an inlaid, mahogany billiard table, attributed to John Shaw, the Annapolis cabinetmaker, and made between 1790 and 1800*

377. *Below: a lithograph of a billiard parlor, published about 1830*

378. *Opposite: gentlemen's musical soirée, detail of drawing, 1827*

379. *Opposite, below: a piano, "John Geib Jun'. Patent New-York"*

Bowling alleys and billiard parlors (377) became popular resorts in America's towns and cities, although looked upon with heavy disapproval by strait-laced citizens. A female devotee of the billiard table, however, wrote to *The Ladies' Billiard Messenger* that the game made her forget all her troubles, and she could play it confident that she was not sacrificing health to a morbid appetite for amusement. Among the more homespun pleasures acceptable to American moralists was music. Downing was pleased to note that the pianoforte was found "even in simple cottages, where such a thing would excite astonishment in Europe," and he hoped that "by-and-by, we may be as musical a people as the Germans." Meanwhile, musical get-togethers (378), in towns such as Charleston, were enjoyed by local gentlemen who met "to beguile away the time" with a drink and a tune.

Card games continued to be a favorite pastime in all levels of society, and poker was introduced by way of New Orleans and the Mississippi river boats. A royal flush (381) is from an English deck of cards, with a young George Washington as the king of spades, an Indian squaw as the queen, and an Indian brave as the jack. Gambling, again an issue to draw the wrath of press and pulpit, was a widely pursued pleasure. The extraordinary craze for lotteries eventually led to a ban on such games of chance in most areas of the country. Betting, however, was a traditional and exciting adjunct to flat racing, trotting races, professional foot races, rowing and sailing regattas attended by "multitudinous and vociferous citizens," and to cockfighting, still openly held in some parts of the country. Baseball, soon to be the national sport and fostered by impromptu games behind the lines during the Civil War, would shortly have its season of disrepute, in the 1870's, because of the activities of professional gamblers.

380. *Left: boatman at cards, by George C. Bingham*

381. *Opposite, above: playing cards printed in 1827*

382. *Opposite: Chinese or Indian ivory game board, designed with western motifs, a China trade import*

Some Domestic Sciences

◄◆►

The Functioning Home

In the central court of New York's Crystal Palace, under "the largest dome in the Western World," stood a monumental statue of George Washington on horseback modeled by the Anglo-Italian sculptor Carlo Marochetti. Had Washington himself visited the fair he would hardly have recognized the nation he had fathered but two generations earlier. The quantity and variety of merchandise on display reflected a world of circumstances remarkably different from those that had prevailed in his lifetime. For one thing, the assortment of household gear at the exhibition was unlike anything the first President had known. Like other cultured Americans of his time, Washington paid scrupulous attention to the architectural design, the decoration, and the furnishing of his own home—matters to which he brought an informed, personal taste, an easy familiarity with the fashions of the day, and an adequate purse. Over the course of almost half a century he developed Mount Vernon from an unpretentious farmhouse into a stately, handsomely furnished southern mansion. By the 1850's, however, such craftsmen as had satisfied Washington's exacting demands were playing a diminishing role in American society; they were losing their place in the economic world to skilled mechanics. The independent artificer was becoming, increasingly, a wage earner. Manufacturers were taking their place beside merchant princes as commanding figures in the world of affairs. And the common man was becoming something of a prince in his own right, with means enough to build his own home and furnish it amply with factory-made goods.

For those many who needed counsel in adapting themselves to improved or enlarged domestic circumstances there appeared a spate of manuals devoted to the problems of housekeeping, differences in styles, and matters of etiquette, as well as to the actual construction and planning of the house itself. In the preface to one of his several books Downing reminded his readers that his intention was "to develop the growing taste of the people"; and, asking that he be allowed "to prose a little," he cautioned his public not to confound fashion with taste. Among other household hints, he pointed out that "the furniture of the hall, however correct, would not be in good keeping with the dining-room, nor the furniture of the dining-room in keeping with the library." After that, for the benefit of all, he provided an illustrated survey of the bewildering variety of styles and new forms in furniture which were available for consideration by the well-intentioned householder.

Quite aside from matters of style and taste, the American home was undergoing functional changes of novel sorts, at least in urban areas. For one thing, the city kitchen was taking on a new character. The cast-iron cooking range was re-

Opposite: a detail from the ormolu and glass candelabrum shown above in its entirety

placing the hearth in progressive homes. An early model was patented in 1815. Years later, Harriet Beecher Stowe reminded her readers that "it was the memory of the great open kitchen-fire...its roaring, hilarious voice of invitation, its dancing tongues of flame," that helped the veterans at Valley Forge endure that agonizing winter. "Would our Revolutionary fathers have gone barefooted and bleeding over snows to defend air-tight stoves and cooking-ranges?" she asked; and answered, "I trow not." However, such cast-iron contraptions had come to stay for quite a while, and the industrialization of the kitchen was fairly begun.

In other rooms of the house, as well, the open fire as a heating device was giving way to the cast-iron stove. As the Pennsylvania mines were more extensively worked during the early decades of the nineteenth century, as railroads and canals facilitated distributing and marketing, and as the use of anthracite coal became better understood, patents were filed for parlor stoves in a multitude of forms, most of them ornamented in one or another of the prevailing "period" styles. Ironically, about the time those devices were approaching a peak of elaboration, a new stage in domestic progress was removing them from living quarters altogether, putting the source of heat out of sight in the basement, and piping hot air or water throughout the house. Central heating was not a new idea. As early as 1608 in London Sir Hugh Platt had suggested (as "a mere conceit") piping heat from a single source "into what place you shall think mete." In 1808 a Philadelphian was prepared to warm and ventilate public buildings by hot air, and as the century advanced progressive homeowners yearned increasingly for such a convenience. Downing recommended warming houses by hot water, but cautioned that it cost about five times as much as heating by air. It was an expatriate American inventor in England, Jacob Perkins, who developed a practical system for domestic central heating by steam and hot water—a system that found a more responsive public in his native country than in England, where the natives have always distrusted a "fyre secret felt but not seene." In 1845 or 1846 the Eastern Hotel in Boston became America's first steam-heated building.

Meanwhile, more and more American cities were providing their inhabitants with abundant running water. By 1850 eighty-three urban communities had public water supplies. In the early 1840's New York reached almost forty miles into the countryside to tap the Croton River and channel its waters to local reservoirs. "Nothing is talked of or thought of in New York but Croton water...," wrote Philip Hone in 1842. "The moral as well as the physical influence of water pervades everything." A few years later Boston inaugurated its first city-wide public water system with a ringing of bells, a firing of cannon and skyrockets, and the singing of James Russell Lowell's "Ode," which began: "My Name is Water." And with water pouring out of faucets from city mains—and with adequate sewer drainage—that "glory of the plumber's art," the ubiquitous and well-appointed American bathroom, started to develop in earnest. The new conveniences were making the weekly bath a simple operation for Americans.

The American's ready acceptance of mechanical conveniences in the home, parlor stoves and central heating, along with Dover beaters and other gadgets, was influenced by the continuing need to save labor and time. Cotton Mather's proposition "that if God will bless me with Good Servants, I will serve him with more Fidelity and Activity" was a prophetic complaint about the servant problem in America. Even George Washington's advertisement for a cook and coachman ran in the New York papers for a month and a half before it was withdrawn. The Father of his Country may have expected too much, for he required only

A domestic interior in the Gothic Revival style

servants who were "perfect in the business," and such were not easily had.

To some it almost seemed that the American considered his house more as a piece of equipment than as a home in the traditional sense. Beyond that, most Americans had little intention of settling down for any length of time. Speculation on a different and better future, and on real estate, spiraled upward. In this country, Dickens wrote, everything and everybody was in a state of everlasting motion. Even the buildings "looked as if they had been built and painted that morning, and could be taken down on Monday with very little trouble." On one of his journeys he actually saw a house on the move, "coming downhill at a round trot, drawn by a score or more of oxen." In city and country alike the spring of the year brought about a surge of restlessness. To some witnesses of the urban scene, on the first of May the entire population appeared to be in a state of total confusion as families made their annual move from one set of quarters to another. And in the hinterland, it was claimed, the chickens were so accustomed to moving on every year, farther westward usually, that they came up to the house of their own accord in the spring to have their legs trussed. A man's home, in short, was where he hung his hat.

Out on the prairies where heavy timbers, labor, and carpentering skills were all in short supply, home builders were obliged to do with makeshifts to get a home at all. The cities that mushroomed in that region could never have risen as fast as they did without the introduction of a new type of building known as the balloon frame—a construction of light two-by-four studs nailed in a close, basketlike manner, the studs rising continuously from foundation to rafters. When cheap, machine-made nails became generally available, as they were by the 1830's, the balloon frame was widely adopted. No expert carpenter was needed to practice the mysteries of mortise-and-tenon joining of huge timbers, and in spite of its fragile-looking, nailed-together skeleton the balloon-frame construction was actually exceptionally strong. The method has been generally used throughout the country since it was first conceived. Meanwhile, newly designed steel plows were cutting through the tough sod of the prairies (and scouring cleanly). Cyrus McCormick's mechanical reapers, which were being mass produced, were revolutionizing the harvesting of wheat. Such improved implements were helping to turn the infant city of Chicago, almost overnight, into the greatest primary grain market of the world, and into a lusty metropolis hundreds of miles in the interior of the continent—far beyond the western lands Washington had bought and sold on speculation in the eighteenth century.

As the pace of travel quickened by way of railroad and steamboat more specialized institutions for the accommodation of transients replaced the old-fashioned tavern at key points along the road. In the larger cities, where the concentration of travelers was greatest, the city hotel developed into a peculiarly American establishment. Such places anticipated every need and convenience of the guest, including many he was slow to recognize. At New York's celebrated Astor House, completed in 1836, plumbing was carried throughout the building, each floor having its own bath and toilet rooms. (Shortly after, the first cabs were stationed at the front door to ease intra-urban transit.) In some such public places, Englishmen were astonished to learn, they could have their shirts washed and ironed while they bathed. And the "musical tinkling" of ice water, another especially American convenience, became the most characteristic sound of the better hotels in every season of the year. Many Americans were thus introduced to amenities of bedrooms and baths they had not known at home.

Stages in the building of a balloon-frame house

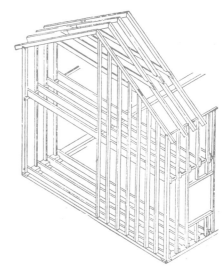

Isometric perspective view of a balloon frame

295

Mostly on the Brighter Side

In spite of new lighting techniques developed between the Revolution and the Civil War, the candle retained its accustomed role in most American homes until kerosene became widely available around 1860. Good candles were never really cheap. In the eighteenth century such eminent householders as Edward Holyoke, president of Harvard College, and George Washington kept careful account of the cost of candlelight as a matter of essential economy. Candle-holding devices, in any case, remained basic and often handsomely fashioned equipment. In the decades following the Revolution, bronze- or brass-mounted glass shades, sometimes handsomely cut and engraved (383), were often used to steady the flame of candles hung in halls. At the same time other glass shades, in the form of shaped cylinders open at both ends and commonly called hurricane shades, were often placed over standing candles to protect them from drafts. Lamp shades enjoyed a growing vogue in America during the early decades of the nineteenth century. The so-called *bouillotte* candelabrum (385), with its adjustable shade of painted tin or tinned iron (toleware), took its name from a French prototype, which was often placed in the center of a table used for a popular card game of that name. Wired for electricity, the form is still popular.

383. *Opposite: a cut-glass, brass-mounted lantern*

384. *Above: a Sandwich pressed-glass candlestick*

385. *Right: candelabrum with an adjustable shade*

386. *Opposite: glassware salesroom, London, 1823*

387. *Above: ormolu candlestick with glass prisms*

388. *Right: one from a pair of ormolu candelabra*

Although cut-glass chandeliers were being made in America early in the nineteenth century (see page 129), for decades after the Revolution, England continued to be the main source for such fixtures. They were costly to use. In 1793 a theatre in Federal Street, Boston, lighted by "3 glass chandalears," among other devices imported from London, consumed 56 pounds of spermaceti and tallow candles each night. In public places, as in private homes, the styles of candleholders followed the prevailing fashions in other furnishings. The chandeliers illustrated (386) are in the Regency style; one of a pair of candlesticks (387) has a miniature Gothic cathedral in ormolu at the base; one of another pair (388) is an exuberant concoction of natural forms recalling the carvings of Belter furniture.

Candlelight was not only relatively expensive, but at best it was inefficient, and by modern standards inadequate for most practical purposes. But throughout history it remained the most satisfactory artificial illumination until the invention of the Argand lamp, by the Swiss Aimé Argand, in 1783. The Argand burner consisted of two concentric tubes enclosing a tubular wick. A current of air played upon the inner surface of the circular flame. The addition of glass chimneys materially improved combustion of the oil, which was fed by gravity from an elevated reservoir. This provided a far stronger light than a candle or any earlier form of lamp. As the American physicist and adventurer Benjamin Thompson (Count Rumford) observed in 1811, "no decayed beauty ought ever to expose her face to the direct rays of an Argand lamp." It enjoyed continued success for more than two generations, and was the parent form of subsequent, improved oil lamps.

389. Above: one of a pair of Argand lamps made in Boston. Opposite: 390. English silver wall lamp from Mt. Vernon. 391. chandelier with Grecian design font. 392. double lamp by Baldwin Gardiner, N.Y.

390

391

392

301

393. *Above: woodcut showing a whale-oil lamp with one wick*

394. *Right: blown-glass, whale-oil lamp with two wicks, 1830–50*

395. *Opposite, above: in quest of oil; crew harpooning a whale*

396. *Opposite, below: a britannia ship lamp by Yale and Curtis*

For millenniums, until well into the nineteenth century, simple oil lamps consisting of a cotton or tow wick resting in almost any kind of illuminant, from fish oil and kitchen grease to whale and vegetable oils, provided a feeble, cheap alternative to candles. In 1787 John Miles of Birmingham, England, patented a lamp in which the oil well was enclosed and the wick was held upright, instead of hanging over the side. Advertisements referred to it as an "agitable" lamp, "so constructed as to prevent oil from spilling, although the lamp be overturned or thrown in any direction." Such lamps, burning whale oil, gave no less light than a small candle and at a reasonable cost. They were immensely popular in America. In the middle of the last century an English commission referred to them as "lamps peculiar to the country." Most were made with double burners, following Benjamin Franklin's advice that two small wicks close together gave more light than one large wick. To supply the increasing demand for oil, American whalers found their way, as Melville said, to "the remotest secret drawers and lockers of the world."

303

The most popular improved variant of the Argand burner in the 1830's and 1840's was the astral, or *sinumbra* (without shadow), lamp (400), a French development quickly adopted in America. Here the oil font, fitted under a ground-glass shade, formed a ring about the burner, which minimized the shadow cast. In the Carcel lamp (397), still another French innovation, a clockwork mechanism pumped oil up from the reservoir to the wick above. Meanwhile, the search for better and cheaper illuminants continued. In the 1830's a method was worked out for combining turpentine and alcohol, and a variety of such "burning fluids" appeared on the market. They were also called "liquid gunpowder," because they tended to explode with careless handling. A solar lamp (398), designed to burn oil pressed from lard, was claimed as "The Greatest Luminary in the World, except the Sun." But, the cost of both lard and whale oil remained high, ranging up to $2.50 per gallon.

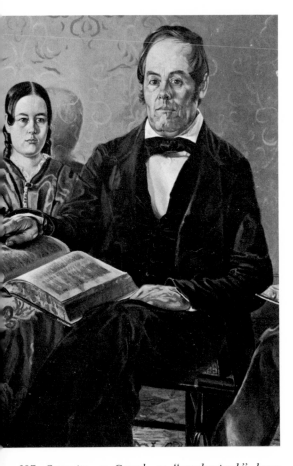

397. *Opposite: a Carcel, or "mechanized," lamp*

398. *Above: the Atwood family about a solar lamp*

399. *Top: Mrs. Zebidu Ring seated by an astral lamp*

400. *Right: an astral, or sinumbra, lamp, around 1840*

Steamboats and railroads with their nighttime operations and traffic signals, factories with their new and special demands, and the growing desire for improved lighting for city streets all called for stronger light than candles or burning fluids could provide. Experiments with gas lighting were made in Philadelphia in 1796; gas was used to light certain cotton mills during the War of 1812; and in 1816 Baltimore organized a company for the distribution of lighting gas. In 1824 *The New-York Evening Post* reported that gas was far superior to oil or candles for lighting homes and public buildings as well as streets. But the public remained wary of using "smoke" as an illuminant. Philip Hone wrote that at a fashionable New York ball in 1836 "the gas suddenly gave out in the midst of a cotillion," causing merriment and some embarrassment. He concluded it was liable "at all times to give the company the slip, and [was] illy calculated for the ordinary use of a family."

401. *Above: lighting a gas lamp in New York, about 1835*

402. *Opposite: gas chandelier, originally installed in the Van Rensselaer Manor House, Albany, New York, 1844*

Sewing Kits
& Quilting Bees

In every household, rich or poor, women sewed. Although a lady of means did not have to address herself to such practicalities as clothing for the family, needlework remained a domestic tradition and leisure time was consumed in delicate and exacting tasks of an artistic nature—from microscopic embroidery stitches on handkerchiefs of gossamer Indian cotton to needle-point slippers and suspenders for the gentlemen. The fire screen, an elegant and not altogether utilitarian piece of furniture in itself, became even more elegant when finished with an embroidered panel. This one (403), made about 1809, was carved by Samuel McIntire; the oval gilt frame, in which the silk embroidery is mounted, was made by

John Doggett of Roxbury (see page 211). And for a lady of means, her sewing accessories were often as decorative as her needlework. A sewing table (406), possibly made by the Seymours (see page 54) in Boston, is of veneered and inlaid mahogany, and the workbag is embroidered satin. It may well have held such choice items as a gold thimble, ivory winders for silk threads, and scissors with enameled or mother-of-pearl handles. For women too busy to sit in their parlors and sew a fine seam, pocket-aprons (or "pockets" as they were known) served as sewing kits. Pockets were usually made of leftover fabric, sometimes thriftily sewn together in a patchwork. An example (405) made in Connecticut was decorated with crewelwork.

403. *Opposite: detail of silk-embroidered fire screen*

404. *Above: Mrs. Richard Yates, a portrait by Stuart*

405. *Above, right: an embroidered linen pocket-apron*

406. *Right: a work table made in the Sheraton style*

407. *Above: world globe worked in silk*

408. *Right: embroidered pastoral scene*

409. *Left: a young woman flanked by her suitors attends to her sewing; a workbasket is at her feet.*

410. *Opposite: an embroidered memorial picture*

Fashions in needlework can be as indicative of their period as styles in furniture or architecture. At the turn of the eighteenth century, with Americans exploring uncharted western territories and the American merchant marine sailing to ports all over the world, embroidered maps became a needlework fashion of the times. Generally they were made of satin embroidered with silk, then mounted in a picture frame. An unusual example (407) of the new enthusiasm for geography was worked in the form of a globe by Mary Dickinson, who entered the Westtown School in Pennsylvania in 1814. Westtown, a Quaker school, gave particular emphasis—as did all schools in those days—to sewing lessons for the girls enrolled. The Moravian school in Bethlehem, Pennsylvania, which John Adams described as a "remarkable institution for the education of young ladies," is credited with initiating the fashion for mourning, or memorial, pictures (410), which were

also, as a rule, silk-on-satin embroideries. Mourning pictures were melancholy views of the bereaved at the tombs of the departed, usually shaded by weeping willows. These memorial embroideries reflected the neoclassic modes of the day in such details as Grecian urns atop monuments stitched in Greek Revival patterns, the women dressed in the draped, Grecian gowns of the period. With the rise of romanticism, embroidered pictures depicted a host of sentimental subjects—lovers' trysts, lovers' partings, Biblical and mythological scenes, shepherds, and shepherdesses (408). The popularity of silk needlework typified the times for, until the bubble burst around 1840, a mania for silk culture swept America, with speculators investing heavily in the new industry and mulberry trees selling for highly inflated prices. Silk-embroidered taffeta sewing aprons also were in vogue during the silk craze; one was apparently worn by the young woman (409) in Mount's picture.

Quilting, an antique form of needlework, is believed to have originated with the Chinese, who have worn quilted garments for untold centuries. In Europe, quilting was variously used—for padding under armor, for coverlets and bed hangings, for elaborately stitched petticoats and waistcoats. The bedquilt of patchwork, however, is uniquely American. During the early colonial period, when textiles were a precious commodity, patchwork quilts were purely utilitarian, contrived from carefully hoarded scraps of cloth. With leisure and prosperity the patchwork quilt became an ornament and an artistic achievement, usually made in flowing patterns imitative of imported chintzes. The geometric designs, so fondly associated with American quilts, appeared in the early 1800's. Here, the "Mariner's Compass" (411), with each figure made of sixty-four symmetrical pieces, exemplifies this type of painstaking needlework. There are thousands of such designs, all with fanciful names: the Bear's Paw, Drunkard's Path, Jacob's Ladder, Whig's Defeat, and Mrs. Cleveland's Choice, to name but a few. Quilts, of course, were also made in a less formal fashion with appliqués of animals, flowers, and figures (412). In rural areas, the quilting bee continued as a festivity, with the day's work celebrated in music and dancing at nightfall.

411. *Opposite: Mariner's Compass quilt*

412. *The encircling pictures are examples of patterns and figures appliquéd to quilts.*

413. Top: woman with sewing box, about 1850
414. Above: Winding Up, drawn by Mount
415. Right: needle-point bag, made about 1850

Knitting, an ancient needlecraft of the Middle East, was a masculine occupation comparable to weaving during the heyday of the European guilds. In the hands of American women knitting needles produced everything from rugs to bands of lace. (In William Mount's sketch (414) a knitter winds a skein of wool in the time-honored manner.) Crocheting, which also lent itself to the creation of innumerable forms, was brought to America from Ireland in the 1840's by immigrants fleeing the famine in their homeland. Needle point was revived about this time, to become the craze of the Victorian period. Pre-patterned canvas backings and bright, soft worsteds made from the fleece of merino sheep were exported from Berlin; hence the term "Berlin work" for the innumerable pillows, pictures, mottoes, seat covers, shawl straps, cigar cases, "foot muffs," antimacassars, doilies, and carriage bags (415) stitched by indefatigable Victorian ladies. As a "convenient receptacle of various articles of needle work," Downing liked the useful basket-stand (416), "easily lifted and carried about." Some were "curiously carved, for the villa." Others were described as rustic, "in the Swiss manner," or made of bamboo, a Chinese fashion, "for the cottage."

416. Basket-stand, "suitable to the parlor"

Hand-weaving did not immediately vanish from the American scene, despite the advent of the power loom. In fact, the family loom in many instances was given a new lease on life, thanks to factory-spun yarns which obviated the time-consuming tasks of carding and spinning raw wool by hand. In many country districts homemade textiles were an unshakable tradition, whether made by housewives or professional weavers. Many of the latter were Scottish, Irish, and German immigrants, trained in their craft by master weavers in the old country. Woven coverlets in geometric patterns of stripes and squares are most typical of homespun. The weaver's skill at its finest is illustrated with the intricately loomed detail (417) from a coverlet, made between 1840 and 1850, with a design of alternating eastern and western villages, which is righteously entitled: "The Heathen and Christian Religion." Again, despite factory-produced blankets and bedding, quilts continued to be made by hand. One patchwork pattern (418), for example, is identical to a design used by Dwight D. Eisenhower's mother, and he has recalled sleeping under just such a quilt as a boy. The brilliant red squares, shown here, were known as "Turkey red," achieved by an almost colorfast dye introduced from the East and made from madder, a Eurasian herb.

417. *Above: detail from a double-woven coverlet of indigo-blue wool and unbleached cotton*

418. *Opposite: a quilt, fashioned in a popular optical-illusion pattern, made in mid-century*

Machine Made & Ready to Wear

The development of a practical sewing machine (419) in the 1850's challenged one of the most ancient forms of human art and drudgery. As a contemporary periodical observed, the family Singer was a tireless seamstress; one that was "always at home when you want work done, never troubled with beaux, nor with aching shoulders, nor with mumps, nor mopes." Some years later *Harper's Bazaar* pointed out that 20,530 stitches were required to make a shirt, a statistic the editors hoped might induce some gentleman to provide his wife with one of the new labor savers. At the same time textile machinery was being remarkably improved. A power loom (421) for weaving fancy cottons, patented by William Crompton in 1840 and soon adapted for manufacturing equally fancy, figured cassimeres (woolens), cheapened production to the point where such fabrics became the fashion about the world. Both mechanical developments encouraged the ready-made clothing industry (420) to turn out everything "from the rough garments of the boatman and the ditch digger to the elegant...apparel of the nabob."

419. Opposite: the sewing machine's contribution to domestic felicity

420. Above: an advertisement for ready-made clothing, Illinois, 1855

421. Below: Crompton power loom for manufacturing fancy woolens

Hot & Cold Running Water

Henry Thoreau was inclined to believe that bathing was one of the necessities of life, but many of his contemporaries were diffident about the matter. Before hot running water was generally available within the home, for one thing, allover bathing was a chore and a nuisance. Even such a limited, if elegant, convenience as the Sheraton-style dressing table (425), with its Staffordshire pottery bidet and washbowl, its "pot cupboard" in the center, and its various other appointments, presupposed servants to haul hot water from the kitchen to the bedroom and to perform disposal operations. As early as 1810 the Markoe house in Philadelphia incorporated a bathroom, complete with tub, basin, and water closet. Later in the century, as other cities were provided with public water systems, the urban bathroom became mechanized (422), although for most country folk bathroom and toilet facilities (423) long remained primitive.

422. *Opposite, upper: a mechanized bathroom; an advertisement, 1844*

423. *Opposite, lower: country outhouse; from a painting by Mount*

424. *Above: young lady at her toilet*

425. *Right: Sheraton dressing table*

321

Parlor Stove & Kitchen Range

The thought of a New England meetinghouse relying on heat from a cast-iron stove rather than the fire and brimstone of the customary sermon moved one old-timer to lament in the Boston *Evening Post:*

> Extinct the sacred fires of love,
> Our zeal grown cold and dead,
> In the house of God we fix a stove
> To warm us in their stead.

However, in many sections of America, the winter's cold was more severe than English immigrants had known at home, for one thing, and from the beginnings of colonization special measures were taken to keep it out of doors. In the course of the nineteenth century, especially after the widespread availability of anthracite coal and before common reliance on central heating, the cast-iron range became virtually an American institution —"a particularly dreadful institution," according to Oscar Wilde who, later in the century, resented the stoves' machine-made ornament. No other country produced so many and such varied types of stoves for all purposes, "planned with the view of supplying the wants of the million" and "designed to be useful as well as ornamental."

426. *Opposite: detail from a painting by W. S. Mount, 1837*

427. *Upper left: classical style open stove with dunce-cap dome*

428. *Above: highly ornamented parlor stove in the form of a house*

429. *Upper right: base-burning coal stove with Gothic decoration*

323

As many different kinds of stoves were devised for the kitchen as for the parlor. In both areas ventilation diminished with the elimination of the open fire on the hearth, sucking air into the room to feed its flames. There were other drawbacks. For another thing, spitting, that common custom among American males that so annoyed Mrs. Trollope and other visitors, was a less acceptable practice when a man hit the iron range instead of a blazing fire. And it was not so easy to dump trash and refuse into the small enclosed fire of a stove. However, such kitchen conveniences proliferated. One model (432), dating from about 1833, was designed with a revolving top so that any one of several pots could be turned to a place over the direct heat for fast cooking. Two flues ran through a cylindrical oven. In 1844 an up-to-date kitchen range (431) provided hot water that could be pumped to the adjoining sink and an upstairs bathroom.

430. *Opposite: laundry stove for heating flatirons*

431. *Below: a kitchen with range and sink, 1844*

432. *Left: cook stove with rotating top; oven above*

Homes Away from Home

Americans were on the move, and homes away from home were a new and significant aspect of the bustling young nation. The sudden proliferation of the boardinghouse was a phenomenon of the times, created by housing shortages, increasing rents, and the chronic servant problem. It has been estimated that at least 70 per cent of the population during the 1800's lived in boardinghouses at some time of their lives. The boardinghouse was everywhere, from fashionably-run households (433) in mansions of the newly poor, to company-owned lodgings for workers in industrial areas. Guardians of domestic virtue deplored boardinghouse life as one of the social evils of the century. Mrs. Trollope also disapproved: "A great number of young married persons board by the year....I can hardly imagine a contrivance more effectual for ensuring the insignificance of a woman, than marrying her at seventeen, and placing her in a boarding-house."

With the expanding network of turnpikes and roadways, the roadside inn (434) offered temporary quarters for travelers. Not only were inns a social institution for local residents, but for passing guests they served as a clearinghouse for mail, gossip, news, and business, and as a place of general entertainment. James Fenimore Cooper described the American innkeeper as something more than an ordinary publican. "He is often a magistrate, the chief of a battalion of militia, or even a member of a state legislature. He is almost always a man of character." As to inns and taverns in far-flung outposts, Mrs. Basil Hall was not impressed. "There is no carpet or curtains, of course, and no glass on the windows," she wrote from Georgia. And in Indiana she remarked: "It is never for a moment supposed that our party is to occupy more than one sleeping room, and a chicken is all we get besides the eternal pork...on every American table."

433. Above: a fashionable boardinghouse scen

434. Opposite: the interior of a Philadelphia in

435. Left: the Delphian Club of Baltimore celebrating its first anniversary

436. Below: a Boston eating house, that served meals "All hours of the Day"

437. Opposite: the Gem Saloon, New York, with the largest mirror in the city

As cities grew larger and the distance greater between a man's home and his place of work, eating houses (436) specializing in the "quick-lunch" at a modest price became a fixture on the American scene. The national habit of bolting a meal in grim silence was summed up by one European visitor as "gobble, gulp, and go." A visiting Englishman described one such short-order restaurant in New York as a long dark room with rows of boxes large enough for four persons, "an amazing clatter of knives and forks; but not a word audible to us was spoken by any of the guests." The silence, however, was made up for by the waiters who "bawled out in a loud voice, to give notice of what fare was wanted," and to the visitor's wonder, the food arrived piping hot within a few seconds.

After working hours, there was the leisure and conviviality of the saloon, whether in a gilt, mahogany, and cut-glass setting (437), the neighborhood grogshop, or the whiskey mill of a frontier town. In urbane circles the gentleman who chose to relax among his peers retreated to his club, those redoubtable masculine strongholds adopted from the English. There were eating clubs, drinking clubs, sporting and fishing clubs, or such thoroughgoing homes away from home as New York's Union Club. Formed in 1836, it was "similar in its plan and regulations to the great clubs of London," wrote Philip Hone, who added that it was a "resource for bachelors and 'men about town'...an excellent lounging place for old and young beaux, each of whom would fain to be thought what the other is."

"All the world is here," wrote the ever-observant Philip Hone in 1839 on a visit to Saratoga, New York State's most popular spa. "Politicians and dandies; cabinet ministers and ministers of the gospel; office-holders and office-seekers; humbuggers and humbugged; fortune-hunters and hunters of woodcock; anxious mothers and lovely daughters." With increased wealth, more leisure, and the prodigious advances in transportation, Americans of all classes thronged resort towns for a holiday away from home. Summer vacations and pleasure jaunts had become acceptable pursuits for the workingman, as well as for those with money. The annual summer exodus from New York prompted one editor to comment, in 1845, that "the city will soon be abandoned to the dog-killers, cabmen, and police justices at the Tombs." A foreign visitor, marveling at so many Americans on the move, wrote: "There is scarcely an individual so reduced in circumstances, as to be unable to afford his 'dollar or so,' to travel a couple of hundred miles from home, 'in order to see the country.'" The wealthy, on the other hand, were accused of carrying their craving for travel "to a passion and a fever." Meanwhile, entrepreneurs in resort towns and cities were building luxurious hotels to accommodate trippers and tourists.

The Tremont House in Boston (439), designed by Isaiah Rogers and opened in 1829, so impressed Charles Dickens with its architectural splendors, that he wrote: "It has more galleries, colonnades, piazzas, and passages than I can remember, or the reader would believe." The Astor House in New York, again an Isaiah Rogers design, was famed for its sumptuous cuisine and a grand *salon* reminiscent of the chapel of Henry VII in Westminster Abbey. Saratoga Springs was famed for the number and lavishness of its hotels, such as Congress Hall (preferred by "the more ancient families") and the United States Hotel (patronized by "the rich mercantile class") with its accommodations for two thousand. The lush and extravagant decor of these establishments evoked a few words from Downing on the vulgarization of furnishings hitherto reserved for the palaces of royalty or the nobility of Europe. "When the proprietors of our great steamers and hotels can afford...to lavish far more in the furniture, gilding, and decoration of their saloons, than our best private fortunes will allow...the only resort for a gentleman who wishes his house to be distinguished by good taste, is to choose the opposite course, viz. to make its interior remarkable for chaste beauty, and elegant simplicity."

438. *Left: High, Iodine, and Empire springs at Saratoga, New York, 1848*

439. *Below: the Tremont House, Boston, a water color by George Harvey*

440. *Bottom: dancing the quadrille in the ballroom of Tremont House*

441. *Top: Baltimore and Ohio coach heated by a cast-iron stove*
442. *Above: seats made into berths; a sleeping car of the 1850's*
443. *Opposite: a ladies' saloon on a Long Island Sound steamer*

Steamboats varied, of course, from "the very filthiest of all filthy old rat-traps," to floating "fairy palaces" that amazed and dumfounded Americans and Europeans alike. A gentleman in Ohio declared the Mississippi boats to be as comfortable as "a first rate hotel. You will have a large bar for refreshment—also a hair dressers and shaving store (first rate and no mistake)." However, the separation of the gentlemen's and ladies' saloons led one European visitor to point out that the men, left to their own devices, were reduced to cards, drinking, chewing tobacco, and talking politics. In train travel, which was apt to be a rough, dusty ride, there was no space for such refinements as the ladies' saloon of a first-class steamboat—much to the distress of one female correspondent, who was appalled at the lack of privacy in the sleeping cars (442). "It is rather hard...," she wrote, "that young girls should have to be thus familiarized with that unattractive object, a sleepy and unwashed man. That trial should be postponed until marriage has rendered it inevitable."

Patterns on Paper

444. *Opposite: window shade with a painted vista*

445. *Top: a Boston newspaper advertisement, 1830*

446. *Above: bandbox, from Hartford, about 1824*

Until about 1850 the better wallpapers used in America continued to be European imports, as were the majority of paper products, whether cheap news- and book papers or expensive writing paper. (In the early 1800's, for example, the United States Senate used an import watermarked "Napoléon, Empereur et Roi, 1813.") Patterned wallpapers of domestic manufacture were generally copied from such French and English designs as stripes, floral and geometric motifs, simulated drapery, and scenic views. Comparable motifs were popular on painted cambric window shades (444), made from about 1830 to 1860. Bandboxes (446), in vogue for storing or transporting hats and other bits of finery, were covered with papers often specially made for this market. The designs, in a New York shop or on a New England peddler's wagon, ran the gamut from General Zachary Taylor on horseback, to a winged cupid riding a goat, or a view of Istanbul.

Until mid-century panoramic wallpapers, which presented a continuous, nonrepeating landscape, were a highly fashionable (and costly) import from France. Interestingly enough, more of these papers survive in their original locations in American houses than in houses in France itself. Shown here (447, 448) are views from "Scenic America," a series that includes prospects of New York, West Point, Boston harbor, and an Indian dance. This particular set was rescued from a Maryland house, about to be demolished, and can now be seen at the White House. "Scenic America" was first produced in 1834 by the wallpaper firm of Jean Zuber, at Rixheim, Alsace, and reissued several years later as the "War of Independence," with the same background, but with new figures illustrating events of the American Revolution. Despite the introduction of machines that produced "endless" rolls of paper and the increasing perfection of color presses, panoramic wallpapers, by their very nature, had to be block printed, a technique which often needed thousands of engraved blocks for one series. The individual sections were usually six feet in height, explicitly numbered in their proper order, and designed with a surplus of sky that could be trimmed away, if necessary. Wallpaper dadoes, or footings, imitating balustrades were generally hung beneath the panorama.

447. *Opposite: Natural Bridge, Va., with a stagecoach*
448. *Above: the Falls at Niagara, "a sublime spectacle"*

Forms
of
Tradition

*American
Folk
Art*

Someone has defined man as an art-producing creature. The truth of that statement rests in the fact that the creative urge in man is continuous and irrepressible. As children so often and so happily reveal in their uninhibited expressions with paints and crayons, we are all born artists with more or less talent, which we find more or less occasion to develop in the course of our lifetimes. For ages the creative efforts of the common man, the folk arts, have provided an undercurrent to the history of the fine arts, in America since its settlement as elsewhere—with differences.

The typical folk art of Europe was rooted in racial or class traditions; it largely depended on old, inherited patterns of design that were worked by skilled and specialized craftsmen. It tended to be a static, timeless art, such as the decorative painting on Sicilian carts. With some exceptions, American folk art was geared rather to the shifting demands of a democratic society in constant ferment. In any case, as the term is applied in this country, it refers to the work of men and women (and of youngsters, at times) who expressed themselves with little or no benefit of academic training in the arts and with small regard for the sophisticated fashions of their day. These artists and artisans included professionals and amateurs alike. Some pictures, sculptures, and other objects were the work of men who were just as much professionals as were members of a national academy, but who served a simpler public and were primarily concerned with the useful purpose of their products, were they shop signs, house decorations, ships' figureheads, or whatever. Other forms of folk art were the output of nonprofessionals working primarily for their own gratification or bent on pleasing others, with no thought of the trade value of their work. As the term is commonly used, it generously includes the handiwork of young ladies bent on pleasing their parents and instructors with their embroidered and painted fabrics, the decorative patchwork of other (usually older) ladies, as well as decorative painting applied by countrymen to furniture and the walls of houses. Examples in these latter categories have already been shown in this book in separate contexts.

Actually, in this country no sharp line divided the ranks of such relatively untutored persons and those of the especially trained and highly skilled practitioners. Sometimes, indeed, there was a continuity that can be traced in the work of a single individual from one level of expression and achievement to another. In late colonial days Benjamin West progressed from a virtually self-taught young "primitive" to become historical painter to King George III and president of England's Royal Academy. He was probably the most celebrated American-born painter in history, at least until the time of James McNeill Whistler a cen-

Opposite: detail from The Peaceable Kingdom, *shown above, painted by Edward Hicks*

tury later. The *émigré* John James Audubon, another self-taught artist (although he sometimes claimed, rather implausibly, that as a lad he had studied in Paris briefly with Jacques Louis David), worked up his incipient talents over the years by unremitting self-criticism and industry to become the greatest bird painter in the western world. (His first essays in portraiture had been the simple profiles that are common among examples of folk art.) Some artists who won lasting reputations in their maturity, such as Charles Willson Peale and Chester Harding, grew to manhood before they became aware of the art of painting. Peale had been trained as a saddler, Harding as a country chairmaker.

However, a sizable number of other painters and craftsmen never developed their native endowments to such heights of recognition and were content to satisfy a relatively limited, local public by adapting their skills to their opportunities and circumstances. In this area of American life, as in others, conditions did not favor intensive specialization. An abundance of fresh opportunities constantly tempted the artist and the craftsman, like the mechanic and the merchant, to turn from one vocation to an ever more alluring one, or to practice several vocations at once for that matter. Few rural communities in nineteenth-century America could support a full-time resident portrait painter, and those who practiced portraiture either combined such work with other pursuits or took to the road in search of commissions. Early in the century one Luther Allen, "limner" of Enfield, Connecticut, advertised that he not only painted portraits "from busts to full figures" in oil, pastel, or crayon, but also did "hair work," coach, carriage, and sign painting, lettering, and clockface decoration—a range of capabilities that must have assured him a reasonably steady income. The itinerants, sometimes called "travelers" by their contemporaries, wandered from community to community offering their services to each so long as they were required. Legend asserts that at times they carried with them "stock" canvases, figures that were already completed except for the face which was dubbed in when a commission was made. However, it is more likely that they "took" the face on the spot and filled in the costume and other accessories by one or another set formula at home.

When hard cash was scarce on either end of the bargain a deal by barter could be consummated. In 1835 William Prior painted a likeness of his barber in exchange for "three months' shaves." Or, in return for his accommodations at an inn, the itinerant might decorate the walls of the establishment for the proprietor or paint his portrait. In Belleville, Illinois, Dickens noticed painted decoration that had been done by a traveler who got along by "eating his way." In the best room of the hotel at his next stop he saw "two oil portraits of the kit-cat size [somewhat less than half-length], representing the landlord and his infant son; both looking as bold as lions, and staring out of the canvas with an intensity that would have been cheap at any price. They were painted, I think, by the artist who touched up the Belleville doors with red and yellow; for I seemed to recognise his style immediately." If need be, the painter might accommodate his style to the purse of his client, as did Prior, who charged much less for a portrait "without shade or shadow" than for one that included such embellishments. Occasionally, the itinerant ran into competition from female amateurs who had been schooled in art at a seminary, as in the case of one immigrant painter who went from house to house in Cincinnati in search of work only to learn that there was "a lady artist in every family."

American folk art is variable and diversified; it manifests a broad range of

Portrait drawn by John James Audubon in 1819

individual expression; and it varies widely in its levels of accomplishment. At its best it reveals a straightforward, functional simplicity and a basic understanding of design and composition, of material and color. At the other extreme it displays an appealing naïveté, a charm enhanced by our growing familiarity with and appreciation of the primitive arts of other distant and earlier cultures. The fact that the folk artist, either from incompetence or willfulness, often showed scant respect for formal rules of perspective and proportion does not disconcert those of us who have come to accept the freely distorted forms so characteristic of much modern art. (In passing, it is interesting to note that the revival of interest in folk art coincides roughly with our exposure to the advanced art of the last number of decades.)

In nineteenth-century America there were societies-within-societies where something closer to the traditional European folk arts were practiced; societies which for a time, at least, remained apart from the surging mainstream of American life. The Pennsylvania Germans were the most notable example of such groups whose artists and craftsmen tended to perpetuate centuries-old forms and designs, picturesque survivals in a land otherwise so largely dedicated to everlasting change and progress. But even those folk were inevitably affected by the different atmosphere of the New World, and modifications and improvisations progressively altered the character of their output. Thus, also, the crude but expressive nineteenth-century paintings and carvings, holy images for the most part, of the natives in the Southwest relate back to the baroque art of Spain hundreds of years earlier. And these, too, tended to lose their traditional character with the intrusions of a mechanized, democratic world.

The various communities of Shakers that flourished in this country more than a century ago constituted a separate, aloof society within the fabric of American life, and one that produced forms and designs that were modest in pretension but highly distinctive in realization. With a burning religious ardor the Shakers had re-examined the problems and responsibilities of men and women who must live together in a human society, and had stripped these matters to what they considered fundamental necessities. Their austere concept of what made for a good life on earth (with heavenly rewards) was reflected in everything they produced. Order and use were basic considerations in all that was done, and to labor faithfully, meticulously, and diligently was to pray. As two of their announced precepts pointed out, "order is the creation of beauty" and "that which has in itself the highest use possesses the greatest beauty." The severe simplicity of their work—their folk art—and the scrupulous workmanship that was insistently practiced, resulted in an esthetic standard that anticipated the popular functionalism of twentieth-century American art and architecture.

Painted tavern sign from Brooklyn, about 1830

An evening school for young ladies, about 1840

341

Hooks & Braids for Underfoot

449. *Opposite: embroidered wool carpet, detail*
449a. *Left: embroidered bird from same carpet*

There was no apparent limit to the ingenuity of the American women who made their own carpets, whether through choice or for reasons of thrift. "Mother herself cut flags [rushes] in the marshy places," wrote a Connecticut woman, born in 1824, "and having colored linen yarn blue, red, yellow, for warp, wove some homemade matting. This was for the best room." Painted floorcloths also provided bright and inexpensive floor coverings. Lyman Beecher's mother made one about 1800, decorating it with "roses and other flowers," the carpet nailed to the garret floor while she worked. Another later memoir recalled the lady of the house spinning and weaving the linen herself, nailing it to the side of the barn, and there applying her painted patterns. For a more leisurely and elegant creative effort, an embroidered carpet could be several years in the making, as was this fine example (449) by Zeruah Guernsey Caswell of Castleton, Vermont. Completed in 1835, Zeruah's handiwork was made from wool sheared from the family sheep, then spun, dyed, and woven at home. The carpet, twelve feet wide and thirteen and a half feet long, is made up of squares, each carrying its own rich design.

450. *Left: knitted rug trimmed with braided border*

451. *Below: a hooked rug finished with a wool fringe*

452. *Opposite:* The Talcott Family, *painted in 1832*

453. *Opposite, below: a hooked rug with a "Turkish" design copying an imported Oriental Ghiordez rug*

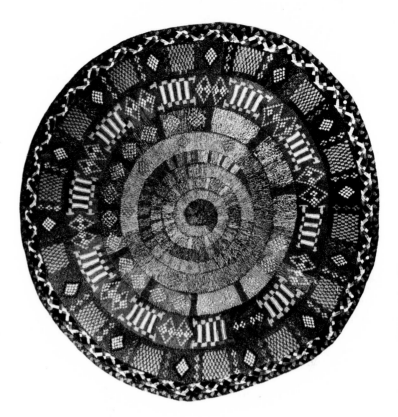

Woven striped carpets, generally with a warp of wool and a weft of cotton, comprised a comparatively simple pattern, easily achieved on a home loom. The example on which the Talcott family posed for their portrait (452) illustrates the vivid colors often used. (As an interesting footnote to this water color, the painter was Miss Deborah Goldsmith, of North Brookfield, New York, who journeyed forth at the age of twenty-one to be an itinerant painter, as a means of supporting her aging parents. Deborah met her future husband when he sat for his portrait in 1831.) Another version of the striped floor covering, the rag carpet, as it was called, was woven from strips of leftover materials, again with a weft of cotton threads. Miscellaneous fabric scraps were also braided, then coiled, and stitched into round rugs. This knitted rug (450) was made by the Shakers, whose ascetic surroundings were often brightened by colorful homemade carpets. The hooked rug (451, 453) became popular around 1840 and was made throughout the Victorian period in limitless variations of size and design.

454. *An intricately carved scrimshaw brooch*

455. *Center: a painted wooden toy whale, with articulating jaw*

456. *Scrimshaw ditty box, for holding the paraphernalia of a seaman*

From Humble Hands on Distant Seas

No folk art is associated with such wild adventure and sordid horror as those objects carved from whale teeth and bone by American seamen and known as scrimshaw, or scrimshander. (The origin of the term is obscure, and it took various forms.) The man who for the first time found himself "putting into the charmed churned circle of the sperm whale" at the climax of the pursuit, wrote Herman Melville, felt stronger and stranger emotions than any recruit going into his first battle or any "dead man's ghost encountering the first unknown phantom in the other world." But then there was the bloody and slimy business of cutting up the whale's carcass and the filth and stench of boiling down the masses of blubber, and in general the foul, oppressive condition of life on shipboard month after long, trying month. A whaling voyage might last more than three years, and to alleviate the boredom of seemingly endless hours of enforced leisure, the whaler took to his jackknife and other tools to carve and cut the tooth and bone of his prey into any one of a wide variety of objects to bring home as a remembrance or a keepsake. In 1844 one whaler wrote in his journal: "Got up a couple of Sperm Teeth, scraped them off Smooth ready to polish. Have some idea of Scratching a little something on them to make them Look as Curious as possible."

Ivory carving is an ancient art practiced by many people in various parts of the world. Scrimshaw was, on the whole, a distinctively American variant. Naturally, the carving and engraving on the examples that have survived vary in quality as well as in design. But in general the results attract the eye and excite the imagination. They bring to mind the remark of Augustus Welby Pugin, the famous English architect and critic: "In matters of ordinary use a man must go out of his way to create a bad thing." To produce such results took patient and careful labor. The teeth of the sperm whale, for example, had to be cut from the gums of the massive lower jaw, then dried, soaked in brine, filed and smoothed with sharkskin or some other abrasive, and then polished. When the chosen design, either copied from prints or freely invented, was ultimately cut into the tooth with one or another sharp implement, ink or some other coloring was rubbed into the incised lines by thumb or palm. The final products were infinitely varied. "The Captain, officers, Boatsteeres and foremost hands Busily employed," recorded one whaleman, "Sawing up Bone for Canes, Swifts, Busks, fids, Gilmet and Chisel handles, etc."

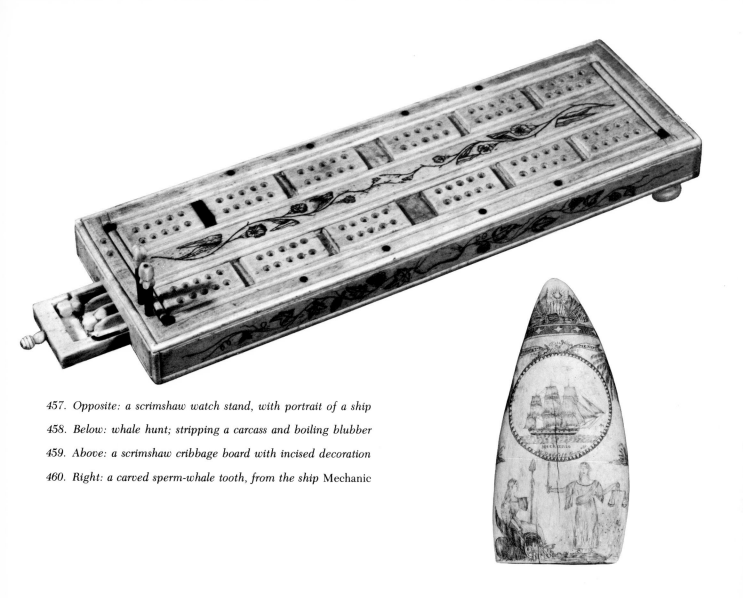

457. *Opposite: a scrimshaw watch stand, with portrait of a ship*

458. *Below: whale hunt; stripping a carcass and boiling blubber*

459. *Above: a scrimshaw cribbage board with incised decoration*

460. *Right: a carved sperm-whale tooth, from the ship* Mechanic

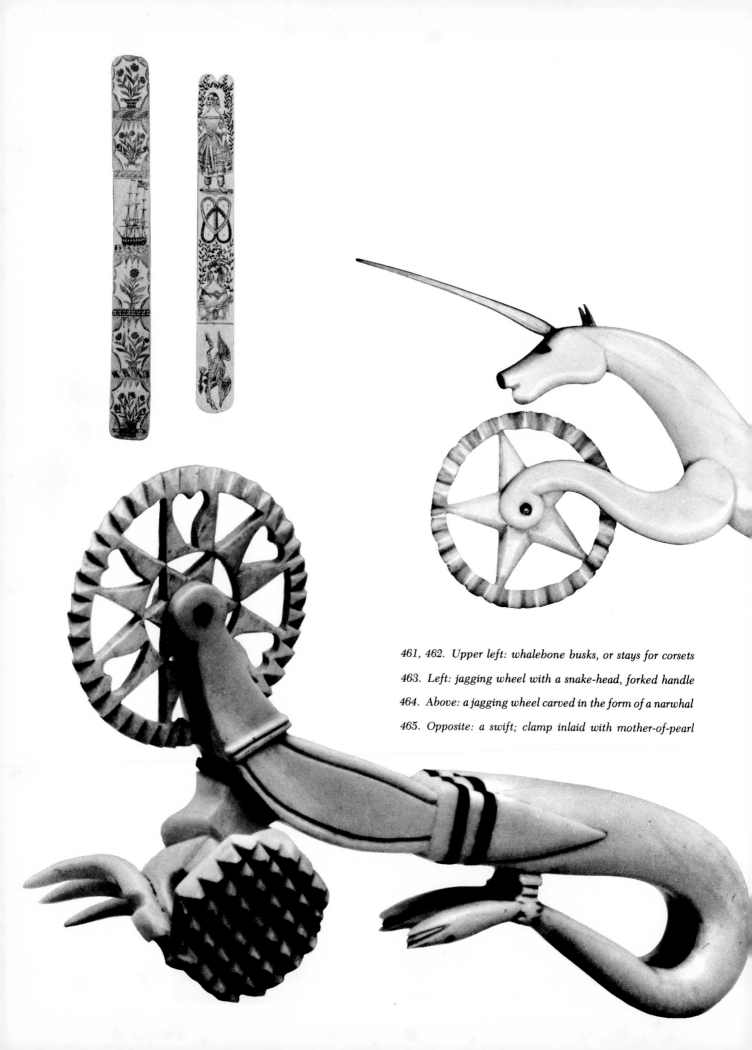

461, 462. *Upper left: whalebone busks, or stays for corsets*

463. *Left: jagging wheel with a snake-head, forked handle*

464. *Above: a jagging wheel carved in the form of a narwhal*

465. *Opposite: a swift; clamp inlaid with mother-of-pearl*

Jagging wheels (463, 464), with their zigzag edges, for cutting pastry or pie dough were made from the jawbone of a whale. With their intricate cutting and imaginative, graceful designs, they include some of the masterpieces of scrimshaw. Even more complicated in structure was the swift (465), an ingenious apparatus which opened up like an umbrella and about which yarn was wound to form a hank for knitting or other ladies' handiwork. Busks (461, 462), frontal stays for women's corsets, were simpler but more romantic tokens of a whaler's ocean reveries. A bit of doggerel on one example sums up the matter:

> *Accept, dear Girl, this busk from me*
> *Carved by my humble hand.*
> *I took it from a Sperm Whale's jaw,*
> *One thousand miles from land.*
>
> *In many a gale, has been the whale,*
> *In which this bone did rest,*
> *His time is past, his bone at last,*
> *Must now support thy breast.*

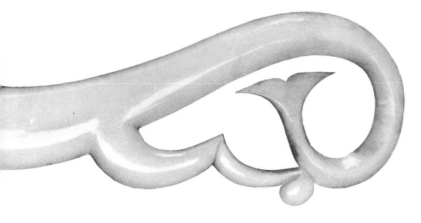

Limners & Likenesses

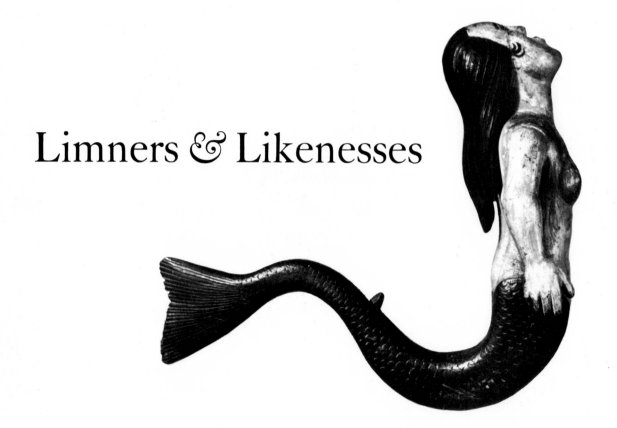

More often than not the names and individual histories of the American folk artists whose work we now enjoy and admire have been lost with time. In those cases, the examples that have survived, often quite by accident, must speak for themselves without the personal associations that add to our interest in viewing the works of artists with illustrious names. The identity of the person who carved the graceful little mermaid (466) has long been forgotten. The figure once served as part of a garden fountain in Baltimore. Water ran through a tube in the center of her body to spout out of her mouth in a liquid curve corresponding to the curve of the figure itself. Thus, too, we may never know who painted the portrait of Agnes Frazee and a child (467) in 1834. And we will surely never know whether the elaborate headdresses of both adult and child were proud possessions of the subjects or studio props of the anonymous artist, which he freely disposed about the two faces to create a pleasing and colorful pattern. In the case of the view of Poestenkill, New York, shown overleaf (468), the artist has been identified as Joseph H. Hidley, a man who intimately knew the small crossroads town he painted.

466. *Above: painted wood mermaid, from a fountain*

467. *Opposite: a portrait of Agnes Frazee and child*

468. OVERLEAF: *View of the town of Poestenkill, N.Y.*

469. *Upper left: painted-wood shop figure*

470. *Left: a water color by Emma Cady*

471. *Above:* Meditation by the Sea, *1850's*

Hidley was a man of many parts, a woodcarver, a taxidermist, a maker of artificial flowers, and a cabinetmaker, as well as a competent professional painter of varied subjects. About the same time as he painted Poestenkill, in the 1850's, another, unidentified artist painted the pensive little figure in *Meditation by the Sea* (471), gazing at the crisp, curling surf; a scene he depicted with somewhat less mastery than Hidley brought to his art. However, the mood of lonely reverie is hardly diminished by the painter's apparent limitations. Over the past two generations we have learned to look at art in new ways; to realize that even the most able realists among artists do not include in their canvases everything they can see of a subject, and rarely do they paint things precisely as they greet the eye. Some distortion and abstraction of natural appearances is the essence of art at any level. Often enough the rather

vague approximations of reality by the folk artist remind us of the studied compositions of modern art. The delicate water color (470), painted by a young lady named Emma Cady about 1820, for example, recalls the highly sophisticated arrangements of such twentieth-century artists as Charles Demuth.

Long after an American "school" of sculptors had struck roots, largely in Florence and Rome, woodcarvers at home continued to turn out a wide variety of decorative and useful forms—notably ships' figureheads and store-front figures. The gaily painted caricature of a navigator (469) stood before the shop of James Fales, nautical instrument maker of New Bedford, Massachusetts, a century or more ago—the same sort of "little timber midshipmen...," remarked by Dickens, "eternally employed...in taking observations of the hackney coaches" on the London streets.

Our age is so accustomed to think of art as primarily a form of free self-expression, we tend to forget that throughout history the finest artists have often borrowed their themes, compositions, and even details from the work of others. With the proliferation of engravings in the seventeenth and eighteenth centuries, this practice was made much easier and it became more common. Large numbers of American paintings of the colonial period, for example, were virtual copies of English prints. The *santeros* of New Mexico used Mexican prints as their guides. Much American folk art was derivative in this same manner, and is none the less interesting on that count. Young ladies who were taught to paint in water colors on silk, a desirable social accomplishment in the early nineteenth century, were usually provided with such models. It is altogether likely that *Venus Drawn by Doves* (473), an example of this kind of genteel art, was based on a contemporary engraving and accommodated to the young lady's competence. Writing masters also demonstrated their calligraphic skills in pen drawings (472) and flourished designs intended to attract students and to serve as models for emulation. With the mass production of steel pens with slit nibs, which began in the 1820's, and with the advent of the Spencerian style about the same time, the art of penmanship developed a broad and popular base in this country.

472. *Above: penmanship drawing in ink of a deer*

473. Venus Drawn by Doves, *water color on silk*

The Way the Wind Blows

In a land that was still largely rural, as America was throughout most of the nineteenth century, the promise or threat of rain or shine were matters of constant and common interest. Benjamin Franklin had been wise enough to take advantage of this widespread concern by incorporating comments on the weather in his *Poor Richard's Almanack* and thus reaching a large audience (in a sort of tie-in sale) with ideas that otherwise would never have been heeded. But aside from the audacious prophecies of almanacs, for on-the-spot forecasting the countryman depended, as he had in ages past, on the daily appearance of the skies and the direction of the wind. Vanes of infinite variety, from figures of the cock (476) of ancient tradition to wood-burning locomotives (474) of fairly recent memory, were hammered, cast, and whittled into shape throughout the land. Cocks were commonly used above churches to recall Peter's denial of Christ. Picasso once remarked that cocks have never been so well seen as in American weather vanes.

474. *Opposite: a vane combined with a lightning rod*

475. *Above: wrought-iron vane in form of a serpent*

476. *Right: vane with cast body and sheet-metal tail*

Images of
the Southwest

477. *Left:* bulto, *Our Lady of Guadalupe*

478. *Opposite: figure of Saint Raymond*

At the end of the sixteenth century the Spanish explorers made their historic march from Mexico into the territory that is now our American Southwest in search of legendary cities of fabulous wealth. They found only humble Indian pueblos, but they lingered and in New Mexico (an area today comprising Texas, Arizona, Colorado, and New Mexico) established a northern outpost of the sprawling Spanish empire, and of the crusading Catholic faith. To the isolated frontier they brought up from Mexico those carved and painted wooden figures and colorful altarpieces that were symbols of their religion. It was a provincial art, but one that was directly, if remotely, derived from Spanish tradition of the baroque period.

From an early date, it seems, the Franciscan fathers encouraged their Indian converts to help in the construction and decoration of local mission churches. It was reported that the Indian workmen were entirely responsible for altar screens in such churches as San Miguel in Santa Fe, San Esteban del Rey in Acoma, and others. In any event, with time the influence of native artisans reduced the sophisticated concepts of the Spanish or Mexican prototypes to "primitive" versions that constituted a distinctive regional folk art, one that flourished in relatively changeless fashion from about 1750 to about 1850. In a figure of Saint Raymond (478)—who was born by Caesarian section, was the patron of midwives, and was revered by expectant mothers—the assertion of an indigenous spirit is more apparent than in the image of Our Lady of Guadalupe (477), the highly revered patroness of Mexico, with its obvious carryover of a borrowed cultural tradition.

479. *Left: Our Lady of Sorrows* (Mater Dolorosa)

480. *Above: altar screen from Our Lady of Talpa*

481. *Opposite: Saint Michael overcoming Lucifer*

As it is commonly used, the term *santos* refers to those carved, painted, and otherwise delineated representations of holy persons or objects. Those who made them are called *santeros*, some of whom traveled from community to community to satisfy local demands. Figures in the round are known as *bultos*, painted altarpieces and other panels as *retablos*. *Bultos* were often carved of cottonwood roots in several parts that were pegged together, with small regard for anatomical niceties, and at times adorned with draperies made of cotton cloth dipped in wet gesso. An image of Our Lady of Sorrows (479) has such an overgarment, painted black. A brightly painted effigy of the archangel Saint Michael (481) stands poised to slay the singularly appealing Lucifer he has just subdued. Many of such carvings and paintings were commissioned by pious families for their private use and display, as was the altar screen (480) shown here from the chapel of Our Lady of Talpa, built about 1820 for the family of Leandro Duran. The representations of holy personages are here reduced almost to symbolic patterns. As in children's paintings, they suggest ideas meaningful to their audience, with lines drawn around them.

Hands to Work, Hearts to God

"Whatever is fashioned, [let] it be plain and simple,...unembellished by any superfluities, which add nothing to its goodness or durability. Think not that ye can keep the laws of Zion while blending with the forms and fashions of the children of the unclean!" With such ascetic precepts as a guide, the Shaker communal societies—frugal, industrious, and celibate—were at their height from the 1790's to about the time of the Civil War. Their prosperity, their architecture, and the quality of their furniture and artifacts drew comments from every side. "Each of these communities," wrote a traveler in 1844, "is a well-built, handsome village...surrounded with beautiful and well cultivated kitchen and flower gardens, vineyards, orchards, and farms, the very best that are to be seen in the United States." Miss Martineau declared that the Shakers had the finest furniture and house linen in the country, as well as the finest habitations, frame dwellings "finished with the last degree of nicety, even to the springs of the windows and the hinges of the doors." And yet another visitor exclaimed on the immaculate order of Shaker interiors, detailing halls and rooms "lined with rows of wooden pegs, on which spare chairs, hats, cloaks, bonnets and shawls are hung."

482. *Opposite: Shaker chairs hung on wall pegs*

483. *Left: a tripod table, Mount Lebanon, N.Y.*

484. *Below: a rocking chair, Canterbury, N.H.*

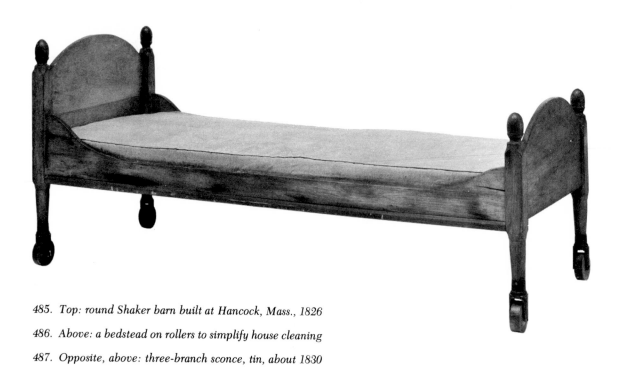

485. *Top: round Shaker barn built at Hancock, Mass., 1826*

486. *Above: a bedstead on rollers to simplify house cleaning*

487. *Opposite, above: three-branch sconce, tin, about 1830*

488. *Opposite: "Sewing desks" had sliding shelves, useful for both sewing or writing. This one is from Enfield, N.H.*

The Shaker movement began in eighteenth-century England, where the members were known as the "Shaking Quakers" because of the physical ardor of their worship. A young Manchester woman named Ann Lee, slum-born, illiterate, and a millworker, became a leader among the members of this sect and "was acknowledged as *mother* in Christ, and by them was called *Mother Ann.*" With a few faithful followers, Mother Ann came to America in 1774; the following year she founded the first Shaker community at Watervliet, New York. By 1840 some thirty colonies had been established from Maine to Indiana. In building their precisely planned villages, the laws of the society forbade "fanciful styles" or "beadings, moldings, and cornishings." Shaker architecture, therefore, was the epitome of functional design. Interiors were reduced to the final essentials—peg boards from door to door, built-in shelves and cupboards, and undecorated plaster walls—all wrought by flawless, unhurried workmanship. A Shaker community, primarily an agricultural enterprise, designed its barns with care. This one (485) has an inside driveway circling the hayloft; a wagon could drive in, unload, circle, and drive out by the same door it had entered.

369

The style of Shaker furniture was rooted in colonial practices in workmanship and design that had been perpetuated by country craftsmen. Because Shaker membership was largely drawn from rural areas, cabinetmakers who joined in the early days brought provincial traditions to their tasks. The customary, unpretentious furniture forms of such country men were further distilled into a purity of design untainted by the ''deception'' of superfluous or worldly decorations. ''The Shakers believe,'' wrote one visitor to the Watervliet community in mid-century, ''that their furniture was originally designed in heaven, and that the patterns have been transmitted to them by angels.'' Because of the Shakers' apprentice system and rules of uniformity governing every aspect of life, standard designs continued to be reproduced over the years. Shaker furniture was marketed to the outside world, as were other of their products—brooms, herbs, garden seeds, leather goods, fabrics, silk-lined straw bonnets, and baskets (490).

489. *Left: a spindled settee from Enfield, N.H.*

490. *Above: a basket in a typical Shaker design*

491. *Below: a tripod stand, New Lebanon, N.Y.*

492. Left: sewing desk, before 1850

493. Above: swivel chair made in New Lebanon, N.Y., about 1850–75

494. Below: box, the "fingers" of the maple band held by rivets, the base and cover fitted with discs of pine

495. Opposite: table made of cherry, from Canterbury, N.H., early 1800's

The Shakers, generally viewed as a sight-seeing attraction in their respective neighborhoods, received innumerable visitors, most of them curious to attend the Shakers' public worship, famed for its ritual of marching, singing, clapping, and dancing. Reactions to Shaker villages were diverse: "The Church is a large handsome room eighty-four feet by ninety, with the best kept and most beautifully polished floor I have seen in this country," wrote Mrs. Basil Hall on her visit to New Lebanon, although she deplored the Shaker church service as "folly." Another guest in 1844 spoke of "the cheerfulness and contented looks of the people [that] afford the reflective mind continual pleasure." Charles Dickens, however, found the atmosphere "grim," the men "wooden," and as for Shaker furniture, he wrote: "Ranged against the wall were six or eight stiff, high-backed chairs, and they partook so strongly of the general grimness, that one would have much rather have sat on the floor." Clearly, Mr. Dickens' Victorian eye did not recognize the delicacy and subdued elegance so frequently achieved by the cloistered Shaker cabinetmakers.

496. *Above: "A Present from Mother Ann to Mary H.," an inspirational drawing done in color on pale blue paper at New Lebanon*

497. *Encircling page: symbolic details from other inspirational drawings of the period*

498. *Opposite: the Tree of Life was a favorite design for Shaker pictures; this one, "Seen and painted by Hannah Cohoon" in the "City of Peace," (Hancock, Mass.)*

374

Fifty-three years after Ann Lee's death at Watervliet in 1784, the Shakers experienced an intense revival of mysticism and religious emotion, which they perceived to be "Mother Ann's Second Appearing." Her divine presence was first revealed in 1837 in the songs, whirling dances, and visions of a group of Shaker schoolgirls. Similar manifestations—including trances, the gift of unknown tongues, the "laughing gift," and possession by Indian, Eskimo, or Chinese spirits—swept through Shaker communities for almost ten years. Heavenly messages and testimonials (496, 497, 498) were rapturously transcribed and illustrated with symbols of spiritual gifts: golden chains, crowns, "diamonds of charity," doves, exotic fruits and trees, angels, celestial bowers, and "sweet-scented manna on shining plates." As hallowed messages, they were exempt from Shaker bans against superfluous decoration and the prodigal use of color; but because the display of pictures was forbidden, the drawings were never on exhibit.

Zeitgeist in Zoar

Among the many religious communities founded before the Civil War, the Separatists Society of Zoar, Ohio, was one of the most successful "holy experiments." Established in 1817 by Germans who had emigrated from Württemberg, Zoar prospered under the leadership of Joseph Bimeler. By 1852 the self-contained village, largely made up of hard-working peasant stock, was valued at one million dollars, with a brickyard, iron foundry, and woolen mill among its industries. The economy, however, was primarily agricultural. A brisk trade, for example, grew up from plants and seeds developed in a vast central garden that was laid out in a radial plan of the New Jerusalem envisioned in the Apocalypse. In making furniture, Zoar craftsmen continued for years to work in the folk patterns of their homeland. This chair (500) is an early European type, the back and seat joined by the ancient device of mortise and tenon. The chair (501) with a heart-shaped piercing and punched designs again reflects a strong German tradition, while the red and black invalid chair (499) shows the encroachment of more sophisticated styles in the Sheraton details of the fretwork trim.

499. *Opposite: a four-wheeled invalid chair or wagon*

500. *Above: a plank chair in the German tradition*

501. *Right: a side chair of walnut, made about 1850*

Art of a Children's World

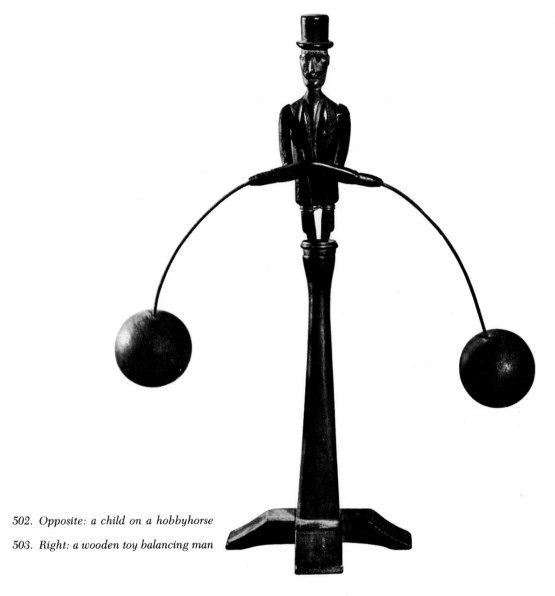

502. *Opposite: a child on a hobbyhorse*

503. *Right: a wooden toy balancing man*

Shortly after he first undertook to make a living by his brush, John James Audubon was called upon to record the likeness of a recently dead child whose little corpse was disinterred for the purpose. He gave the portrait to the parents, he recalled, "as if still alive, to their intense satisfaction." Such a macabre incident is a compelling reminder that, a century and more ago, the rate of infant mortality was many, many times greater than it is today. Visitors from other lands noted that, in general, American children were indulged by their parents. One early French traveler wrote that "nowhere is so much tenderness shown toward children as in Virginia; all their whims are indulged." In 1785 an immigrant cabinetmaker in Philadelphia advertised that he made "Rocking-Horses in the neatest and best manner, to teach children to ride and give them a wholesome and pleasing exercise." Such toys were not inexpensive. In 1800 Charles Swift of Philadelphia paid twenty-seven dollars for "One middle size Hobby-horse" bought from John and William Wigglesworth, local toy dealers.

In 1804 a New York toy merchant advised the public that among the general assortment he offered for sale were "jointed Dolls, elegantly dressed, of all sizes...intended to amuse and instruct the rising generation." Some years earlier Charles Willson Peale painted *Little Miss Proctor* (506), showing the young lady holding her treasured doll, which has survived (507) along with the portrait. Children, after their baby garments were put aside, were customarily dressed like miniature adults until the nineteenth century, and dolls followed suit. So it was both with Miss Proctor and her fashionably attired doll. It was not until about mid-century that "baby dolls" were introduced. Until well into the nineteenth century the more elaborate dolls and other toys were generally imports. Meanwhile, native artisans working in wood, largely, continued to provide their local markets with highly individual playthings, such as the ingenious sled with a single runner and handgrips on the seat (505) and the winsome little painted boy doll (504)—a rare presence in what was primarily a child-woman's world. In the late 1830's one Yankee carpenter and sometime toymaker, William S. Tower of South Hingham, Massachusetts, observing that his fellow woodworkers were occasionally producing more toys than they knew how to sell, organized them into a toymakers' guild. It was the beginning of a thriving trade.

504. *Left: a rare example of a carved, painted boy doll*

505. *Right: a one-runner wooden sled, made in Vermont*

506. *Above:* Little Miss Proctor *holding her doll*

507. *Right: the doll shown in the painting above*

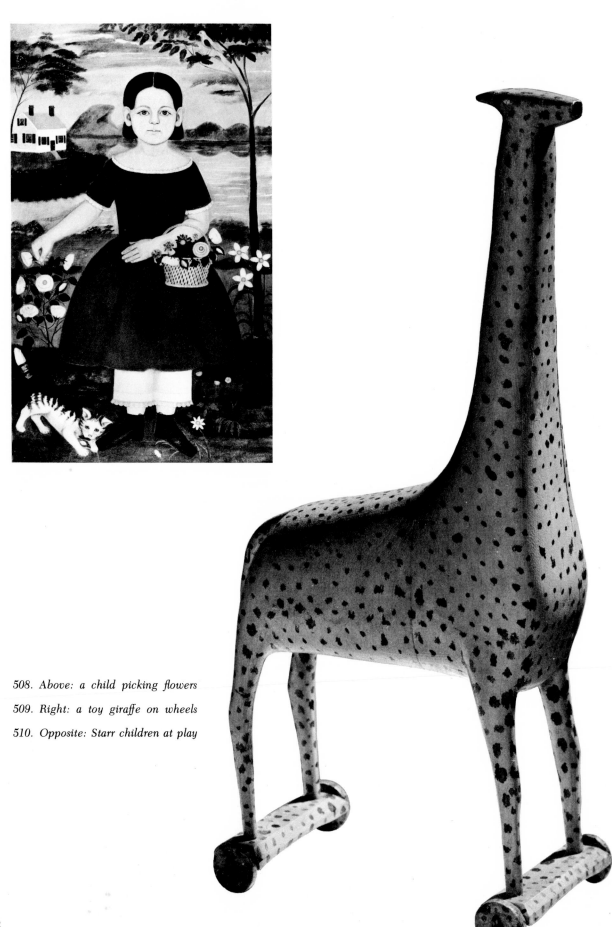

508. Above: a child picking flowers

509. Right: a toy giraffe on wheels

510. Opposite: Starr children at play

A pair of Hungarian revolutionaries who accompanied Louis Kossuth to America in 1852 thought that children in this country largely had their own way. "They run in and out and play," the couple observed, "tumbling and dragging about books and cushions and chairs and climbing up and down just as they please." As a consequence of this sort of freedom, they concluded, the children grew "strikingly sharp" and self-dependent. Each generation of American children was expected to do better than its parents in the race for success. To some witnesses it seemed that by their willful self-assertion they were bent on eliminating their parents from the race altogether. However, in deference to convention they were rarely portrayed other than as little models of innocence, grace, and propriety as in the portrait, by an unknown artist, of a little girl picking flowers in a field (508). The folk artists who took their juvenile likenesses were not always able to picture the essential childishness of their subjects. As in the work of much earlier artists in the development of western painting—medieval miniaturists, for example—the youngsters in their pictures often resembled small adults in children's garb engaged in childish pursuits. In 1835 Ambrose Andrews painted the children of Nathan Starr (510) of Middletown, Connecticut, with hoop and stick and playing battledore and shuttlecock across a room or the hall of their home. Less pretentious, and less expensive, toys than the prancing hobbyhorse shown on page 378 were often whittled out of wood and gaily painted, either by itinerant artisans or by the handiest man of the house. As ever, small children were often satisfied by the simplest toys (509).

511. OVERLEAF: *A nineteenth-century ivory carving of an eagle*

Glossary
of
Terms

ACANTHUS A carved ornamentation patterned after acanthus leaves, used decoratively on furniture (119); used in architecture principally on Corinthian and Composite capitals

ACORN CLOCK Connecticut shelf clock, so-called because its shape suggests an acorn (291)

ALARM TIMEPIECE See EDDYSTONE LIGHT-HOUSE CLOCK

AMBROTYPE A positive photograph on glass, made by the collodion process, to be shown against a dark background

Anthemion

ANTHEMION A conventional design of flower and leaf forms derived from ancient Greek art, used as an ornamental motif in Greek Revival architecture and on Empire furniture, silver, glass; also called Greek honeysuckle pattern

ARGAND LAMP A lamp with tubular wick, fed from an elevated reservoir, creating an air current inside and outside the flame; invented 1783 by the Swiss Aimé Argand (389)

ARMOIRE A tall cupboard or wardrobe, with one or two doors, used for storage of linens and garments (232)

ASTRAL LAMP A type of Argand lamp, made so that the flattened, ringed cistern holding the oil does not throw a shadow; also called *sinumbra* lamp (400)

BACCARAT GLASS Fine crystal glass made at the manufactory of La Compagnie des Cristalleries de Baccarat, in the town of Baccarat, France

BALLOON FRAME A frame for building, adopted in America in the middle of the 19th century, in which light two-by-four studs were nailed together in a tight, basketlike manner, rising continuously from foundation to rafters of the structure (page 295)

BALLOON-BACK CHAIR A chair with an open back and transverse splat, the top

rail rounded so as to be continuous with incurved uprights and thus assuming a roughly balloon-shape outline (343)

BALUSTER An upright support, usually turned and vase shaped, topped by a rail; also called a banister

BANDING A narrow edging or border of veneer; a contrasting band of inlay. See also Stringing

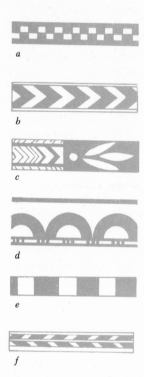

Banding and stringing patterns characteristic of: a. Massachusetts. b. New Hampshire. c. Massachusetts. d. Massachusetts. e. Connecticut. f. Maryland

BANJO CLOCK Wall clock invented by Simon Willard and patented in 1802, with a circular dial over a flaring shaft, flanked by scroll brackets. Underneath is a rectangular pendulum door. Shaft and pendulum door often decorated with *églomisé* panels and dial surmounted with cone or eagle; also called an improved patent timepiece (289)

BAR-BACK CHAIR Side or armchair having a square back with carved and reeded spindles and turned and reeded supports. Made in Philadelphia in the early 19th century by Ephraim Haines and Henry Connelly (16)

BAROQUE A style of art and architecture developed in the late 16th and 17th centuries in Europe, featuring dynamic curved elements and extravagantly and dramatically contorted classical forms

BASKET STAND A work stand with two tiers surrounded by galleries made up of turnings or spindles (416)

BEADING A fine-scale, beadlike, semicircular convex molding (39)

BELLFLOWER Floral ornament, carved or inlaid, with bud of three or five pointed, narrow petals

BENNINGTON WARE An earthenware with a mottled or streaked brown glaze properly called Rockingham ware, but popularly known in America as Bennington ware because of its extensive manufacture at the Vermont potteries

BERLIN WORK Wool embroidery, popular in the mid-19th century, so-called from the prepatterned backgrounds and soft worsteds exported from Berlin for American needleworkers (415)

BEZEL A grooved rim; in clockmaking the rim into which a clockface glass is secured

BILBAO MIRROR A classical style mirror with marble veneer or marble and wood frame, so named after the Spanish city from which such forms were exported

BISCUIT WARE Unglazed pottery or porcelain; also called bisque

BLOWN-MOLDED GLASS Glass impressed with a design from a small patterned mold and then expanded (160)

BLOWN THREE-MOLD GLASS Glass impressed with a design from a full-size, three-part, hinged mold; popular from about 1815 to about 1830 (276)

BOBECHE A plain or ornamental disk, often of glass, set on the candle socket of a candlestick, chandelier, or sconce, to catch the drippings

Bellflower

BOHEMIAN GLASS A trade name for mid-19th-century glass with one or more layers of colored glass cut away in patterns revealing the clear glass body; also called cased or overlay glass (356)

BONHEUR-DU-JOUR A desk, originating in France, designed for ladies' use, with an oblong recessed structure and doors opening into smaller drawers and compartments. It is usually surmounted by marble and a pierced metal gallery and has a hinged or pull-out writing board.

BOSTON ROCKER A rocking chair, developed from the Windsor chair and introduced in America about 1835, with wooden seat curving down at the front and up at the back and a high back made of vertical spindles beneath a crest rail (252)

BOUILLOTTE CANDELABRUM A table lamp with dish-shaped base supporting a shaft fitted with two or three candle brackets and a metal shade surmounted by a finial. The name comes from the French card game of *bouillotte* (385).

BRACKET FOOT A foot shaped like a bracket with mitered corners, often scrolled on the free sides, and found on case furniture

Bracket foot

BREAKFRONT A large case piece with a projecting center section, usually surmounted by a pediment; a form often used in bookcases and secretaries (10)

BRITANNIA WARE A trade name applied to a form of pewter; a silverlike alloy consisting of tin, antimony, and copper, which lent itself to mass production by spinning and stamping (264)

BULTOS Figures in the round representing holy persons or objects, made in Mexico and New Mexico (now New Mexico, Arizona, Colorado, and Texas) from about 1750 to about 1850 (477)

CABOCHON A plain round or oval surface, without ornamentation

CARCEL LAMP A variation of the Argand lamp, with a clockwork pump to keep the burner filled with oil from the reservoir below; also called a mechanized lamp (397)

CASED GLASS See BOHEMIAN GLASS

CASTELLATED Pierced in a regular pattern, as on the parapets of fortified structures; used also on some Gothic and Gothic Revival furniture as an ornamental device

CARYATID A supporting column in the form of a female figure developed in ancient Greece and since used in architecture and furniture

CENTRIPETAL CHAIR See SPRING CHAIR

CHAISE GONDOLE See GONDOLA CHAIR

CHEVRON V-shaped design of inlaid and other decoration

CHINESE EXPORT PORCELAIN Ceramic ware made and decorated in China for export to the Occident from the early 16th to the mid-19th century; often misleadingly termed Lowestoft (86)

COMMODE A low chest of drawers, or a cabinet on legs (244); a term also used for a form enclosing a chamber pot

Conch

CONCH Inlaid or painted ornamentation resembling such a shell often appearing on Federal style furniture

CONNECTICUT SHELF CLOCK See ACORN CLOCK

CONNECTICUT WALL CLOCK See LYRE CLOCK

CONSOLE TABLE A side table without back legs, the top supported by one or more brackets or consoles; often fixed to the wall and beneath a mirror (152). See also Pier Table

CONVERSATIONAL See TETE-A-TETE

CORNER BLOCK Triangular block set in the corners of chair and other frames as reinforcement

CORNER TABLE A table shaped to fit into a corner, often made in pairs and frequently decorated during the federal period with marquetry or lacquer work and fitted with a marble top; also called an encoignure (291)

CORNUCOPIA Carved, inlaid, or painted ornamentation resembling a horn of plenty often appearing on furniture of the Federal and Empire styles (below)

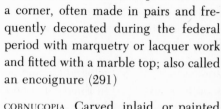

COURTING MIRROR Term for a small mirror with crudely painted glass insets in the wooden crest and frame, originally fitted into a shallow box with a sliding cover; imported from northern Europe in the late 18th and early 19th centuries

CREST RAIL The top rail of a chair, settee, or any other seating form

CROCKET A carved, projecting ornament, of curved and bent foliage, used on the sloping edge of spires and gables in Gothic and Gothic Revival architecture; sometimes used to decorate furniture in those styles

CROSS-BANDING Decorative bands of veneer in which the grain runs transverse to that of the general surface

CRYSTAL A term used for clear, brilliant glass of excellent quality, commonly containing lead oxide

CURULE CHAIR A chair with a cross-base support, termed "Grecian Cross" legs, derived from the folding stool of an ancient Roman magistrate (129)

CUSP A Gothic ornamental detail, consisting of a point or knob frequently carved, projecting from the intersection of two curves

CUT GLASS Glass ornamented by grinding and polishing to produce more or less elaborate designs, principally geometric (170)

Crocket

Cusp

CYMA A double curve; a cyma recta is concave above and convex below, a cyma reversa, convex above and concave below; also called an ogee

DAGUERREOTYPE A photograph made by a process developed in France by Louis J. Daguerre, in which a silver or silver-covered copper plate is made sensitive to light by the action of chemicals (256)

DRAPED URN Carved, inlaid, or painted ornamentation of a classical urn shape draped with a simulated swag of fabric, used principally on furniture in the Federal style

DRESSER A type of bureau or chest of drawers with an attached mirror (321)

DRESSING BUREAU See DRESSING CHEST

DRESSING CHEST A chest of drawers, the top one fitted with compartments for cosmetics; sometimes also fitted with a mirror or a writing-slide; also called a dressing chest of drawers (54)

DRESSING GLASS A framed mirror, often on a swivel, made to stand on or be attached to the top of a small chest with drawers or table; also called a dressing stand (61)

DRESSING STAND See DRESSING GLASS

DRESSING TABLE A small table or stand with a mirror attached (344)

DRUM TABLE A library table with a circular revolving top, often inset with a tooled leather panel, over drawers or compartments for books (155)

EAGLE-HEAD FOOT Terminal of the leg of a table, sofa, or case piece, carved to resemble the head of an eagle

EARLY VICTORIAN STYLE A general and loosely used term referring to the varieties of styles popular during the early years of Queen Victoria's reign (from 1837); especially those of a more or less elaborate and eclectic character, such as the variations of earlier French designs

Draped urn

Fan light

Eagle-head foot

EDDYSTONE LIGHTHOUSE CLOCK An alarm timepiece, patented by Simon Willard, 1822, with a tapering wooden base suggesting a lighthouse in form and an alarm dial and bell in a glass case above (290)

EDGING Thin strip of solid wood at the edge of a veneered panel, to protect the veneering

EGLOMISE See VERRE EGLOMISE

ELIZABETHAN REVIVAL STYLE A furniture style of the mid-19th century, characterized by ball and spiral-twist turnings derived from the baroque style

ENCOIGNURE See CORNER TABLE

ESCUTCHEON Shaped surface on which armorial bearings are displayed; also a decorative plate about a keyhole

ETAGERE See WHATNOT

FANCY FURNITURE Furniture painted or japanned with pictorial scenes or other decorative designs (27). See also Hitchcock Chair

FAN LIGHT Elliptic or half-round window over a door, with radiating design of mullions or leading

FAUTEUIL French term for a chair with open arms (132)

FEATHEREDGE Edge of a board thinned off, as in paneling and sheathing

FENTON'S ENAMEL See FLINT ENAMEL

FERROTYPE See TINTYPE

FESTOON Painted or carved decoration in the form of scalloplike series of loops, as a rope, chain of flowers, drapery (65). See also Swag

FINIAL A device used as a terminal ornament

FLINT ENAMEL A ceramic formula patented 1849 by Christopher Webber Fenton, of Bennington, Vermont, that provided an improvement in the application of color to Rockingham ware. Powdered metallic oxides were dusted on a transparent glaze, the piece was then fired again, producing an enamel-like finish; also called Fenton's enamel

FLINT GLASS Glass of a heavy, brilliant quality containing lead; also called lead glass or crystal

FOLIATED Ornamented with leaf forms

Foliate

FREE-BLOWN GLASS Glass blown without molds, given form by the use of hand tools

GALLERY A decorative railing, often of metal, around the edge of a piece of furniture, a shelf, or a tray (104)

GALLOON Narrow tape used as a binding, a trim, or a gimp in the finishing of upholstery

GARLAND Floral decoration, freely arranged

GAUDY DUTCH WARE A popular name for gaily decorated pottery made in Staffordshire especially for the Pennsylvania German trade (197)

GIRANDOLE A wall mirror with candle branches attached. Those introduced in the late 18th century were circular with a convex glass, the gilt frame decorated with gilt balls and usually topped with an eagle (125)

GIRANDOLE CLOCK A wall clock with a round dial and pendulum door set in gilt moldings, decorated with gilt balls, as were girandole mirrors of the Federal period (235)

GONDOLA CHAIR A side chair with open back, solid center splat and top rail, and uprights curved forward to rest on the seat rail; also called a *chaise gondole* (307)

GOTHIC CLOCK See STEEPLE CLOCK

GOTHIC REVIVAL STYLE A term used to refer to architecture and furnishings featuring pointed arches, cusps, crock-

ets, and other design elements associated with the medieval past; popular in America largely in the several decades after 1840

GRANDFATHER CLOCK See TALL CASE CLOCK

GRANDMOTHER CLOCK A modern term for a miniature tall case clock

GREEK HONEYSUCKLE PATTERN See ANTHEMION

Greek key

GREEK KEY A repeating, geometric motif derived from ancient Greek art

GREEK REVIVAL STYLE A term referring to architecture and furnishings, especially from about 1820 to about 1850, in which ancient Greek forms and ornamental details were used in more or less free interpretations

GUERIDON A small round table, originally a decorative candlestand made in the likeness of a young Negro holding a candle. Also applied to a variety of small occasional tables or candlestands (144)

HITCHCOCK CHAIR Mass-produced versions of "fancy chairs," with stenciled and painted decorations, made by Lambert Hitchcock in Hitchcocksville, Connecticut, and in other factories largely in the second quarter of the 19th century (253)

HURRICANE SHADE A cylindrical shade of glass, open at either end, placed over a candlestick to protect the flame from drafts. Also earlier called a wind glass

Hurricane shade

INLAY Decoration formed by contrasting materials set into the surface of a piece

INNOVATIVE FURNITURE Machine-made furniture of the 19th century employing such technical advances as lamination, metal and tubular construction, or using mechanical devices like the metal-coil spring for upholstered pieces and various types of reclining or folding chairs (371)

KLISMOS A side chair derived from an ancient Greek type shown in vase paintings and grave monuments. The seat and rail uprights are united by a continuous line which flows into the incurved or saber leg

Klismos

KNIFE BOX A highly decorative box-case for silverware, often made in pairs and displayed on sideboards; introduced at the close of the 18th century. Also called a knife case (14)

KYLIX A form of shallow, footed, two-handled bowl used by ancient Greeks as a drinking vessel at banquets

LACY PRESSED GLASS A mechanically pressed glass with complicated relief designs on a finely stippled, lacelike ground (285); made in the United States about 1828–40

LANCET A sharply pointed arch of a window or a window light; also an arch so shaped

LEAD GLASS See FLINT GLASS

LEAF AND SCROLL DESIGN A serpentine acanthus leaf motif used to decorate 19th-century pressed glass (280)

LILY PAD Applied decoration formed by superimposing a layer of glass in a pad-like form about the base of a blown-glass vessel; used on South Jersey type glass (156)

LION-HEAD DRAWER PULL A furniture mount, usually brass or ormolu, with a ring suspended from the lion mask

LION-PAW FOOT A foot resembling the paw of a lion, used on chairs, sofas, and case pieces, most frequently in the Empire period

Lion head

Lion-paw foot

LITHOGRAPH A print made by offsetting onto paper an image drawn with grease on a flat stone or metal surface; when the surface is wetted it rejects the oily printer's ink except for the greased areas

LIVERPOOL POTTERY A generic name given to creamware made both in Liverpool and other Staffordshire potteries; particularly applied to wares with black transfer-printed decorations, often of American historical subjects (85)

LOLLING CHAIR See MARTHA WASHINGTON CHAIR

LONG CASE CLOCK See TALL CASE CLOCK

LOVE SEAT A small upholstered sofa or settee designed to seat two people. See also Tête-à-tête

LOWESTOFT See CHINESE EXPORT PORCELAIN

LYRE Ornamental motif resembling the classical stringed musical instrument, often used on furnishings of the federal period

Lyre

LYRE CLOCK A Connecticut wall clock with square face surrounded by foliate wooden border and with a lyre-shaped wooden pendulum case and small pendant (304)

MARTHA WASHINGTON CHAIR Armchair with tall upholstered back, usually serpentine arched, and curved open arms. Said to have been used by Martha Washington at Mount Vernon; also called a lolling chair

MASSACHUSETTS SHELF CLOCK A clock with thirty-hour or eight-day movement of brass made by the Willards and others, mainly in Massachusetts, shortly after the Revolution (287)

MASSACHUSETTS WALL CLOCK A relatively small and inexpensive clock with a light, thirty-hour movement made in the last decades of the 18th century (286)

MECHANIZED LAMP See CARCEL LAMP

MEMORIAL PICTURE See MOURNING PICTURE

MERIDIENNE A French term for a sofa or day bed having one arm lower than the other (306)

MONOPODIUM A support derived from an ancient design, consisting of an animal leg surmounted by an animal head in a single composition

MOUNT A piece of decorative hardware or metal ornament on a piece of furniture (137)

MOURNING PICTURE An embroidery, usually silk on satin, or painting depicting an urn or monument often with a name or epitaph, a willow tree—emblem of mourning—and figures that may have been intended to represent the bereaved family. Usually framed under glass and displayed like a painting; also called a memorial picture (410)

OGEE See CYMA

OGEE-CROSS SPLAT Open-back chair splat composed of two conjoining ogee-curved elements

OGIVE A Gothic style pointed arch

ORMOLU Gilded brass or bronze used for furniture mounts and other purposes; also called gilt-bronze

OTTOMAN A long or circular, low upholstered seat (336)

OVERLAY GLASS See BOHEMIAN GLASS

OYSTERING Veneer showing cross-sectional grain in irregular concentric rings, resembling the shape and markings of oyster shells

Ormolu mount

PARIAN WARE Fine-grained, waxy porcelain resembling white marble, used chiefly for portrait statues and parlor ornaments in the mid-19th century. First produced in America at Bennington by C. W. Fenton and later at many other American manufactories; also called statuary ware (367)

PATERAE Flat, circular ornaments resembling the classical saucers used for wine in libations; usually in low relief, ornamenting a frieze or other element of architecture or furniture

Ogee-cross splat

Paterae

PATTERN MOLD A mold with depressions or protuberances forming patterns on the interior surface into which glass is forced or blown, then removed and expanded

PEDIMENT In architecture, a triangular or arched section above the entablature; in cabinetmaking, a similar top, either straight, or curving, for case pieces

PEMBROKE TABLE A small, rectangular drop-leaf table usually having straight slender legs (34)

PETIT POINT A fine-stitch embroidery worked upon a canvas mesh and used chiefly for upholstering seating furniture and screens

PIER TABLE A table designed to stand against a pier, that section of a wall between two windows or doors, usually beneath a pier glass; a side table (309). See also Console Table

PILLAR AND SCROLL FURNITURE Furniture featuring flat-section scroll supports, frequently attached to the upright members in the form of pillars; a popular style of the 1830's and 1840's

PILLAR AND SCROLL SHELF CLOCK A shelf clock with slender feet and pillars, with a broken arch or double scroll at the top. Sometimes called Terry-type clocks after Eli Terry, the first to produce them in quantity about 1816 (292)

Pillar and scroll support

PLATE Term used for forms made of solid silver or gold of standard or sterling quality

PLATEAU A long, low decorative centerpiece for the dining table, generally of a gilt-bronze or silver, mounted on short feet or a plinth. Usually made in several short pieces so that its length could be adjusted. In France, also called a *surtout* (104)

PLATED WARE Forms made of a thin layer of silver over a heavier base of copper, either manually fused (as in old

Sheffield plate) or, later, chemically electroplated

PRINCE OF WALES FEATHERS Motif consisting of decorative carved or painted feathers, sometimes set within an oval chair back in the Federal style; commonly associated with the insigne of the Prince of Wales (236)

Prince of Wales feathers

PUNCHED WORK Decoration, in relief, wrought by closely set dots punched into metal or wood (501)

QUILLING Ribbon of glass applied and pinched into wavy lines; also called pinched trailing

RECAMIER A day bed or couch, originally without a back, with head and foot scrolled outward and of equal height. Its name came from the portrait of Juliette Récamier by Jacques Louis David in which this type of couch is shown. The form derived from couches used in classical times for sleeping or reclining at meals (136). See also Triclinium

REEDING A motif, in semicircular relief, resembling straight, stylized reeds

Reeding

REGENCY An English development of the classical revival, from 1795 to 1820

RESTAURATION Relating to developments of the classical revival style in France during the reign of Louis XVIII

RETABLOS Pictures of holy persons or objects painted on wood panels over a gesso ground (480), made in Mexico and New Mexico (now New Mexico, Arizona, Colorado, and Texas) principally from about 1750 to 1850. See also *Santos*

RINCEAU Ornamental motif of elaborate scrollings, often worked in a symmetrical design (below)

ROCKINGHAM WARE A ceramic ware with rich brown manganese glaze, named for that produced by the Rockingham kiln at Swinton, England. A term applied to the similar product of potteries in Bennington, Vermont, as well as other American potteries. See also Bennington Ware

ROCOCO A style of art and decoration developed in the 18th century in France, characterized by designs curvilinear in form and imitative of shellwork, scrolls, and foliage asymmetrically arranged.

ROCOCO REVIVAL STYLE A style popular in the middle decades of the 19th century, which freely interpreted French designs of the first half of the 18th century and characterized by S- and C-curves, scrolls, and shell and floral carvings

SABER LEG Chair or sofa leg curved inward in the shape of a saber; see also Klismos

SALEM SECRETARY A breakfront bookcase or cabinet with a writing compartment. The recessed upper section has two or four glazed doors. The projecting lower section is fitted with drawers; also called a gentleman's secretary (76)

SALT GLAZE A hard, rough, transparent glaze produced by introducing rock salt into the kiln during the firing of earthenware or stoneware

SANDWICH GLASS Glass made at the Boston and Sandwich Glass Company. The term is sometimes erroneously used to refer to any American pressed glass, especially of the lacy variety (357)

SANTEROS Makers of *Santos*. See also *Santos*

SANTOS An image in any medium of a holy person or thing, made in Mexico and New Mexico (now New Mexico, Arizona, Colorado, and Texas) principally from about 1750 to about 1850; see also *Bultos, Retablos, Santeros*

SCRIMSHANDER See SCRIMSHAW

SCRIMSHAW Objects carved from whale

teeth or whalebone in decorative shapes and patterns by American seamen in the 18th and 19th centuries; also called scrimshander (454)

SCRITOIRE See SCRUTOIRE

SCRUTOIRE An enclosed writing cabinet or table; also called escritoire

SERRATED Having notched, or toothed, ornamentation

SEWING TABLE See WORK TABLE

Sheaf of wheat

SHEAF OF WHEAT An ornamental motif depicting a bound sheaf of wheat, sometimes with a sickle, appearing most commonly on spoon, fork, and knife handles of the Empire period

SHIELD-BACK CHAIR A chair with an open back in the shape of a shield (47)

SIDEBOARD A dining-room piece for storage and serving, consisting of a wide chest of drawers, generally with cupboard space underneath (19)

SILVERED GLASS Glass in which a deposit of silver is encased between covering layers of clear glass (361)

SINUMBRA LAMP See ASTRAL LAMP

SLIP WARE Red earthenware decorated by the application of colored slip (diluted clay) to the glazed surface

SOLAR LAMP A modified Argand lamp designed for burning lard oil. The fuel supply was usually placed under the burner of a lamp constructed as a metal or marble column surmounted by a large globe the base of which was often decorated with prisms (398)

Shield back

SPADE FOOT The foot of a tapering, square-section leg, somewhat wider than the leg itself, in profile suggesting a spade; often shown in Hepplewhite's designs (47)

Spade foot

SPANDREL The triangular space formed by the outer curve of an arch and the angle lines enclosing the arch

SPATTERWARE A cheerful Staffordshire export pottery made for provincial American trade, the sponged or spattered patterns in lively designs (198)

SPLAT The upright, center support in a chair back

SPOOL TURNING Continuously repeated bulbous turning suggesting rows of spools (below)

SPRING CHAIR A chair with metal coil springs, made to rock and/or revolve. Patented by the American Chair Company of Troy, New York and first shown at the Crystal Palace Great Exhibition in London in 1851; also called centripetal chair (371)

S-SCROLL A scroll carved in the form of the letter S

STATUARY WARE See PARIAN WARE

STEEPLE CLOCK A Connecticut shelf clock with pointed top and pillars terminating in pointed finials, introduced about 1845 and made in many sizes and varieties; also called Gothic clock (328)

STERLING A term applied to a standard of silverware indicating a proportion of 925 parts fine silver and 75 parts fine copper in each 1000 parts

STILES The upright side supports of a chair back

STONEWARE A form of hard, nonporous pottery made of clay fired at high temperatures; often salt glazed

STOPPED FLUTING Fluting in which the lower parts of the furrows or channels are fitted with reeding

STRAWBERRY-DIAMOND PATTERN On 19th-century pressed or cut glass, an allover diaper pattern made up of diamonds enclosing smaller ones suggesting the shape of strawberries (281)

STRINGING In furniture, a line or thin band of wood used as an inlay set in a contrasting ground. See BANDING for illustration

SURTOUT *See* PLATEAU

SWAG Swinging or suspended decoration, representing drapery, ribbons, garlands of fruit and flowers; also called festoon

SWELL FRONT Convex curved front, as in a chest or commode or any case piece

TABERNACLE MIRROR A mirror of Sheraton type having a flat cornice with a row of gilt balls beneath it, surmounting a scene painted on glass, with applied columns at its sides (128)

TALL CASE CLOCK A clock incorporated within a tall, standing case to protect the works and accommodate the pendulum; also called long case clock and grandfather clock (48)

TAMBOUR A form of sliding door consisting of narrow strips of wood with convex surfaces which are glued beside each other on a canvas backing (63)

TEARDROP MOTIF Ornamental motif in the shape of an elongated tear (38)

TETE-A-TETE S-shaped love seat designed so that two people may sit face to face; also called a conversational (334)

TILT-TOP TABLE A table, usually with tripod support, the top of which is hinged to tip to a vertical position (245)

TINTYPE A positive photograph on a thin iron plate, made by a collodion process, having a darkened surface; also called a ferrotype

TOBY JUG A figure jug or jar representing Toby Phillpot, the toper, or another comical character. Originated in mid-18th-century England. Toby jugs and bottles were made at Bennington and other American factories in the mid-19th century.

TOILETTINETTE A lady's toilet table of the Victorian period

TRACERY Originally the delicate decorative openwork in Gothic windows, then copied by wood carvers as an ornamental detail, either solid or pierced

TREFOIL A stylized, three-lobed design, often used in Gothic and Gothic Revival patterns

Trefoil

TRICLINIUM A couch or sofa derived from the Roman banquet couch. Greek Revival examples frequently have rolled ends of unequal height and saber legs. Sometimes called a Récamier couch, but the couch in David's portrait of Mme Récamier in the Louvre has equal ends and straight legs

VENEER Thin layers of wood or other materials glued to a solid ground

VERRE EGLOMISE Painted glass used as decorative inserts on furniture. The word *églomisé* came from the name of an 18th-century French framer and designer, Jean-Baptiste Glomi (29).

WAG-ON-THE-WALL CLOCK A tall-clock movement hung directly on the wall, without a pendulum case

WHATNOT An open stand of shelves, sometimes with drawers beneath, for displaying bric-a-brac; also called an *étagère* (320)

WHIMSEY Term used for odd or unusual pieces of glass, such as hats, slippers, buttonhooks, made by individual workmen; or the adaptation of a conventional form to some odd or unusual shape

WHORL FOOT A foot consisting of an upturned scroll; also called a knurl foot

Whorl foot

WORK TABLE A small table fitted with accessories for needlework, often made with one or two drawers, and frequently a suspended fabric workbag (11)

Style Chart: the Federal Period

In spite of considerable regional variation in furnishings of the federal period, an obvious and consistent spirit of design characterizes the output of those years. Straight lines and suave curves, inset or low-relief ornament, graceful proportions, relatively light construction, and restrained, symmetrical outlines all reflect the prevailing classicism of the times—a classicism derived from designs of the late Roman Empire as interpreted principally by Robert Adam, modified by Hepplewhite and Sheraton, and further adapted to local taste by American craftsmen.

Hepplewhite sideboard

Silver sugar urn

New England tambour desk

Tilt-top candlestand

Gilt looking glass

Sheraton work table

Sheraton dressing bureau

Chinese export teapot

Ogee-cross armchair

Tall case clock

Cut-glass goblet

Silver and glass Argand lamp

Square-back side chair

Pembroke table

Duncan Phyfe sofa

Martha Washington chair

Sheraton secretary

Shield-back side chair

Hepplewhite chest of drawers

Sheraton card table

Style Chart: the Empire Period

In the second, third, and fourth decades of the nineteenth century American styles reflected the influence, either directly or through English adaptations, of those popularized in France during Napoleon's reign. The classical vein continued, but with closer regard for archaeological evidence from ancient Greece and Rome in both forms and details. Proportions became heavier, carving deeper, ornament more elaborate. Late in the period the style dwindled off into highly simplified variations of the basic models that lent themselves to quicker, less costly production.

Pier table with glass

Récamier style sofa

Tucker porcelain coffeepot

Klismos chair

Scroll-support card table

Marble-top center table

Duncan Phyfe window seat

Silver, anthemion motif

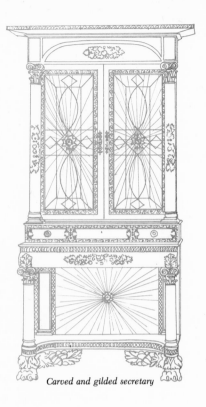

Carved and gilded secretary

Silver cream pitcher

Work table on pedestal

Cut-glass compote

Card table with eagle supports

Gondola chair

Lyre-back armchair

Tabernacle mirror

Four-poster bed

Style Chart: the Early Victorian Period

By the time Queen Victoria ascended to the British throne in 1837 the classical tradition had largely spent its force in America. What remained of its influence was overshadowed by the development of different styles; styles that, for the most part, reached back to other periods of history for models and ideas. Forms and designs associated with the Middle Ages and eighteenth-century France were two major sources of inspiration. Side by side, at times mingling in a single piece, those and other stylistic interpretations of the past competed for public attention.

Rococo Revival sofa

Cast-iron mirror

Baroque design glass pitcher

Rococo Revival whatnot

Balloon-back chair

Hound-handled pitcher

Eclectic chair

Eclectic gaming table

Elizabethan Revival dressing table

Gothic Revival chair

Ruby-glass compote

Rococo Revival chair

Silver sugar bowl

Gothic steeple clock

Rococo Revival dressing table

Astral lamp with glass shade

Rococo Revival table

Metal-frame chair

Acknowledgments

The editors wish to express their deep gratitude to the institutions and individuals mentioned below for their generous help in providing pictorial material from the collections in their custody and for supplying information and advice.

Antiques Magazine
Ruth B. Davidson

Avery Architectural Library, Columbia University
Adolf K. Placzek
Eleanor Thompson

Baltimore Museum of Art
William V. Elder, III

Colonial Williamsburg
Marguerite Gignilliat

Corning Museum of Glass
Paul N. Perrot
Kenneth M. Wilson
Jane S. Shadel

Essex Institute
Huldah Payson

George Eastman House
Beaumont Newhall
Robert Bretz

Ginsburg & Levy Inc.
Benjamin Ginsburg

Henry Ford Museum and Greenfield Village
Dr. Donald A. Shelley
George O. Bird
Katharine Hagler
Walter E. Simmons, II
Charles Miller

Metropolitan Museum of Art
James Biddle
Janet S. Byrne
Margaret Nolan
Harriet Cooper
Berry B. Tracy
Mary C. Glaze
Nada Saporiti
Dianne Hauserman

Museum of the City of New York
Ralph Miller
Margaret Stearns

Museum of Fine Arts, Boston
Wendy O. Goodell
Anne P. Parker

National Trust for Historic Preservation
John N. Pearce

Newark Museum
J. Stewart Johnson
Helen G. Olsson

New-York Historical Society
Dr. James J. Heslin
Caroline Scoon
William DuPrey

New York Public Library
John Miller
Karl Kup
Elizabeth Roth

New York State Historical Association
Dr. Louis C. Jones
Jeri Sleeper
Sybil Ann Frank

Old Sturbridge Village
Henry J. Harlow
Etta Falkner
Robert Chase
Elizabeth Royce

Peabody Museum of Salem
Philip C. F. Smith

Philadelphia Museum of Art
Calvin Hathaway
Elvira L. Honoré
Alfred J. Wyatt

Shelburne Museum
Bradley Smith

Sleepy Hollow Restorations
Joseph T. Butler

Smithsonian Institution
C. Malcolm Watkins
Rodris Roth
Margaret B. Klapthor
Richard E. Ahlborn

The White House
James R. Ketchum

White House Historical Association
Hillory A. Tolson

Henry Francis du Pont Winterthur Museum
Ian M. G. Quimby
Helen M. Schlatter
E. Marie McCafferty
Gilbert Ask

Grateful acknowledgment is made for permission to quote from the following publications:

Edward Deming Andrews and Faith Andrews, *Shaker Furniture*, copyright 1937 by Edward Deming Andrews, Dover Publications, Inc., New York

The Diary of William Bentley, D.D., Vol. IV, American Antiquarian Society and the Essex Institute, Salem, Massachusetts, 1914

J. P. Brissot de Warville, *New Travels in the United States of America, 1788*, ed. Durand Echeverria, copyright 1964 by the President and Fellows of Harvard College, The Belknap Press of Harvard University Press, Cambridge, Massachusetts

Kathryn C. Buhler, *Mount Vernon Silver*, copyright 1957 by The Mount Vernon Ladies' Association of the Union, Mount Vernon, Virginia

Roger Burlingame, *Backgrounds of Power*, copyright 1949 Charles Scribner's Sons, New York

Carl C. Cutler, *Greyhounds of the Sea*, copyright 1930 by Carl C. Cutler, G. P. Putnam's Sons, New York

James Thomas Flexner, *Gilbert Stuart, A Great Life in Brief*, copyright 1939 by James Thomas Flexner, Alfred A. Knopf, New York

Albert TenEyck Gardner, *Yankee Stonecutters*, copyright 1945 Columbia University Press, published for the Metropolitan Museum of Art by the Columbia University Press, New York

Helmut and Alison Gernsheim, *L.J.M. Daguerre, The History of the Diorama and the Daguerreotype*, copyright 1956 by Helmut Gernsheim, Secker & Warburg, London, 1956

Gilbert Stuart, Portraitist of the Young Republic, National Gallery of Art, copyright 1967 by Museum of Art, Rhode Island School of Design, Providence, Rhode Island. Eliza Quincy excerpt taken from section by William B. Stevens, Jr.; John Adams excerpt from section by Mrs. Mary E. Burnet

Mrs. Basil Hall, *The Aristocratic Journey*, ed. Una Pope-Hennessy, copyright 1931 by Una Pope-Hennessy, G. P. Putnam's Sons, The Knickerbocker Press, New York

Oscar Handlin, *This Was America*, copyright 1949 by the President and the Fellows of Harvard College, Harvard University Press, Cambridge, Massachusetts

Elizabeth A. Ingerman, "Personal Experiences of an old New York Cabinetmaker," *Antiques Magazine*, November, 1963. Excerpts taken from the notebook, *Personal Experiences of an Old New York Cabinet Maker* given by Mrs. Halsey to the Henry Francis du Pont Winterthur Museum in 1956

Oliver W. Larkin, *Art and Life in America*, copyright 1949 by Oliver W. Larkin, Holt, Rinehart and Winston, Inc. New York

Marvin Lowenthal and Frank Monaghan, *This Was New York*, copyright 1943 Doubleday, Doran and Company, Inc., Garden City, New York

Samuel Eliot Morison, *The Maritime History of Massachusetts*, copyright 1921 by Samuel E. Morison, Houghton Mifflin Company, Boston

Charles Merrill Mount, *Gilbert Stuart, A Biography*, copyright © 1964 by W. W. Norton & Company, Inc., New York

Kenneth Roberts and Anna M. Roberts, *Moreau de St. Méry's America Journey, 1793–1798*, copyright 1947 by Kenneth Roberts and Anna M. Roberts, Doubleday & Company, Inc., Garden City, New York

Edouard A. Stackpole, *Scrimshaw at Mystic Seaport*, The Marine Historical Association, Inc., Mystic, Connecticut, 1958

Alexis de Tocqueville, *Democracy in America*, Vol. II, ed. Phillip Bradley, translated by Francis Bowen, copyright 1945 by Alfred A. Knopf, Inc., Vintage Books, New York, 1957

Picture Credits

The color plates for the frontispieces on pages 8, 96, 166, 226, and 292 were made from photographs taken specially for this book by Lee Boltin. Also by Boltin, figures: 13, 97a, 108, 162, 164, 182, 240, 279–282, and 334. Photographs reproduced on page 169 and in figures 28, 37, 75, 77, 87, 116, 181, 289, and 510 by Geoffrey Clements; in figure 74 by Eric M. Sanford; in figures 301 and 323 by Edward Prince, Prince Studio, Natchez, Mississippi; in figures 248, 255, 292, 294, and 474 by Einars J. Mengis; in figure 505 by Morton Rosen.

The drawings on pages 385-403 were executed by Ray Porter.

Front jacket: South Jersey type glass candlestick, figure 164 (MMA)—Belter style love seat, figure 334 (MMA)—Classical style silver sugar urn by Paul Revere, figure 97a (MMA). These photographs were taken by Lee Boltin.

Back jacket: Tall case clock in Federal style from Pennsylvania, figure 24 (HFM)—Parian porcelain pitcher from Vermont, figure 367 (HFM)—Gold freedom box presented to John Jay from City of New York, figure 108 (MMA, photograph, Lee Boltin)

Endsheets: Engraving, *Broadway and City Hall, New York, 1819*, by Akrell after an aquatint by Baron Axel Klinckowström, NYHS

Front matter. Half-title page: Carved dolphin arm support from a chair in the Empire style made for James Monroe. Ginsburg & Levy Inc. Title page: Detail of the crest rail of a Hepplewhite sofa carved by Samuel McIntire for the Derby family, Salem, Massachusetts, 1790–1800. MFA, M. & M. Karolik Collection. Table of contents page: Carved and gilded lyre motif from a card table in the Federal style, Philadelphia. WINT. Preface: Carved detail of an apron from a rosewood table in the Victorian style by John Henry Belter, New York, about 1850. HFM

The location of each of the objects illustrated in this volume is listed below. Special photographic credits appear in parentheses; the other photographs were supplied by the institutions and individuals mentioned. Unnumbered illustrations are described after the page number; numbered illustrations follow the figure number. Both page and figure numbers are in boldface type. Where two or more illustrations appear on one page, the references are separated by dashes. To simplify the listings the following abbreviations are used:

AAS: American Antiquarian Society
AIHA: Albany Institute of History and Art
BM: Brooklyn Museum
CMG: Corning Museum of Glass
CW: Colonial Williamsburg
EI: Essex Institute
FAH: Museum of Fine Arts, Houston
HFM: Henry Ford Museum and Greenfield Village
IAD: Index of American Design, National Gallery of Art
LC: Library of Congress
MCNY: Museum of the City of New York

MFA: Museum of Fine Arts, Boston
MHS: Maryland Historical Society
MMA: Metropolitan Museum of Art
MWP: Munson-Williams-Proctor Institute
NM: Newark Museum
NYHS: New-York Historical Society
NYPL: New York Public Library
   R. B. Div.: Rare Book Division
   A. & A. Div.: Art & Architecture Division
NYSHA: New York State Historical Association, Cooperstown
OSV: Old Sturbridge Village
PM: Philadelphia Museum of Art
PMS: Peabody Museum of Salem
SHR: Sleepy Hollow Restorations, Inc.
SI: Smithsonian Institution
SM: Shelburne Museum
WHHA: White House Historical Association
WINT: Henry Francis du Pont Winterthur Museum

Republican Modes
The Federal Style (1783–1815)

UNNUMBERED ILLUSTRATIONS LISTED BY PAGE:

8, 9 Silver sauceboat. MMA, Fletcher Fund, 1959 **10** Detail of advertisement for a mail stage. AAS—Painting of Susquehanna River crossing. MMA, Rogers Fund, 1942 **11** Painting of Charles Towneley. Towneley Hall Art Gallery and Museum Committee, Burnley, England **12** Design for a pier table from *The Cabinet-Maker and Upholsterer's Guide*, 1794. NYPL, R. B. Div. **13** Detail of view of Genesee Falls by Comte de Beaujolais. NYHS—Portrait of Mrs. Bingham. Courtesy of Dr. Francis Fisher Hart **14** Engraving of Federal Hall by Amos Doolittle. NYPL, Stokes Collection **15** Drawing of White House. LC **16** Nathan Ruggles' label. WINT **17** Porcelain saucer. MMA, Rogers Fund, 1928—Painting of naval battle. New Haven Historical Society **64** Gilbert Stuart self-portrait. MMA, Fletcher Fund, 1926—Portrait of Stuart by John Neagle. Boston Athenaeum (photograph, MFA) **65** Engraving of Washington after Stuart portrait. U.S. Treasury Department, Bureau of Engraving & Printing **86** Detail from advertisement for craftsmen association. Rhode Island Historical Society—Pewterer's banner carried in New York's Federal Procession of 1788. NYHS **87** Advertisement for cabinet and chair factory. AIHA

FIGURE NUMBERS:

1 *The Works in Architecture*, 1773. NYPL, R. B. Div. **2** MFA, M. & M. Karolik Collection **3** Plate 2, Hepplewhite, *The Cabinet-Maker and Upholsterer's Guide*, 1788. MMA **4** EI **5** Plate 33, Sheraton, *The Cabinet-Maker and Upholsterer's Drawing Book*, 1792. NYPL, R. B. Div. **6** Israel Sack, Inc. **7** EI **8** NYPL, Stokes Collection **9** MMA **10** WHHA **11, 12** WINT **13** MMA, Fletcher Fund, 1962 **14** Ginsburg & Levy Inc. **15, 16** HFM **17** WINT **18** Collection of Mr. and Mrs. Harry Connelly

Groome, Jr. (photograph, PM) **19** PM **20** Taft Museum, Cincinnati, Ohio **21** HFM **22** AIC **23** MMA, The Crosby Brown Collection of Musical Instruments, 1889 **24** HFM **25** MHS **26** WINT **27a, b** Baltimore Museum of Art **28** MMA, Fletcher Fund, 1934 **29, 30** WINT **31** MFA **32** HFM **33** WHHA **34** MFA **35** MFA, M. & M. Karolik Collection **36** David Stockwell, Inc. **37** MMA, Gift of Mrs. Russell Sage, 1909 **38** HFM **39** WINT **40** MMA, Kennedy Fund, 1918 **41** NYHS **42** NYPL, Stokes Collection **43** MCNY **44** Art Commission, City of New York **45** NYHS **46** HFM **47** WINT **48** AIHA **49, 50** WINT **51** NYHS **52** AIC **53** Peter Hill, Inc. (photograph, Adams Studio, Washington, D.C.) **54** MMA, The Sylmaris Collection, Gift of George Coe Graves, 1931 **55** MFA, M. & M. Karolik Collection **56** WINT **57** Massachusetts Historical Society **58** MFA, Gift of Mrs. Horatio A. Lamb in memory of Mr. and Mrs. Winthrop Sargent **59, 59a** MFA, M. & M. Karolik Collection **60** MMA, Gift in memory of Mr. and Mrs. Andrew Varick Stout, 1965 **61** MFA, M. & M. Karolik Collection **62** Ginsburg & Levy Inc. **63** FAH, Bayou Bend Collection **64** MFA, M. & M. Karolik Collection **65** MMA, Fletcher Fund, 1926 **66** MFA, M. & M. Karolik Collection **67** HFM **68** MFA, M. & M. Karolik Collection **69** HFM **70, 70a** MFA, M. & M. Karolik Collection **71** National Gallery of Art, Gift of Col. Edgar William and Bernice Chrysler Garbisch **72** HFM **73** MMA, Gift of Mrs. Russell Sage, 1909 **74** Currier Gallery of Art, Manchester, New Hampshire **75** MMA, Sansbury-Mills Fund, 1956 **76** WINT **77** MMA, Rogers Fund, 1907 **78** Worcester Art Museum **79** National Gallery of Art, Gift of Mrs. R. Homans **80** Coll. Mrs. E. Lewis (photo., National Gallery of Art) **81** MFA **82** Estate of Robert Morris VI (photograph, PM) **83** Collection of Dr. Francis Fisher Hart **84** MMA, Gift of William H. Huntington, 1883 **85** MMA, Rogers Fund, 1951 **86** MMA, Harris Brisbane Dick Fund, 1934 **87** MMA, Gift of Col. Edgar William and Bernice Chrysler Garbisch, 1964 **88** HFM **89** WINT **90** MFA **91, 92** WINT **93** MMA, Rogers Fund, 1935 **94** CMG **95** Ginsburg & Levy Inc. **96** Collection of Marshall B. Davidson **97a, b** MMA, Bequest of A.T. Clearwater, 1933 **98** Virginia Museum of Fine Arts **99** MFA, Gift of Joseph W.R. Rogers and Mary C. Rogers **100** WINT **101** MCNY **102** MMA, Gift of Mrs. J. Insley Blair, 1942 **103** MFA, M. & M. Karolik Collection **104** Collection of Mr. and Mrs. Samuel S. Schwartz **105a, b** MMA, Bequest of A. T. Clearwater, 1933 **106** EI **107** NYHS, Bella C. Landauer Collection **108** (photograph by courtesy of MMA) **109** MMA, Bequest of Charles Allen Munn, 1924 **110, 110a** SI **111** MFA **112** MMA, Rogers Fund, 1946 **113** Missouri Historical Society **114** AIHA **115** WINT **116** NYHS **117, 117a** MMA, Rogers Fund, 1922 **118–120** WINT **121** HFM **122** MMA, Purchase, 1938, Joseph Pulitzer Bequest **123** Ginsburg & Levy Inc. **124** WINT **125** HFM

American Empire
The Classic Summation (1815–1840)

UNNUMBERED ILLUSTRATIONS LISTED BY PAGE:

96, 97 Card table by Lannuier. MMA, Funds from various donors, 1966 **98** Water color of the Capitol by Charles Burton. MMA, Joseph Pulitzer Bequest, 1942 —Colored aquatint of Fort McHenry by John Bower. Chicago Historical Society **99** Engraving of South Street from Maiden Lane by William J. Bennett. NYPL, Stokes Collection—Water color of Erie Canal by John W. Hill. NYHS **100** Chinese porcelain pagoda. WINT **101** Detail of water color of the *Paragon* by Paul Svinin. MMA, Rogers Fund, 1942 **102** Wash drawing of the Bank of Pennsylvania. MHS—Engraving of a door, Plate 63, from *The Modern Builders' Guide* by Minard Lafever, 1833. Avery Architectural Library, Columbia U. **103** Marble bust of Andrew Jackson. MMA, Gift of Mrs. Frances V. Nash, 1894 **104** Latrobe's drawing for White House chairs. MHS **105** Portrait of Juliette Récamier by Jacques Louis David. Louvre **130** Brass quadrant. PMS—India-ink drawing of the shop of Pynchon and Lee, Springfield, Mass., about 1860. Museum of Art, Rhode Island School of Design—Water color from the log of the *Belisarius*. PMS **131** Lithograph of "slaying seals" by George Endicott and Moses Swett from *Voyages Round the World* by Edmund Fanning, 1833. New York Society Library **162** Bust of Hiram Powers by Horatio Greenough. MFA—Marble statue, *Greek Slave*, by Hiram Powers. NM **163** Engraving of *Greek Slave* at Düsseldorf Gallery. NYPL

FIGURE NUMBERS:

126 MMA, Rogers Fund, 1933 **127** Photograph, Taylor & Dull, Inc. **128** MMA, Gift of Mrs. Russell Sage, 1909 **129** MCNY **130** MFA **131** MHS (photograph, NM) **132** From *Receuil des Décorations Intérieures* by Charles Percier and Pierre Fontaine, 1812. MMA, Dick Fund, 1925 **133** HFM **134** PM **135** MMA, Fletcher Fund, 1930 **136** MMA, Gift of Mrs. Maynard Verplanck, 1940 **137** AIHA **138** MFA, Gift of the Misses Aimee and Rosamond Lamb **139** PM (photograph, NM) **140** AIHA **141** WINT **142** NYHA **143** *Antiques Magazine* **144** WHHA **145** MMA, Gift of Mrs. William W. Hoppin, 1948 **146** Collection of Joseph T. Butler **147** HFM **148** MMA, Rogers Fund, 1945 **149** WINT **150** MWP **151** NM **152, 153** HFM **154** WINT **155** HFM **156** OSV **157** MMA, Bequest of Edward C. Moore, 1891 **158** MMA, Gift of J. Pierpont Morgan, 1917 **159** MMA, Bequest of Constance R. Brown, 1940 **160** MMA, Gift of F. W. Hunter, 1914 **161** MMA, Bequest of Edward C. Moore, 1891 **162** MMA, Rogers Fund, 1910 **163** MMA, Gift of J. Pierpont Morgan, 1917 **164** MMA, Rogers Fund, 1935 **165, 166** CMG **167** MMA, Rogers Fund, 1935 **168** MMA, Rogers Fund, 1940 **169** Carnegie Museum, Pittsburgh **170** CMG **171** WINT **172** MMA, Rogers Fund, 1941 **173** MMA **174** HFM **175** WINT **176** PMS **177** Victoria & Albert Museum, London **178** Ginsburg & Levy Inc. **179** HFM **180** PMS **181** Ginsburg & Levy Inc. **182** MMA, Rogers Fund, 1941 **183, 184** WINT **185** Museum of Art, Rhode Island School of Design (photograph, MMA) **186** MMA, Gift of Gustavus A. Pfeiffer, 1948 **187, 188** WINT **189** HFM **190, 191** Carl

H. Boehringer Collection **192–194** NYHS **195** WINT **196** HFM **197, 198** NYHS **199, 200** PM **201** HFM **202** NM **203** WINT **204** BM (photograph, NM) **205** NM **206** MCNY (photograph, Taylor & Dull, Inc.) **207** Museum of Art, Rhode Island School of Design **208** Samuel Kirk & Son, Inc., Baltimore **209** White House Collection **209a** White House Collection (photograph, NM) **210** Collection of Mr. and Mrs. Mark Bortman (photograph, NM) **211** NYHS **212** MMA, Whittelsey Fund, 1953 **213** PMS **214** AAS **215** LC **216** SI **217** Pennsylvania Academy of the Fine Arts **218, 219** From *History of the United States Capitol* by Glenn Brown, Washington, 1900. MMA **220** Collection of Forrest Home (photograph, PM) **221** MMA, Edward W. C. Arnold Collection (photograph, MCNY) **222** Photograph, Daniel Farber **223** From *Green-wood Illustrated* by James Smillie, New York, 1847. MMA **224** Boston Athenaeum **225** MMA, Gift of William Backhouse Astor, 1872 **226** MMA, Gift of John Taylor Johnston, 1888 **227** MMA, Gift of the Children of Jonathan Sturges, 1895 **228** The Huntington Library, San Marino, Calif. **229, 230** Museum of New Mexico, Santa Fe **231** Museum of New Mexico, Santa Fe **232, 233** Missouri Historical Society, St. Louis **234** Archdiocese of Detroit (photograph, Detroit Institute of Arts)

Short Cuts to Style
Craftsmen & Mechanics

UNNUMBERED ILLUSTRATIONS LISTED BY PAGE:

168, 169 Pressed lacy-glass plate. MMA, Gift of Mrs. Charles W. Green, 1951 **170** Statue of George Washington by Horatio Greenough. SI **171** Engraving of gristmill from *The Young Mill-Wright and Miller's Guide* by Oliver Evans, 1795. NYPL, R. B. Div.—Engraving of "Colossus" [Fairmount] Bridge from Baron Axel Klinckowström's *Atlas*, Stockholm, 1824. LC **172** Sketch of Philadelphia waterworks from Latrobe's Journal III, July 1796. MHS **173** Hitchcock chair. HFM—Advertisement for clocks. Former collection of Carl Drepperd **174** Pressed-glass candlestick by Boston and Sandwich Glass Company. MMA, Rogers Fund, 1936 **175** Water color by Benjamin J. Harrison. MCNY **177** Daguerreotype of John Quincy Adams by Nathanial Southworth and Josiah Hawes. MMA, Gift of I. N. Phelps Stokes, Edward S. Hawes, Alice Mary Hawes, Marion Augusta Hawes, 1937 **190** Self-portrait of Samuel F. B. Morse in his late teens. National Academy of Design—Daguerreotype of Morse by an unknown American photographer. George Eastman House **191** Morse's sketch of his code, 1837. LC—Japanese print of a telegraph transmitter. Norfolk Museum of Arts and Sciences

FIGURE NUMBERS:

235 OSV **236** MMA, Gift of Mrs. Samuel Auchmuty Tucker, 1947 **237** MFA, Charles Hitchcock Tyler Residuary Fund **238** WINT **239** HFM **240** MMA, Sansbury–Mills Fund, 1954 **241, 242** HFM **243** Cooper Union Museum for the Arts of Decoration **244** Collection of Donald R. Preckel (photograph, NM) **245, 246** HFM **247** Abby Aldrich Rockefeller Folk Art Collection, CW **248** SM **249** HFM **250** John Gordon, Ameri-

cana **251** Ginsburg & Levy Inc. **252, 253** HFM **254** MMA **255** SM **256, 257** George Eastman House **258** Los Angeles County Museum of Natural History **259, 260** George Eastman House **261** NYHS **262** From *Photography and the American Scene* by Robert Taft, New York, The Macmillan Company, 1942, page 214 (photograph, Peale Museum) **263** NYHS **264** WINT **265** George Eastman House **266–268** HFM **269** NYHS **270** WINT **271** *Antiques Magazine* **272** WINT **273** MMA, Gift of Mrs. Stephen S. FitzGerald, 1962 **274** WINT **275** CMG **276** Photograph, Taylor & Dull, Inc. **277** OSV **278** CMG **279–282** MMA, Gift of Mrs. Charles W. Green, 1951 **283** Toledo Museum of Art **284** NYHS, Bella C. Landauer Collection **285** CMG **286** MMA, The Sylmaris Collection, Gift of George Coe Graves, 1930 **287** Israel Sack, Inc. **288** *Antiques Magazine* **289** Seamen's Bank for Savings **290** WINT **291, 291a** HFM **292** SM **293** NM **294** SM **295–300** CMG **301** Rosalie, State Shrine of Mississippi D. A. R., Natchez (photograph, Prince Studio) **302** MMA, Gift of Mrs. R. W. Hyde, 1943 **303** Collection of Richard Darlington Patterson (photograph, *Antiques Magazine)* **304** Collection of Mr. and Mrs. Vincent Versage (photograph, NM) **305** Lyman Allyn Museum **306–308** MMA, Gift of L. E. Katzenback Fund, 1967 **309** NM **310, 311** MMA, Gift of Mrs. R. W. Hyde, 1943 **312** NYHS **313** MHS

Heir to the Ages
Victorian Eclecticism (1840–1860)

UNNUMBERED ILLUSTRATIONS LISTED BY PAGE:

226, 227 Belter style rosewood chair, New York, mid-19th century. MMA, Gift of Mrs. Charles Reginald Leonard, 1957, in memory of Edgar Welch Leonard, Robert Jarvis Leonard, and Charles Reginald Leonard **228** *Outward Bound*, lithograph by T. H. Maguire after a drawing by J. Nichol, 1854. State Street Trust Company (photograph, Chicago Historical Society)—Lithograph of New York's harbor, with incoming liner, by Thomas Thompson, about 1828. Collection of Harris D. Colt **229** Lithograph of San Francisco, about 1851, by M. & N. Hanhart after a sketch by F. S. Marryat. NYHS **230** Lithograph of a Shaker dance. Worcester Art Museum **231** Illustration from *Ten Nights in a Bar-Room, and What I Saw There* by Timothy Shay Arthur, 1854 **232** Plate XVIII from *Strawberry Hill Accounts* by Horace Walpole, 1927. NYPL, A. & A. Div.—Portrait of Sir Walter Scott. National Portrait Gallery, London **233** Oil painting of Sunnyside, by George Inness, Sr. SHR **235** Advertisement from *Godey's Magazine and Lady's Book*, 1850. MMA **252, 253** Engravings of details from the oak buffet by Gustave Herter. From *The World of Science, Art, and Industry* by Benjamin Silliman, Jr. and Charles R. Goodrich, 1854. New York Society Library

FIGURE NUMBERS:

314 From *The World of Science, Art, and Industry* by Benjamin Silliman, Jr. and Charles R. Goodrich, 1854. NYPL, R. B. Div. **315** MCNY **316** From *Gleason's Pictorial Drawing-Room Companion*, October 22, 1853. Bennington Museum **317** NYHS **318** MMA, Harris Brisbane Dick Fund, 1924 **319** Collection of Mr. and

James Biddle **320** BM **321** SI **322** NM **323** Collection of Mrs. Annie Vaughan, Natchez, Mississippi (photograph, Prince Studio) **324** MMA, Harris Brisbane Dick Fund, 1924 **325** Avery Library, Columbia University, A. J. Davis Collection **326, 327** Lyndhurst, National Trust for Historic Preservation **328** Collection of A. A. Adams (photograph, *Antiques Magazine*) **329, 330** MWP **331** From *Gleason's Pictorial Drawing-Room Companion*, Nov. 11, 1854. NYPL **332** HFM **333** MCNY **334** MMA, Gift of Mrs. Charles Reginald Leonard, 1957, in memory of Edgar Welch Leonard, Robert Jarvis Leonard, and Charles Reginald Leonard **335–337** WHHA **338** NYHS **339** Virginia Museum of Fine Arts, Richmond **340** MHS **341** HFM **342, 343** SHR **344** Louisiana State Museum, New Orleans **345** BM **346, 346a** MWP **347** MCNY **348** HFM **349, 350** MCNY **351** SHR **352** Toledo Museum of Art **353** NM **354** MMA, Gift of George Lowther, 1906 **355** NM **356, 357** HFM **358** Toledo Museum of Art **359–361** HFM **362–364** Bennington Museum **365** WINT **366** Bennington Museum **367** HFM **368, 369** Bennington Museum **370** SHR **371** Collection of Edgar Kaufmann, Jr. (photograph, MMA) **372** Cooper Union Museum for the Arts of Decoration **373** MMA **374** AAS **375** Former collection of Paul Magriel **376** WINT **377** Historical Society of Pennsylvania **378** Carolina Art Association, Gibbes Art Gallery **379** WINT **380** St. Louis Mercantile Library **381** Collection of Dr. Allan J. Ryan, Wallingford, Connecticut **382** MMA, Rogers Fund, 1962

Some Domestic Sciences
The Functioning Home

UNNUMBERED ILLUSTRATIONS LISTED BY PAGE:

292, 293 Glass and ormolu candelabrum. MMA, Gift of Mary E. Steers, 1961 **294** Engraving of a Gothic style drawing room. Figure 179 from *Cottage Residences* by Andrew Jackson Downing, 1842. NYPL **295** Engraving of construction of a balloon-frame house by William W. Wilson from *The Modern Architect* by Edward Shaw, 1855. MMA—Engraving of a perspective view of a balloon frame from *Woodward's Country Homes* by George E. Woodward, 1865. NYPL

FIGURE NUMBERS:

383 Ginsburg & Levy Inc. **384** OSV **385** WINT **386** Illustration from *Ackermann's Repository* by John Gelland, April, 1823. MMA **387** SHR **388** MMA, Gift of Mrs. F. Carrington Weems, 1955 **389** WINT **390** Mount Vernon Ladies' Association **391** MMA, Joseph Pulitzer Bequest, 1942 **392** Collection of Joseph T. Butler **393** MMA **394** MMA, Gift of John Palmer Gavit, 1932 **395** SM **396** WINT **397** SHR **398** MFA, M. & M. Karolik Collection **399** NYHS **400** SHR **401** MCNY, Bequest of Mrs. J. Insley Blair **402, 403** MFA **404** National Gallery of Art, Mellon Collection, 1940 **405** OSV **406** WINT **407** Chester County Historical Society **408** Ginsburg & Levy Inc. **409** Suffolk Museum, Stony Brook, New York **410** NYSHA **411** SM **412** Clockwise starting from top center: Eight-pointed star, MMA, Posthumous gift of Miss Eliza Polhemess Cobb through Mrs. Arthur Bunker, 1952; Flower, SM; Mother and child, SM; Flowers, SM; Gossips, IAD; Bowl of flowers, SM; Lady on horseback, SM;

Flower, MMA, Also gift of Miss Cobb; Elk, SM; Flower, SM Upper left: Bird, SM. Upper right: Tree, SM **413** Abby Aldrich Rockefeller Folk Art Collection, CW **414** Collection of Lt. Col. H.W. Williams, Jr. (photograph, Corcoran Gallery of Art) **415** HFM **416** SHR **417** HFM **418** SM **419** AAS **420** Old Print Shop, Kenneth M. Newman **421** AAS **422** LC **423** MMA, Gift of Louise F. Wickham in memory of William H. Wickham, 1928 **424** Lithograph from *Domestic Manners of the Americans* by Mrs. Trollope, 1832. MMA **425** WINT **426** Corcoran Gallery of Art **427, 428** HFM **429** Schaffer Library, Union College, Schenectady, New York **430** HFM **431** LC **432** HFM **433** MCNY **434** Toledo Museum of Art **435** MHS **436** AAS **437** Kennedy & Co. **438** NYPL, Eno Collection **439** Boston Athenaeum **440** AAS **441** From *Illustrated London News*, April, 1861. NYPL **442** Transportation Library, University of Michigan **443** NYHS, Bella C. Landauer Collection **444** NYSHA **445** Boston Public Library **446** Cooper Union Museum for the Arts of Decoration (photograph, IAD) **447, 448** The White House (photographs courtesy of Maria de Kosenko)

Forms of Tradition
American Folk Art

UNNUMBERED ILLUSTRATIONS LISTED BY PAGE:

338, 339 *The Peaceable Kingdom* by Edward Hicks, 1830–40. Abby Aldrich Rockefeller Folk Art Collection, CW **340** Portrait of James Berthoud by John James Audubon, 1819. J.B. Speed Art Museum, Louisville, Kentucky **341** Tavern sign from Brooklyn, New York, about 1830. HFM—Pencil and water color drawing of *Girls' Evening School* by an unknown artist, about 1840. MFA, M. & M. Karolik Collection

FIGURE NUMBERS:

449, 449a MMA, Gift of Katharine Keyes, 1938, in memory of her father, Homer Eaton Keyes **450** Shaker Museum (photograph, Alexander Bender; courtesy of *Antiques Magazine*) **451** Collection of Nina Fletcher Little (photograph, OSV) **452** Abby Aldrich Rockefeller Folk Art Collection, CW **453** Collection of Nina Fletcher Little (photograph, OSV) **454** PMS **455** Abby Aldrich Rockefeller Folk Art Collection, CW **456** PMS **457** MMA, The Sylmaris Collection, Gift of George Coe Graves, 1930 **458, 459** PMS **460–462** Mystic Seaport, Marine Historical Association, Mystic, Connecticut **463** MMA, The Sylmaris Collection, Gift of George Coe Graves, 1930 **464** Old Dartmouth Historical Society and Whaling Museum, New Bedford, Massachusetts **465** Mystic Seaport, Marine Historical Association, Mystic, Connecticut **466** NYSHA **467, 468** Collection of Col. Edgar William and Bernice Chrysler Garbisch **469** Old Dartmouth Historical Society and Whaling Museum, New Bedford, Massachusetts **470** Abby Aldrich Rockefeller Folk Art Collection, CW **471** MFA, M. & M. Karolik Collection **472, 473** Abby Aldrich Rockefeller Folk Art Collection, CW **474** SM **475, 476** Abby Aldrich Rockefeller Folk Art Collection, CW **477** Museum of New Mexico, Santa Fe (photograph, New Mexico Department of Development) **478–481** Taylor Museum, Colorado Springs Fine Arts Center **482** Milwaukee Art Center

483, 484 PM **485** IAD **486, 487** WINT **488, 489** PM **490** MFA, Shaker Collection **491–493** WINT **494, 495** HFM **496–498** Abby Aldrich Rockefeller Folk Art Collection, CW **499** Ohio State Historical Society **500, 501** HFM **502** National Gallery of Art, Gift of Col. Edgar William and Bernice Chrysler Garbisch **503** Abby Aldrich Rockefeller Folk Art Collection, CW **504** SM **505** Collection of James A. Keillor, Wading River, New York **506, 507** Hammond-Harwood House, Annapolis, Maryland **508** NYSHA **509** PM **510** Collection of Mr. and Mrs. Nathan Comfort Starr **511** MFA, M. & M. Karolik Collection